Latin American and Caribbean

OVERSEAS FOREIGN DIRECT INVESTMENT IN

China

IN THE TWENTY-FIRST CENTURY

Edited by
Enrique Dussel Peters

LATIN AMERICAN AND CARIBBEAN OVERSEAS FOREIGN DIRECT INVESTMENT TO CHINA IN THE TWENTY- FIRST CENTURY

Enrique Dussel Peters — *Coordinador*
Silvia Jiménez Barba — *Edición*
Socorro García — *Diseño y formación de interiores*

Primera edición: Noviembre 2023
ISBN: 978-607-8937-05-9 (electronic)
ISBN: 978-607-8937-09-7 (paperback)

Distributed by Lynne Rienner Publishers, Inc.
1800 30TH St., Boulder, CO 80301 USA
Tel +1(303) 444-6684, Fax: +1(303)444-0824 and email: questions@rienner.com

Latin American and Caribbean
OVERSEAS FOREIGN DIRECT INVESTMENT IN
China
IN THE TWENTY-FIRST CENTURY

Edited by
Enrique Dussel Peters

CONTENTS

INTRODUCTION

Enrique Dussel Peters

China's foreign direct investment (FDI) has been one of the most outstanding socioeconomic and development events in the last 50 years, increasing from levels below 1% of global FDI during the 1980s to 8.25% in 2010 and 15.51% in 2020; China's share over global FDI (10.50% during 2017-2021) has been second only to the United States (17.67%) (UNCTAD 2023).[1] Acknowledging China's FDI increase in absolute terms until 2021, China's FDI flows achieved its highest levels as a share of GDP and gross fixed capital formation (GFCF) in the midst of the 1990s (of 5.98% of GDP and 16.93% of GFCF in 1994) and have fallen significantly since then to levels below 2% and to 3% since the 2010s, respectively. This impressive performance does not only reflect China's capacity to attract FDI, but also the dynamics of Chinese endogenous processes in terms of innovation, value-added and GDP; this is also the reason why FDI has fallen as a share of domestic variables. There is no question regarding the importance of FDI in China, particularly since reform and opening-up until the 2000s from a macro, meso, and micro perspective, as well as global value chains to modernize China's socioeconomy and to allow for

1 If we include Hong Kong, China's share would increase to 18.46% of global FDI during 2017-2021.

in-depth learning processes (WB and DRC 2012:148-150, 417-418). Regulations, strategic attraction of FDI, overall learning processes, as well as the increasing relevance of China's domestic market and the open confrontation between the US and China since 2018 have all played important roles in China's FDI in the 21st century.[2]

The goal of the book is to examine Latin American and the Caribbean (LAC) overseas foreign direct investment (OFDI) to China, including macro, meso, and micro perspectives. Rather surprisingly these type of investment flows to China have not received much attention yet, even less so from a historical perspective that includes country-level specificities. Based on chapters on Argentina, Brazil, Chile, the Caribbean, Central America, Mexico and Peru, the book examines the macroeconomic and historical features of their OFDI to China and including several firm-level case studies. While Chinese OFDI to LAC have been examined at least for a decade, particularly at the Academic Network for Latin America and the Caribbean on China (Dussel Peters 2014, 2023; ECLAC 2010, 2021; Ray and Gallagher 2017), there is no structured analysis on LAC's OFDI to China until today.

The book's seven chapters present an enormous richness regarding each country-study, embed the respective analysis on its OFDI to China within the wider bilateral socioeconomic relationship, integrate several firm-level case studies and include conclusions and respective proposals. Considering the specificities of each country and region, each author emphasizes issues relevant to their relationship with China and conclusions.

At least six topics are important.

First. Statistics matter. Each of the seven chapters of the book highlights enormous differences in the methodology of registration and resulting statistics between Chinese and LAC official sources, in addition to efforts by UNCTAD (United Nations Conference on Trade and Development) and other academic and non-

2 As we shall see below, a detailed analysis on China's FDI goes beyond the scope of this book. For a discussion on the recent performance of Chinese FDI from different perspectives, see: Gereffi, Bamber, and Fernández-Stark (2023); MOFCOM (2022/a/b); Wang *et al.* (2021) and WTO (2021).

governmental organizations. As a result, statistics on LAC's OFDI to China are particularly weak: in most of the countries in LAC there are no OFDI statistics by country and to China. The chapters on the Caribbean and the Cayman and Virgin Islands —as discussed in detail in chapter 3 by Jevon Minto, Chevano Baker and Noel Young— are an important contribution of the book for understanding the methodological differences and specificities according to different sources, in this case regarding the significant role of the Caribbean as an offshore financial center, parallel to homegrown OFDI flows. Any future analysis on FDI and OFDI should be aware of these differences.

Second. According to the last public official statistics on Chinese FDI by country (NBS 2022), LAC's share accumulated almost $210 billion up to 2021 (or 10.27% of China's accumulated FDI until 2021), particularly concentrated on the Cayman Islands and British Virgin Islands (with a 95.85% of China's FDI from LAC for the same period). As discussed throughout the chapters, however, LAC's potential for OFDI is substantial: During 2003-2021, LAC carried out an OFDI of $270 billion or an annual average flow of $12.3 billion; the annual average OFDI from LAC has constantly increased until the last period (2018-2021). In addition, 58% of LAC's OFDI was concentrated in LAC (or intraregional OFDI) during 2003-20021 and only 2.94% to China (Dussel Peters 2022). However, and as discussed in detail in each of the respective seven chapters, the "reorientalization" of the global economy, including LAC's, has been particularly profound in terms of trade, and will deepen in the future in terms of bilateral capital flows, with an enormous potential for bilateral cooperation between LAC and China.

Third. From a national perspective, the chapters of this book examine that in regions such as Central America and countries such as Peru (in addition to many other countries that have not been included in the book), OFDI to China is minimal or nonexistent. The larger countries in the region like Brazil, Mexico and Argentina present an important dynamic in their OFDI to China; Chile is an outlier regarding its exceptionally high levels of OFDI in general, including to China (see chapter 5 of this book). Until today, no LAC country has developed specific instruments to enhance OFDI in general or to China. An important development issue discussed in several chapters of this book refers to the topic of the implications of OFDI for developing countries, and specifically in LAC, characterized as net capital importers and acknowledging OFDI by industrial groups and according to their increasing global activities.

Fourth. Implications of case studies. The 15 detailed firm-level studies in the respective countries allow for an enormous richness of future analysis of the same company and others. Several topics stand out: a. All firms are large multinational corporations (MNCs) or *translatinas* with prior internationalization process before beginning OFDI processes in China, b. In all the examined cases, LAC's MNCs began their OFDI operations at least in the early 2000s, i.e. they account for two decades of experiences in China, c. In all examined cases, LAC's MNCs in China began their activities through trade and representation offices before starting with OFDI processes and larger investments in China either in production sites and/or offering services, d. All cases reflect substantial learning or adaptation processes through their OFDI processes in China, particularly in their initial stages; in some cases these learning processes were interrupted by the cancellation of their activities, such as in the case of Brazil's Embraer in 2016 (see chapter 2 by Celio Hiratuka), e. From an industrial organization and business perspective, these case studies are extremely rich in highlighting different development paths in spite of high entry-barriers and cultural and market differences with the respective company's origin; in most of the cases, for example, firms began their OFDI activities through joint ventures (Bagó, Catlin, Embraer, and ICC) or merger and acquisitions (M&A) (Bimbo and Suzano), with some exceptions through greenfield OFDI in China (such as Cedrus Investments, Tenaris, and WEG), f. In most of the cases the initial OFDI processes were pursued to take advantage of cheap materials and labor power and to benefit from China's growing domestic demand; with few exceptions all firms in

2023 do not only acknowledge an increasing autonomy of their Chinese subsidiaries (Bimbo, Herbalife, ICC, and Suzano), but their subsidiaries benefit so much from China's innovation capabilities that it is transferred to the rest of the respective global industrial groups. This is the case of Interceramic China (ICC), given China's substantial developments in design, production innovations and showroom facilities in floor tiles (see chapter 6 by Enrique Dussel Peters), g. This first learning phase or wave —that took up to a decade for some of the analyzed firms (Bimbo, WEG)— allowed these firms to further expand, mostly through additional M&A and joint ventures. h. Rather surprisingly, all LAC firms doing OFDI activities in China have implemented innovative and state-of-the-art global practices that allowed them to compete in China: from seamless tube (Tenaris, see chapter 1 by Leonardo E. Stanley) to the development of new products and distribution channels (Accenture, Bimbo, Camposol, Codelco, Herbalife and ICC), manufacturing of motors and electrical equipment (WEG) and human and animal health (Biogenesis Bagó), grinding balls to pulverize materials (Elecmetal), automotive components (Tenaris), private wealth and asset management (Cedrus Investment), specialty insurance, reinsurance and other B2B services (Catlin and Peru's Intercorp examined by Alan Fairlie in chapter 7), i. Rather surprisingly, most of LAC's OFDI in China was not carried out in China's largest cities (such as Beijing, Shanghai or Chongqing), but in smaller cities and provinces (such as Baotou, Changchun, Changzhou, Chengdu, Dalian, Foshan, Guangzhou, Hangzhou, Jiangsu, Jiangyin, Nanjing, Ningbo, Qingdao, Shenzhen, Suzhou, Wuxi, Xian, Yangling, Yuling, and Zibo, among many other) that allowed them to benefit from local and regional FDI-instruments and cheaper suppliers; Bimbo, Catlin, Codelco and Embraer are important exceptions of this performance, since they began their OFDI activities with plants and services in Beijing; Suzano is also highly concentrated in Shanghai, and Cedrus Investments in Hong Kong, Shanghai and Beijing. j. Considering the waves and learning processes of these LAC firms in China, several of them have not only been able to integrate into the culture, the suppliers, the clients as well as local, regional and national customers and respective public sectors, but they also use this expertise as a basis for other Asian countries (such as Codelco's recent activities examined in chapter 5 by Dorotea López, Andrés Bórquez and Juan E. Serrano-Moreno and Bermuda's Accenture to provide technology services in China and other Asian markets).

Fifth. Increasingly higher entry-barriers for new LAC OFDI to China. Large LAC MNCs took advantage of "cheap China" since the 1990s, as discussed below. The overall environment for investing in China, however, has changed considerably since the early 21st century. On the one hand, Chinas has become increasingly expensive compared to other Asian countries, also manifested in several cases where LAC firms in China have recently transferred parts and components to other regional suppliers. In addition, while the "cultural distance" remains (see the case of Suzano in chapter 2), the competition in China with Chinese and foreign firms has increased drastically. Finally, the increasing trade tensions between the US and China also generate higher costs and risks, as discussed in chapters 1 for Tenaris and 5 for Elecmetal. The implications of these experiences are profound, including the challenges for smaller firms, or even large firms in LAC with little internationalization experience and without the possibility of having OFDI in China without profits for longer periods, as well as for future LAC OFDI to China, such as highlighted for Central America in agroindustry (and particularly coffee) and services (particularly digital services) by Rafael Arias-Achio and Rafael Arias Ramírez in chapter 4.

Sixth. All firms have been affected by US-China confrontation and the erupting trade war since 2018. However, none have decided to leave China as a result, but rather to follow a "China+1" strategy, i.e. to continue and deepen its OFDI and capacities in China, and to expand OFDI and particular processes, used in some cases for the US-market, to other Asian countries. Such is the case of Chilean Elecmetal (reorienting production to Africa) and Mexico's Italika (substituting motorcycle components from China to India, Thailand, and Vietnam).

The conclusions of the respective chapters are heterogeneous and depend on the respective experiences of the firms and OFDI-flows. At least two topics are relevant in this context. First, all countries in LAC, and LAC as a region, as well as China, should begin with a detailed statistical and structured analysis of LAC's OFDI to China. As discussed earlier, LAC's OFDI in general and to China will continue to increase as a result of specific MNCs strategies, mainly incentivated by China's domestic market and their learning processes in China. So far, however, business organizations and the public sectors in the respective countries have not begun with such an analysis and discussion, despite the increasing macroeconomic relevance and for particular firms.

Second, the topic of LAC's OFDI to China should also be integrated into LAC's regional relationship with China, especially in the LAC-China Business Summit and the CELAC (Community of Latin American and Caribbean States)-China Forum. So far, the issue has not been raised or discussed explicitly neither in regional public and business bilateral institutions, nor in LAC's institutions or Chinese institutions such as MOFCOM (Ministry of Commerce), the Foreign Ministry or the State Administration of Foreign Exchange (SAFE), among others. Overall, specific cooperation in the field of OFDI, preferential treatment, specific benefits, and support for new OFDI from LAC, among other issues, could be discussed in these institutions.

The chapters are an explicit invitation by Red ALC-China for Chinese, LAC and researchers from other countries to continue with this line of investigation, both for new countries and to deepen other aspects of the already included countries and case studies.

References

Dussel Peters, Enrique. 2014. *La inversion extranjera directa de China en América Latina: 10 casos de estudio.* Red ALC-China, UDUAL and UNAM/Cechimex: México.

Dussel Peters, Enrique. 2022. "El proceso de integración de América Latina más allá del comercio: el caso de la OFDI intrarregional". In, Blanco Estévez, Adrián. *Global LATAM 2022. Series Inversión Extranjera.* Madrid: Secretaría General Iberoamericana and ICEX, pp. 57-76.

Dussel Peters, Enrique. 2023. *Monitor of Chinese OFDI in Latin America and the Caribbean 2023.* Red ALC-China: Mexico.

ECLAC (Economic Commission for Latin America and the Caribbean). 2010. "Direct investment by China in Latin America and the Caribbean". In, ECLAC. *Foreign Direct Investment in Latin America and the Caribbean 2010.* ECLAC: Santiago de Chile, pp. 99-130.

ECLAC. 2021. "China´s investment in a changing world: repercussions for the region". In, ECLAC. *Foreign Direct Investment in Latin America and the Caribbean 2010.* ECLAC: Santiago de Chile, pp. 75-122.

Gereffi, Gary, Bamber, Penny and Fernández-Stark, Karina. 2022. *China´s New Development Strategies: Upgrading from Above and from Below in Global Value Chains.* Palgrave Macmillan: Singapore.

MOFCOM (Ministry of Commerce of the People´s Republic of China). 2022/a. *Statistical Bulletin of FDI in China 2021.* MOFCOM: Beijing.

MOFCOM. 2022/b. Report on Foreign Investment in China 2022. MOFCOM: Beijing.

MOFCOM, NBS (National Bureau of Statistics) and SAFE (State Administration of Foreign Exchange). 2022. *2021 Statistical Bulletin of China´s Outward Foreign Direct Investment.* MOFCOM, NBS and SAFE: Beijing.

NBS (National Bureau of Statistics). 2022. *China Statistical Yearbook 2022.* NBS: Beijing.

Ray, Rebecca and Gallagher, Kevin P. 2017. "China-Latin America Economic Bulletin 2017 Edition". *Discussion Paper* 2017-1 (Global Economic Governance Initiative), pp. 1-11.

USTR (United States Trade Representative). 2022. *2021 report to Congress on China´s WTO Compliance.* USTR: Washington, D.C.

Wang, Xinxin, Xu, Zeshui, Qin, Yong, and Skare, Marinko. 2021. "Foreign direct investment and economic growth: a dynamic study of measurement approaches and results". *Economic Research* 35(1), pp. 1011-1034.

WB/DRC (World Bank and Development Research Center of the State Council). 2012. China 2030. *Building a Modern, Harmonious, and Creative High-Income Society.* WB: Washington, D.C.

WTO (World Trade Organization). 2021. "Trends and patterns in FDI". In, WTO. *Trade Policy Review. Report by the Secretariat. China.* WTO: Geneve, pp. 27-31.

1. ARGENTINA'S OFDI TO CHINA

Leonardo E. Stanley

Introduction

The surge of multinationals companies (or MNCs) from the south, in the early 70s, was considered an exceptional phenomenon barely documented but incipiently analysed among Latin American scholars (Ramamurti 2009). In those days, emerging MNCs were basically coming from this region, with Argentinean companies present in an active manner.

By the time catalogued as "third world multinationals", MNCs preferred to establish their business in countries exhibiting lower technological capabilities than their home countries while profiting from host countries' padlocked industrial markets (Stanley 2013). They were better adapted to developing countries as customers than traditional or developed countries MNCs, as their products were already tailored to their necessities and tastes. So, adaptation and imitation became the main technological driver for those manufacturing firms who adventured in less developed markets. Along manufacturing firms, resource-based state-owned companies were beginning its internationalization journey in the 70s, becoming a powerful and disruptive new actor.

By the early 1990s, the economic environment dramatically changed. Most Latin American countries adopted pro-market reforms and managed to stabilize their economies, pushing local groups to external competition. A series of macro and micro transformations led local firms to redefine their business strategies, to reinvent (being competitive) or to die (living the market). Therefore, (a small number of) local groups consolidated, as industrial production reconverted towards low tech specialized sectors, mostly related, or based on natural resource exploitation. This new wave would also permit the internationalization of traditional service sector groups, including retail and finance firms.

This new context, signed by trade liberalization and global markets, made the former argument on companies' international expansion obsolete due to technology distance (Santiso 2008). Those going abroad were now forced to play globally, even if the decision implied adventuring in a neighbour country. A series of institutional changes at home and abroad with the irruption of digital technologies would allow them to innovate and compete on a global level.

In the advent of a new century, a favourable international context led by high prices for its main export commodities and sound macroeconomic policies permitted Latin American companies to flourish and become globally competitive. *Multilatinas* were becoming highly competitive, since they were at the technological frontier profiting from large pools of human capital and management skills. In some industrial segments, such as steel and cement, leading companies are coming from the Global South (India, Brazil, Mexico). Another huge transformation favouring *Multilatinas* relates to their accession to global capital markets. As the cost of capital is reduced, companies become more competitive.

In Argentina a stable and competitive exchange rate (SCER) regime induced a short-lived period of positive rates of growth; employment grew very fast whereas a competitive wage led to many tradable services, manufacturers and agricultural activities to boom and non-traditional exports to expand (Damill *et al.* 2015). Unfortunately, this sound macroeconomic programme would be severely affected in 2008 after the irruption of the global financial crisis, increasingly constrained by the lack of foreign exchange, which would thereafter be definitively disrupted by 2011.

However, despite macroeconomic mismanagement and a recurrent financial crisis, a group of traditional medium and small enterprises (SMEs) were deciding to go global. For much of them, the "new game" implies being part of the technological frontier. Playing in market niches, Argentinean unicorns[1] are becoming global players from the very start in many other latitudes. It also implies international funding, since firms rely on cheap and sound financing sources from global capital markets to internationalise.

Among this segment of start-ups with global funding, a group of them decided to go east, some establishing in China. Other investors have joined them, including firms belonging to traditional industrial sectors, but also a couple from the financial and law services sectors. In analysing MNCs decision to enter a foreign market, knowledge and experience with the local market becomes crucial. Likewise, institutional and cultural factors are also key elements in dealing with such a strategic decision.

A final caveat. Although the phenomenon of service firms internationalizing has been going on for centuries, not years (Jones 2005), the study of productive operations abroad (i.e. factory building) would become the focus of MNEs scholars. Historically portrayed as an economic activity of lesser importance, services-related industries are currently considered essential for development, certainly beneficial in terms of job creation.[2] Therefore, when observing firms that went global in the twenty-first century, those coming from the service sector constitute an important portion (Golub 2009; Capello and Fratesi 2013).

1 The "unicorns" are firms based on an intensive use of technology, which in a relatively short period (7 years on average) reach a price over 1 billion dollars in capital markets.

2 Although until a few decades ago services were considered a characteristic non-tradable sector, several technological and institutional changes permitted the service industry to transform and to go global. Nowadays services constitute the most important share of the global GDP, up to 64.4 % in 2021, according to figures at the World Bank Database (https://data.worldbank.org/indicator/NV.SRV.TOTL.ZS).

1. Literature Review

John Dunning's (1993) 'eclectic paradigm' (OLI theory[3]), explores the underlying rationale for firms to become MNE in an integrated way. OLI advantages, however, describe traditional industrial firms' movements. The digital era is not conducive to observing the emergence of this new type of firm (Menz *et al.* 2021), leading Luo (2021) to introduce a slight change in Dunning's paradigm: open resource advantage (O), linkage advantage (L), and integration advantage (I).

A different perspective to internationalization comes from those adscripted to the International Business (IB) school (Buckley and Carsson 1976; Rugman and Verbeke 1992, 2001, 2008). According to IB scholars, firms go global because either they have some specific advantages (FSAs) or (host) country specific advantages (CSAs) are strong[4]. Advantages, according to the former, arise on firms' ability to organize bundles of activities internally and preventing others from profiting from it. For the latter, advantages basically associate with (mostly, host country) location as in traditional international economic literature. Rugman and Verbeke (1991) further distinguish between non-location-bound firm-specific advantages (NLB FSAs) and location-bound firm specific advantages (LB FSAs).[5]

3 The availability of ownership, locational, or internalization (OLI) advantages encourage firms to become multinational. The first relates, among others, to the presence of brand name, trademark, and superior production mechanism. The second one is explained by the presence of cheap labour, or adequate resources of raw material in the targeted country. The final advantage, internationalization, refers to the benefits that a firm may adopt the market more efficiently and maintain more control in overall strategies rather than entering the market through other firms or through exporting their products to secure the market.

4 CSAs are reflecting Dunning's locational advantage (L), whereas FSAs involves the other two factors (O and I).

5 The former relates to intermediate products, such as product, process or client-specific information and knowledge, brands, marketing, or credit analysis knowledge that can be transferred across borders easily and at low cost (available on the entire network). Advantages in the later are only available to certain affiliates, whether at the host or home country.

Will firms decide to follow a quick or gradual internationalization pattern? For those ascribed to the Upsala model, firms' internationalization journey starts regionally. An alternative explanation comes from an older McKinsey article, in which M. W. Rennie (1993) described the irruption of the "born-global" firm: rather than internationalizing gradually, some firms are born to compete globally from the very start. As borderless businesses gain relevance, firms have greater pressure to go global in order to maintain their competitiveness (Lee *et al.* 2019; Efrat *et al.* 2016; Hennart *et al.* 2021). The pattern is often chosen by techs in the small and medium enterprises (SME) group (Knight and Kim 2008).

A group of Latin American SMEs in technology and knowledge-intensive industries tend to internationalize early and rapidly too, profiting from shrinking physical and cultural distances to install their niche strategy. CEOs and managers of born-global firms engage in building relational trust and social networking, if they want to compete aggressively, they must take risks and innovate, including organizational innovation, in which the development of marketing capabilities is vital.

As born-global firms' competitive advantages associate with intangible assets, which are valuable, rare, inimitable and non-substitutable, entrepreneurs are forced to develop the right set of resources and capabilities that allow them to increase their chance to succeed rapidly in the international market (Lee *et al.* 2019). According to Knight and Cavusgil (2004), innovation capability in offering new product and developing new markets is essential for the success of born-global firms. Advantages might also arise in the production process or knowledge and technological capabilities, permitting firms to internationalize rapidly.

The acceleration theory introduced by Gammeltoft and Cuervo-Cazurra (2021) brings a different perspective. Some firms decide to internationalize in order to acquire competitive advantage (*catch-up accelerator*), particularly those aiming to climb the technological ladder. Others are going global because they are benefited by subsidies and financially assisted by public banks, a helpful policy largely disseminated (but often hidden) among developed countries and emerging economies (*government accelerator*). Another explanation goes that firms go abroad as suppliers to learn the nuances of foreign markets and internationalization *(global value chain accelerator*).

The global value chain literature explains how the revolution in transportation and communication technologies enable retailers (particularly from the US) to establish international production and trade networks, and China to become the world's factory. Retailers might be producing abroad (i.e.: China) but selling their products in the local or regional market, therefore, to be regarded as regional-based MNEs with a global strategy (Rugman and Girod, 2003).

If digital technologies have led to drastic changes in firms, competition, industries and markets (Menz *et al.* 2021), the digital era has also brought back geopolitical nationalism, or (neo) techno-nationalism as suggested by some authors (Shim and Shin 2016; Branstetter 2018; Petricevic and Teece 2019; Luo 2022),[6] with governments around the world often preventing the free movement of flows of data, information and knowledge if coming from competitor nations. Henceforth, some firm's entry would be blocked, whereas the arrival of others would be stimulating as happens with those high-tech Latin American companies going global, aiming to enter the Chinese market.

Beyond commercial disputes, it is true that the present situation is highly complex, it is a moment in which different types of shocks interact, as characterized by a series of conditions, namely: volatility, (deep or radical) uncertainty, complexity, and ambiguity (Shoemaker *et al.* 2018; Petricevic and Teece 2019; Buckley 2020). Dynamic capabilities (DC) are strongly needed, especially for those firms operating in sectors of rapid technological change, and particularly acute for those operating in "any of the strategic

6 Under a techno-nationalism regime states protect the development of their technological capacities. A different case arises under (neo) techno-nationalism, as national economic and security interests is pursued by leveraging the opportunities presented through globalization to gain national advantages.

sectors where China is pursuing breakthroughs", distinctly for those whose ambition is to enter the Chinese market, because "without adequate focus on the DCs related to knowledge buffering as outlined above, there might bring short-term gains, but a long-term weakening of capabilities" (Petricevic and Teece 2019:1503).

A final point relates to cultural and institutional features, similarities and differences that could either enhance or prevent MNCs to invest abroad (Lucke and Eichler 2016; Kirman *et al.* 2017; Beugelsdijk *et al.* 2018; Aguilera and Grøgaard 2019, Kostova *et al.* 2020). Scholars in the IB tradition approached the issue through the concept of distance, portraying the first as differences in values and means of communication. From this perspective, large cultural differences might block the establishment of Argentinean firms: the cost of adapting and integrating into China's business environment and culture is extremely high. Cultural similarities, by contrast, would facilitate entry in mainland China for firms from Taiwan or Hong Kong.

Higher costs of distance are also crucial, like those exemplified by transportation and coordination over time zones. It also involves firms' specific costs as exemplified by the lack of home country diaspora in the host country, the irruption of economic nationalism or by the cost of the home country environment (with restrictions imposed by the host country). All of them are referred to as liabilities of foreigners (LOF), a cultural difference that restrain investors from entering. But MNCs could also have advantages (AOF), often observed among product–differentiated firms.

According to IB scholars, when evaluating companies' strategic decisions, institutions occupy a central role: institutions matter for cross–border investments (Jackson and Deeg 2008; Hoskisson *et al.* 2000; Dunning and Lundan 2008; Peng *et al.* 2008; Cantwell *et al.* 2010). Regarding institutional distance, the concept reflects differences in home and host countries' regulations and norms, formal and informal institutions which adversely affect MNCs entry mode choices. One way to overcome all these disadvantages is to enter via a joint-venture contract with local partners, enabling MNCs to access a diverse, valued, and unique set of practices.

Sometimes it is the host government which impose this venture, because of the technological leapfrogging and advance in the value chain, as has been observed in China.

Despite all variations, like other *Multilatinas*, Argentinean companies were also shaped by the context in which they emerged (Aguilera *et al.* 2018; Cuervo Cazurra 2019). Even if this influence was gradually lost, the education system and knowledge networks remained and influence firms' performance and growth. Henceforth, by the new millennium a group of firms from new industrial service sectors (biotechnology, software, IT) emerged in several Latin American countries, including Argentina.

When analysing the internationalization of emerging MNCs, access to cheap sources of funding becomes key (Claessens and Smuckler 2007; Santiso 2008), although alternatives for cheap financing are widely observed (Ramamurti 2011). Henceforth, cheap financing becomes a sort of necessary but insufficient condition to go global (a firm's own capabilities and competitiveness remains vital). For *Multilatinas*, however, the opportunity to quote in developed stock markets become crucial for obtaining competitive funding. They might also benefit from debt and other corporate financial instruments emitted abroad. Entrance in global financial markets also led to institutional changes, which companies should adopt in their corporate governance rules (Doidge *et al.* 2001). Financial accession (as host country tax benefits incentives) might then explain why some emerging MNCs have abandoned their local address to legally settle their headquarters abroad.

In recent years, China has emerged as one of the world's largest FDI recipient countries. For multiple reasons, the Chinese market represents a golden opportunity for foreign companies deciding to invest abroad. Contrary to previous experiences of development, as observed in Japan, South Korea or Taiwan, MNCs have played a crucial role in China's recent development. The scale of foreign capital utilized has gradually expanded, and the foreign capital became an important force in driving industrial upgrading, increasing taxes and promoting employment (Ministry of Commerce 2022). Relevance does not mean control over the process, as the Chinese government set out the rules and profited from foreigners' experience in upgrading the economy. Consequently, China has become an industrial powerhouse and a technological disrupter, as well as a leader in IT technology.

However, the model of increasing economic interdependence between the West and the emerging world (especially China) was built on assumptions that no longer hold (Garcia–Herrero 2022). A new order is emerging, radical uncertainty keeps rising, and complexity dominates future scenarios. The reasons are varied, ranging from increasing geopolitical tensions to environmental risks. MNCs' longterm decisions are under tension. Many Western companies are seeking to reduce their presence in China, as Chinese firms technological leapfrogging is being contested by governments in the West. Both blocks have decided to block merger and acquisitions operations if perceived as affecting strategic sectors. National foreign investment policies, once friendly and open to foreigners, are being re-oriented towards security issues and sectoral prohibitions. In a fast-fragmenting world, a new locational concept is irrupting in academic circles: *friendshoring*.

The next section considers a group of Argentinean firms who ventured to invest in this remote (geographical) and distant market (cultural and institutional).

2. Argentina's OFDI to China

When analysing emerging MNCs trajectory, companies from Argentina are considered first movers. The literature often mentions the case of Alpargatas, a leading textile and footwear manufacturer, whose investments in Uruguay and Brazil during the 1890s would become the first of a Latin American company adventuring abroad. At the beginning of the twentieth century a new group of Argentinean firms would imitate the experience, including the cases of Bunge y Born (trader services) and Siam (metal-mechanic -manufacturing).

A new wave of MNCs emerged under the process of industrialization by import substitution (ISI process), with most investments to be settled in neighbouring countries, particularly Brazil. At that time, local firms' ownership advantages relied in their ability to adapt imported technology, their better knowledge of host countries' cultures and institutions. As reported by UNCTAD (1993), by the early 1980s Argentinean MNCs occupied a central stage, with the country classified as the second largest outward investor among developed economies. By the end of the decade, however, this wave of internationalisation was losing steam. A decade later, inward-looking policies were definitely abandoned because Carlos Menem's administration decided to accelerate the transition towards a more open and competitive economic environment. The new situation forced local firms either to change and become competitive (to buy) or to leave the market (to be bought) (Kosacoff 1999; Chudnosky and López 2000).

However, this new wave became different in nature. Following a process of restructuring and modernisation, a new wave of multinational companies emerged in the region, including both newcomers and traditional firms. As a result of the creation of MERCOSUR, a regional integration area originally involving Argentina, Brazil, Paraguay and Uruguay, the bulk of Argentina's outward investment flows were directed towards Brazil, the largest market in the region. Nonetheless, new markets were now explored by local companies in South America (Chile, Venezuela, Peru) and elsewhere (US, Indonesia, Malaysia). Although most of the outward funds would concentrate in three firms (Pérez Companc, YPF and Techint), internationalization has also involved an important number of companies as exemplified by ARCOR and Bago.[7]

The arrival of the new century coincided with the largest economic and financial crisis the country experimented for decades,

7 Firms were basically related to the steel, oil, and food industries, although they were also coming from pharmaceutical, petrochemical, information services, banking, telecommunications, construction, and materials. For most of them, limited market size was a crucial factor in explaining the [internationalization] process.

leaving behind several firms, including some historical ones. Henceforth, after the collapse of the convertibility plan the national economy started to recover Argentinean MNCs' relative importance: once again, CEOs were in defence mood.

Ten years later, Argentinean OFDI flows still represent a minor share from Latin America total figures, conceding to Chile and Colombia its former regional home country relevance. Globally, whereas a reduced number of Brazilian and Mexican firms classifies among the group of emerging FORTUNE Global 500, Argentina has no presence (Casanova and Miroux 2021). When considering emerging MNCs with revenues larger than $1 billion (in July 2020), Latin American counts 204 (out of 2339 firms): Brazil 98, Mexico 46, Chile 33, Argentina 14 and Colombia 13. Once again, the Argentine case might be extreme but reflects the regional retraction vis-a-vis the rise of Asian MNCs, particularly, China.

Argentina's attraction as capital importer has also diminished, as investors become less confident in the country long-term perspectives.

Table 1

Argentina and Latin America FDI Flows (2010 - 2021) ($ millions)

	Outflows			Inflows		
	Argentina	Latin America	Share (percentage)	Argentina	Latin America	Share (percentage)
2010	965	46,276	2.09	11,333	171,528	6.61
2011	1,488	44,686	3.33	10,840	209,953	5.16
2012	1,055	49,944	2.11	15,324	214644	7.14
2013	890	51,766	1.72	9,822	206,704	4.75
2014	1,921	50,925	3.77	5,085	190,969	2.66
2015	875	38,926	2.25	11,759	172,797	6.81
2016	1,787	38,944	4.59	3,260	168,429	1.94
2017	1,156	34,862	3.32	11,517	161,521	7.13
2018	1,726	25,771	6.70	11,717	175,632	6.67
2019	1,539	45,754	3.36	6,649	157,689	4.22
2020	1,294	10,705	12.09	4,723	101,486	4.65
2021	1,363	43,046	3.17	6,782	142,794	4.75

Source: Own elaboration based on ECLAC (2023).

With the national economy submerged in a perpetual crisis, surviving firms are certainly in a bad place to go global and compete. However, alongside the new century, new firms emerged in the (highly competitive) service sector (IT, software, financial services),[8] with most of them becoming global from the very start (Artopoulos 2018).[9] An important number of agri-business firms were also emerging and going global, less dependent on natural resources like land, now relying on human capital, organizational capabilities, and frontier technology to gain competitiveness.

A sub-group of traditional and new firms decided to adventure into Asia, few of them went to China.

2.1 Argentinean firms in China

The story of the economic relationship between Latin America and the Caribbean and China is well-known, as it is also the case with Argentina. Whereas most of the research continue to focus on bilateral trade, a group of academics recently decided to focus on Chinese infrastructure contracts arrangements, as well as investments and financial inflows arriving to the region from China (Dussel Peters *et al.* 2018, 2019a/b). A more reduced group of papers came to analyse Latin America's foreign direct investments in Asia, with particular focus on China (Goldstein and Toulan 2007; Dussel Peters 2012; Estevadeordal and Kahn 2012; López *et al.* 2012; Papini and Morinigo 2020).

However, despite recurrent financial crises, macroeconomic instability, and institutional weakness, Argentina maintains a pool of human capital, one of the highest levels of literacy among all Latin

8 As exemplified by companies like Mercado Libre, Grupo ASSA, OLX and Globant. The software development services have experienced outstanding growth since the mid 2000s, after the pass of the Software Industry Promoting Act (*Ley de promoción de la industria del software*) signed in 2004.

9 For firms like ASSA, the end of the convertibility represented a golden opportunity: to sell their services abroad. By exporting their services, the firms dollarized their earnings while most of their salaries were paid in pesos. Globant, on the other hand, would become global from the very start.

American countries, along with a system of public universities and a national system of innovation and competence building. Henceforth, pockets of innovative SMEs and promising frontier sectors had emerged in recent years. As previously mentioned, a solid technical background backed the export strategy of several firms in the service sector. Other die-hard corporations, as was the case of large industrial firms with historical global presence (as exemplified by the Techint group). Born trader firms represent a special niche, which might eventually transform into manufacturing. As a result of changes in global consumer demand patterns, and profiting from technological changes and new sourcing practices, the attractiveness of production centers located in other parts of the world away from China have increased in the past, benefiting traditional manufacturing sectors (e.g., textiles), like for traders and retailers[10].

Table 2. Argentina: OFDI to China

	Investing Project	Destination	Sector	Cluster	Capital invested ($ US million)	Created jobs
2016	Alfaro Abogados	Beijing	Business services	Professional Services	$ 19,30	71
2011	Banco de la Nacion Argentina	Beijing	Financial services	Financial Services	$ 58,60	72
2012	Entaste	Hong Kong	Software & IT services	Agribusiness	$ 5,80	77
2008	Paez (Parathon SA)	Not Specified	Textiles	Wood, Apparel & Related Products	$ 50,80	324
2019	Pampa Corporation	Not Specified	Food & Beverages	Agribusiness	$ 1,13	2
2018	Satellogic	Beijing	Communications	ICT & Electronics	$ 8,30	16
2013	Trapiche	Shanghai	Food & Beverages	Agribusiness	$ 19,00	7
2006	Zecat	Beijing	Consumer products	Consumer Goods	$ 10,30	31

Source: FDI Intelligence Unit.

10 The reference here might fit for companies like Paez or Zecat, but no further information is available.

On top of the list are two service sector firms, one of them in the professional services cluster, the other belonging to the financial sector. In any process of internationalization, service sectors are key: bankers, insurers, or transportation entrepreneurs are enablers of global capitalism (Jones 2005). According to the FDI Intelligence list, financial services continue to play such a role: 37 out of 188 Latin American firms in China belongs to this cluster. Add professional services to the list, often a proxy for boutique finance activities, and the participation climbs to almost 30 per cent of the total.

Banco de la Nación Argentina (BNA), a state-owned bank (SOBs) founded in 1891, is one of the oldest and largest financial institutions of Argentina. BNA conducts its international activity, both commercial and financial, through a (reduced) network of operational branches (Bolivia, Brazil, Spain, USA, Paraguay, and Uruguay). The establishment of a BNA representation office in Beijing brings their financial services to Argentinean firms operating with China.

The BNA case certainly relates to the traditional motive for internationalization: following their customers abroad because its own comparative advantage (FSAs) comes from client-and location specificities. Profiting from Rugman and Verbeke (1992, 2001), it would be argued that the absence of NLB FSAs prevents BNA internationalization, so a representative office in Beijing is convenient to strengthen their LB FSAs located in their domestic market and, eventually, transforming in NLB FSAs (Boehe 2015).

Establishing a foreign presence, in the case of Alfaro Abogados, implies that critical information and knowledge transferred between foreign and domestic locations remain exclusive to the firm and are less likely to disseminate to competitors (Rugman 1981 quoted in Boehe 2015). This law firm is best known for its corporate and finance services, with strong practice in mining, oil, gas (SINOPEC), infrastructure (Gezhouba, Sinohydro-Power China) and pharma. It provides services in a variety of fields, all closely related to MNEs internationalization activities (cross-border transactions, merger and acquisitions, corporate reorganization affecting subsidiaries in other countries, tax planning, and establishing strategic alliances). Two decades ago, AA became the first Argentinean law firm to open in New York, opening the China desk at Beijing in 2016 to expand its representation of Chinese companies in Argentina, particularly those involved in large infrastructure projects. In contrast to the previous case, internationalization allows the law firm to generate NLB FSAs and to differentiate themselves from competitors that solely practice market-based exchange, e.g., by transacting with corresponding foreign partners.

If the picture looks complex for all, it becomes more complicated for SMEs with global intentions, particularly for those operating in the tech-intensive sector. Paradoxically, this group is active and has an operational presence in China as exemplified with the successful case of Satellogic. Founded in 2010 by Emiliano Kargieman, this nanosatellite, earth observation company launched its first spacecraft in 2013, with ambitions to have 300 satellites during the present decade in order to become a worldwide leader in satellite constellations industrial sector (Kulu 2021). Satellogic is a front-runner in the sub-meter resolution Earth Observation ("EO") data collection, offering high-resolution imaging in a micro-satellite platform, with the ability to capture photo data of the Earth at 1-meter resolution and is (almost instantly) delivered to their customers.[11] (Kolovos 2018)

The company belongs to the third generation of satellites,[12] placing their nanosatellites, "a desktop computer hard drive", in low orbits above the surface of the earth. Satellogic obtained $ 123 million from different investors, including $ 27 million funding from Tencent, China in 2018, lists at NASDAQ (NASDAQ: SATL). In 2016, Satellogic started to launch several of its micro-satellites

11 After all satellites are on orbit, Satellogic expect to bring to customers 1 meter resolution imagines in 5 minutes.

12 In contrast to previous satellites only providing imagery, the third-generation ones also offer imagery, and in a high resolution capable of distinguishing the size and shape of a specific object, a key element in intelligence derived from space.

into orbit aboard China's Long March-4B rockets from Jiuquan and Taiyuan Satellite Launch Centres.

A commercial agreement signed in 2019 with ABDAS, a Chinese firm specialized in data science. Per the agreement, which exceeds $ 38 million, Satellogic promises to deliver dedicated satellite constellation for exclusive geospatial analytics in Henan Province, China. The agreement offers access to geospatial analysis and information that contributes to strategic interests but avoiding technical or operational risk for the Argentinean part. According to Emiliano Kargieman, this facility is "a turnkey infrastructure for the collection and analysis of data obtained from Earth observation, with the capacity to strengthen and support key political decisions in the province".

2.2 Tenaris' Investments in China

Techint, a worldwide leading firm founded in 1945 by Agostino Rocca in Italy, had its operation facilities transferred to Argentina the following year and became the leading seamless tubes provider for the State-owned oil company Yacimientos Petrolíferos Fiscales (YPF). This metal firm went international in the 1960s and now has engineering offices in Argentina, Brazil, Mexico, Spain, Italy, Egypt, and India, offering integrated solutions for engineering, construction, procurement, and project management around the world for the oil & gas, energy, mining, downstream and petrochemical segments as well as industry and infrastructure civil works. Techint operates as a global group, including six different firms (Tenaris, Termiun, Techint Engineering and Construction, Tenova, Tecpetrol, and Humanitas), which employ more than 55,000 people from 93 nationalities. The group's global annual net sales totalized $ 27.1 billion for 2021. In over 75 years of activity, the company has successfully completed more than 3,300 projects in more than 45 countries and continues to work on major industrial and infrastructure projects around the world (Techint 2021).

Dalmine-Siderca (later renamed Tenaris), a related Techint company, would be among the earliest *multilatinas* adventuring in China selling seamless tubes during the 1980s (López *et al.* 2012). Ten years later, the company established a sales office in Beijing.

Founded in 2001, Tenaris brand is a subsidiary company of the Techint group.[13] The firm is a leading global manufacturer and supplier of tubular products and services used in the oil and gas industry and a leading supplier for power plants and other specialized industrial and automotive applications. Tenaris is a public company (legally) incorporated in Luxembourg, listed on the México and Milan stock exchanges and American Depositary Securities at the New York Stock Exchange. The company conforms an industrial system integrating steelmaking, pipe rolling and forming, heat treatment, threading and finishing across 16 countries, with a global network of R&D laboratories and product testing facilities on four continents and service and distribution centres in over 25 countries and employs more than 23,000 persons[14].

Tenaris supplies a full range of seamless and welded, high quality casing and tubing as well as premium connections, OCTG accessories, drill pipe, sucker roads and coiled tubing for use in all types of oil and gas drilling and well completion activities (Techint 2019). Tenaris customers are all around the world, distributed in North America (47 %), the Middle East and Africa region (20 %), South America (19 %), Europe (9 %) and Asia Pacific (4 %) (Tenaris 2019). Their customers include most of the world's leading oil and gas companies, as well as engineering companies engaged in constructing oil and gas gathering, transportation and processing facilities.

13 Techint ranks among the oldest investors, exporting since 1976. In 1990 it opened its first manufacture facility at Beijing in 1990. Neither Techint nor Tenaris are included in the above list.

14 See: https://www.tenaris.com/en/contact/tenaris-around-the-world

Since its foundation,[15] Tenaris has created value by following a process of acquisitions and partnerships, a strategy used to expand their operations all around the world (Battisti *et al.* 2020). The M&A wave started in 2004 with the acquisition of Silcotub, a Romanian producer of seamless steel products. The acquisition of the US tube maker Maverick Tube Corporation in 2006 permitted the company founded by Paolo Rocca to capture 20% of the North American (US and Canada) OCTG market and take a leading position for tubular products in the global oil and gas industry (de Paula 2006)[16]. The acquisition valued at $3.18 billion, the largest ever carried out by a Latin American steel company, allowed Tenaris to expand operations in the U.S., Canada, and Colombia. A year later it acquired the US Hydril company ($2.16 billion), a leading manufacturer of premium connections and pressure control products, which permitted Tenaris to expand their presence in the US with its offer to the oil and gas industry. In 2018 the company announced the acquisition of 47,79% of Saudi Steel Pipe (SSP) ($141 billion), which expanded Tenaris' offers to major oil companies in the region (including Saudi Aramco), one of the largest markets for oil pipes. SSPs operate three productions and have a manufacturing capacity of 360,000 tons per year, its facilities are in the Eastern Province of the Kingdom of Saudi Arabia. Finally, during 2019 Tenaris announced the signature of a joint-venture agreement with the Russian company Pao Severstal, to build a welded pipe plant and produce OCTG products in the Surgut area, West Siberia, Russian Federation (Bloomberg 2019). Tenaris will hold a 49% stake in the new company; it invested

15 The strategy precedes Tenaris, being introduced by Techint with the purpose of acquiring leading national producers of seamless steel pipe products. This M&A wave started at June 1993 by the acquisition of Mexican TAMSA (Tubos de Acero de México S.A.). In February 1996, it acquired the Italian Dalmine S.p.A. company, and two years later Techint purchased TAVSA (Tubos de Acero de Venezuela S.A.), the sole Venezuelan producer of seamless steel pipe products. In 1999 it went for the Brazilian CONFAB Industrial S.A. Two more operations in the year 2000: the Japanese producer NKKTubes in August, and Canadian Algoma Tubes Inc., in October.

16 The acquisition expanded to 3.3Mt/y of seamless tubes and 27 Mt/y of welded pipes.

$240 million in the construction of a new plant for the growing market for welded OCTG pipe products.

Tenaris' operations have also expanded by means of green investments. The entry of new manufacturing capacities started in 2011, with the inauguration of a new rolling mill in Veracruz, Mexico. Two years later, Tenaris starts the construction of a seamless facility in Bay City, Texas, commencing operations in 2017. The $1.8 billion investment in a state-of-the-art seamless pipe mill generated more than 600 jobs, incorporated the latest technology to become the company's most environmentally efficient mills (Tenaris 2019/b). The global seamless steel pipeline industry is expected to maintain its ascent trend, keeping a compound annual growth rate (CAGR) of 6.1% until 2028 (Bloomberg 2022). Seamless steel is used by several industries, among others: chemicals, construction, automotive, oil and gas, process industry and aviation. The rise in demand is explained by the growth of the population and rapid urbanization, both phenomena with an epicenter in the Global South. Rapid industrialization (mainly in the South and Southeast of Asia) and government initiatives to boost manufacturing activities (elsewhere) are significant drivers, enlarging the seamless pipe market.

One of the main drivers of Tenaris' investment in China relates to the company's goal of being a world leader in the seamless tube market (López *et al.* 2012),[17] a market in which it competes with many international players. A first group of local companies, including Shanghai Shenhua Steel Tube Co., LTD., Tianjin Pipe (Group) Corporation, TPCO Enterprise, and Shandong Zehong Steel Co. A second group of international players with presence in China are JFE Holdings Inc. (China: Fujian Sino-Japan Metal) and NIPPON Steel Corporation, both from Japan; UMW Holding Berhad from Malaysia; Vallourec from France; Sandvik AB from Sweden; and ArcelorMittal from India. A final group of global players with no presence in China, among others: Jindal SAW Ltd.,

17 Seamless pipes are the pipes that are manufactured using no welding joints or seams, offering greater physical strength and corrosion resistance even under extreme conditions of temperature, pressure and chemical reactions.

and Shalco Industries Pvt. Ltd., both from India; OAO TMK from Russia; Seeberger GmbH & Co. KG from Germany; Tubos Reunidos, SA; and Zaffertec, both from Spain, United States Steel Corporation and Zekelman Industries, both from the U.S.

China would rapidly become the main market in the region (López *et al.* 2012). By the turn of the century, Tenaris invested $ 35 million in a new manufacturing facility in the city of Qingdao in Shandong. Entering operations in 2006, the threading and connection plant allowed the group to strengthen its position in the premium tubes market in the face of growing competition from the high-end market. The election of Qingdao final location was sorted out after a detailed comparison of potential locations were offered by the host country and after a competitive race in terms of tax exemptions involving regional governments (López *et al.* 2012).

A new facility was planned to open by the beginning of this decade, now in joint venture with Mongolia Inner Baotou Steel Union Co. Ltd entering with 40 % of the shares (with Tenaris holding the remaining 60 %). Located in the city of Bautou at the northeast of China (Inner Mongolia), Tenaris Baogang Bautou steel pipe premium facility will be able to produce 220,000 oil and gas drills weighing 70,000 metric tons using high-performance special tubing and casing products, with an annual output value of about 200 million yuan ($ 31.02 million) and a domestic market share of about 10 %. To advance with decarbonization process, Tenaris Baogang aims to advance with the purchase of more eco-friendly technology to adopt hydrogen-based technologies for the steelmaking process.

All the latest investments signal the firm's intention of becoming a major supplier for the Chinese automotive industry. In this direction, during 2016 the company inaugurated a new automotive component centre at Qingdao, a US$ 13 million investment project including machineries of high technological level and an installed capacity of 15 million pieces per year.[18] On March 16, 2023,

18 "Tenaris celebrates the 10th anniversary of its threading facility in Qingdao" by David Bisley - Oilfield Technology.

the automotive division opened an additional production line, a $11 million investment dedicated to airbag inflator components.

Tenaris has a service center in Yulin, Guangxi, which provides Rig Direct® services19 to the oil and gas industry. As main supplier of Shell in its onshore Changbei II Phase I tight gas project (Yulin – Guangxi), Tenaris signed an agreement for the supply of OCTG (Oil Country Tubular Goods)20 products via the Rig Direct® model.

2.3. Argentinean Pharma Groups in China: the Case of Biogenesis Bagó – Grupo Insud

Pharmaceutical industry's competitive advantages are directly related to the industrialisation by import substitution era, where protectionist policies allowed Argentinean firms to accumulate knowledge, to generate their own productive and managerial capabilities (Campins 2015; Campins and Pfeiffer 2017). Starting in the 1970s, an innovation cycle emerged for the industry as the rise of molecular biology indicated the beginning of a new era, leading to the irruption of the biopharmaceutical industrial complex (Niosi *et al.* 2012).[21] The biotechnological complex is science–intensive, an activity based on knowledge and subject to a great speed of technological change, high levels of uncertainty and long maturation. The global market, henceforth, shows a high level of concentration with a reduced number of innovative firms. Although competitive forces are crucial, cooperation efforts

19 An innovative partnership mode of business offered by Tenaris to the oil and gas customers for their drilling projects. More information at: https://www.tenaris.com/en/products-and-services/rig-direct.

20 OCTG an acronym used by the oil and gas industry describes tubular goods used in onshore and offshore operations.

21 Biotechnology involves a large set of technologies, including monoclonal antibodies, genetic engineering, gene therapy, stem cell, and tissue engineering. These technologies have a myriad of applications including human and animal diagnostics and therapeutics, the development of genetically modified bacteria, plants and animals, the separation of metals in the mining industry, model animals for research and many others (Niosi *et al.* 2012).

are also vital, leading to collaborative agreements that will spread risks and take advantage of synergies of knowledge.[22] The global market is led by firms coming from the US, Spain, Germany and South Korea (Stubrin 2022). Biotechnological activity, however, is being deployed in other latitudes as in Argentina (the first firm, Biosidus, was established in 1983).

During the initial years, activity in Argentina associated with non-biotechnological firms from related knowledge areas (biology, chemistry, or agronomy) included Bagó. The industry expansion would then be associated with biotechnological firms, which were gaining ground in the productive network in different application areas (human health, animal health, agriculture, processing industrial). More recently, start-ups and go global firms are explaining the accelerated growth evidenced by the industry as large biotechnological firms (as INSUD) consolidated the harnessing of systemic synergies between company groups.

Here we analyse the experience of Biosidus-Bagó, an Argentinean medium-sized company specialized in the development of vaccines, especially for foot-and-mouth recombinant disease vaccine. Biosidus - Bagó was founded in 2006, when the pharmaceutical group Bagó joined with the leader company in animal health, Biogenesis, to produce vaccines and biotechnological medicines (Campins 2015), with its main manufacturing facilities in the Garin - Buenos Aires Province, alongside modern manufacturing facilities in five other countries. It has become the most important company in Latin America in biotechnological products and veterinary services, its foot and moot vaccine registered in all the countries of the region, with 3 out of 10 bovines receiving the company shots.

Biogenesis Bagó produces more than 90 different products, manufactures more than 450 million doses per year, and it has also certified more than 600 different products of animal health (https://cc.biogenesisbago.com/en/biorabies/). The company is a

22 Cooperation agreements might involve market (other firms, venture capitalists) as well as non-market actors (universities, research centres).

leading exporter of vaccines for bovines, and its products reach more than 40 countries in America, Asia, Europe, the Middle East, and North Africa. Biogenesis Bagó's leading role allowed it to develop a large-scale globalization strategy.

Animal vaccines control the transmission of diseases, thus providing protection for animals and humans. The global animal vaccines market size was valued at $ 12,2 billion in 2022 and was expected to grow by a 9.40 % CAGR by 2030, following the increase in pet ownership (developed countries) and the rise in number of cattle and poultry (developing countries). Rising concerns about the emergence of different animal diseases and the prevalence of zoonotic diseases that can negatively impact human lives push the surge in investments for R&D vaccines. Companies in the veterinary vaccine market are increasingly looking for strategic partnerships and collaborations to enter new geographies and to share research and development projects.

The market is segmented by application (companion animal and livestock vaccines), vaccine type (live attenuated vaccines, inactivated vaccines, toxoid vaccines, recombinant vaccines, other vaccine types), disease type (anaplasmosis, canine parvovirus, foot, and mouth disease, Newcastle disease, distemper disease, influenza, porcine reproductive and respiratory syndrome - PRRS). A reduced group of global players dominates the market, including American companies (Zoetis Inc.; Merck & Co., Eli Lilly and Co.; Flanco Animal Health), Boehringer Ingelheim International – GmbH, from Germany; and the French Virbac. Leading companies' geographical expansion strategies is associates with the launching of new products, merger and acquisitions, and collaborations with local partners. Geographically, North America still represents the largest market, followed by Asia-Pacific.

In China, animal vaccines are mainly for hogs, poultry, cattle, and sheep. The livestock vaccine market experienced a CAGR of 8 % between 2013 and 2017, but it was depressed by the outbreak of African Swine Fever (ASF) in 2018 with the market size edging down 2.5 % on an annualized basis. The industry is currently dominated by local firms, like Jinyu Bio-technology, China Animal

Husbandry Industry Co., Ltd. (CAHIC), Qingdao Yebio Biological Engineering Co., Ltd. (Yebio), Tecon Biology, Keqian Biology, Ringpu Bio-technology and Pulike Biological Engineering. Global firms, like MSD and Boehringer Ingelheim, among others, have presence due to joint-ventures, acquisitions, and greenfield investments.

China is one of the largest markets for Argentinean biotechnology firms.[23] Despite having half of the world's pig population (700 million) and twice the bovine stock of Argentina (110 million), Chinese authorities are still battling with foot-and-mouth disease —a situation that certainly induced the Argentinean group to capitalise. To supply the Chinese market, however, producers need to invest and produce locally. This lead Biogenesis Bagó to open in May 2017 a manufacturing plant in the city of Yangling, Shaanxi Province, to produce the vaccine against foot and mouth disease (FMD)[24].

The Jinhai Biotechnology Manufacturing Plant has received the "Good Manufacturing Practices" certifications from China's Ministry of Agriculture, and the necessary licenses to start producing and marketing the foot-and-mouth disease vaccine for pigs and cattle. Occupying a surface area of almost 15,000 m^2, the manufacturing plant has an annual capacity of 400 million doses (compared to the 300 million capacity display in the Garin plant, Argentina). Equipped with next-generation technology and responsible for production, quality control laboratories, as well as the storage units for raw materials and the finished product, this new industrial facility belongs to Jinhai Biotechnology, a joint-venture agreement with HILE Biotechnology who maintains a majority stake (60 %) as the sector is considered critical by the Chinese government. Biogénesis Bagó contributed with the

23 The Argentine exportable complex referring to bovines is the second most important item in bilateral trade with China and shows a substantial positive variation for the 2018-2019 period.

24 FMD is a highly contagious transboundary disease that mainly affects domesticated animals such as cattle, swine, sheep, goats and buffalo, as well as about 70 other cloven-hoofed wild animals.

technology and knowledge, transformed into a leading case in the company's internationalization strategy as new partnership agreements emerged with companies from Saudi Arabia (MAS) and South Korea (FVC).[25]

Swine vaccines are another promising market: it is expected to reach $ 2.0 billion by 2028. Market growth is driven by a surge in the demand for animal protein, as for the increasing prevalence of diseases. In this sense, the irruption of the ASF bring a new opportunity for Biogenesis - Bagó (Diálogo Chino 2020). ASF irruption slashed China's pig population by a third (around 100 million) because of a surge in the price of pork. Trouble for China might be an opportunity (as a challenge) for biotechnological firms to gain a new market. As many in Argentina become enthusiastic with this idea, Biogenesis - Bagó (in association with the Argentine Association of Pig Producers - AAPP) went a step forward in seeing the crisis as an opportunity to bring new products and develop swine fever vaccines.

Hugo Sigman and Juan Carlos Bago are Biogenesis – Bagó main shareholders, certainly both listed among Argentina's most powerful capitalists[26]. The 1994 anti-foot-and-mouth government campaign gave Sigman an opportunity to form a consortium (Nueva Sociedad, 2020).[27] At the end of the 70s the Argentinean government decided to replace the traditional vaccines with others of an oily type, which were mandatory from 1994. To make the new vaccine, laboratories had to face an expensive conversion, leading Sintyal Chemotechnics to go after a merger with Biogenesis. The new firm, Sintyal Biogenesis, was soon exporting the vaccine to

25 "Con 50 millones de dólares, Biogénesis Bagó expande su negocio a Corea del Sur", Forbes Argentina. 22 July, 2022 (available at: https://www.forbesargentina.com/innovacion/con-50-millones-dolares-biogenesis-bago-expande-su-negocio-corea-sur-n19402).

26 Ranking Forbes 2020: ¿quiénes son y cuánto tienen los 50 argentinos más ricos? (https://www.forbesargentina.com/rankings/ranking-forbes-2020-quienes-son-cuanto-tienen-50-argentinos-mas-ricos-n3469).

27 The foot-and-mouth disease has ravaged the cattle of the region since the beginning of the 20th century, with large local epidemics in 1942 and 1966. A major epidemic affected Argentina during 2001 but was controlled by mass-vaccination and movement restriction (Pérez *et al.*, 2004).

the entire region. Hugo Sigman is the president of Grupo Insud (Chemo, Exelties, mAxience), an international diversity group with a large presence in the pharmaceutical sector[28] (centered on biological drugs[29]). The group has presence in other areas as diverse as: cultural industries, nature and design, as well as agri-business, almost all these businesses are connected to Argentina. With headquarters in Madrid and an active presence in Argentina since the early nineties when Hugo Sigman returned from the exile, INSUD operates 18 production plants and 15 research and development (R&D) hubs around the world.

Insud Pharma invest heavily in R&D and in the continuous improvement of all its processes so as to ensure that the result is of the utmost quality and meets the strictest regulatory agency requirements (Insud Pharma). This diversified biotech group, conformed by Chemo, Exeltis and mAbxience, deals with human and animal health, it presents a global network of alliances and partnerships (Gutman and Lavarello 2014). Large investments in R&D and professional excellence permit CHEMO to manufacture a wide range of active pharmaceutical ingredients (API) and a complete range of finished dosage forms (FDFs), both for human and veterinary use in the main therapeutic areas. Employing approximately 4,000 professionals in over 40 countries, and producing more than 300 pharmaceutical and nutritional specialties, Exeltis is an organization that develops innovative treatments for unmet medical needs of individuals, families, and healthcare professionals.

The global API market size is estimated to grow at a CAGR 6 % rate over the next decade, totalizing earnings at around $ 475 billion dollars. Market expansion is attributed to the prevalence of chronic diseases (cardiovascular, cancer, diabetes), affecting an

28 Chemo is the first company of the group, founded by Silvia Gold and Hugo Sigman in 1977, in Barcelona - Spain.

29 Biological drugs are medicinal substances made from living beings: a hormone, an enzyme or a monoclonal antibody. They are used to treat complex diseases and their cost is very high.

increasing number of people around the world, escalating public health budgets and forcing governments to go after cheaper sources of medicines. COVID-19 has also demonstrated the need for vaccines because of the constraint imposed by relying on traditional pharmaceutical firms. Increasing uncertainty, roaring health complexities and geopolitical tensions, therefore, is also behind market enlargement, as nations aim to guarantee pharmaceutical supply in case of pandemics and chronic diseases. Generic firms have become an efficient, cheap, and safe source for governments to respond to all these challenges.

China and India are expected to play a greater role in the global market, with analysts projecting double digit CAGR growth in these markets. Both countries have also demonstrated excellence in producing drugs and vaccines cheaply and efficiently, a source of cheaper APIs for the global market. Controlling 40 % of global supply, China is the world's leading producer, while India is in third place after Italy, the country where INSUD's first manufacturing plant was established. Chinese firms' competitiveness basically associates with manufacturing costs, which are 20 to 30 % cheaper than in India. Having the lead in manufacturing, however, does not necessarily imply outperforming India in terms of certificates of Suitability (CEP),[30] whose firms triplicate Chinese ones in this field (MundiCare 2020). Leading API producers are, among others, Shenzhen Hepalink Pharmaceutical Group, Zhejian Pharmaceutical and Zhejiang Langhua. Manufacturers, on the other hand, are concentrated in a reduced group of provinces, namely: Zhejiang, Jiangsu, Shandong, Hebei, and Hubei.

The pharmaceutical manufacturing industry is one of China's industries that opened to the outside world at the earliest (Ministry of Commerce 2022). Several reasons attracted foreign pharma firms from the start, including competitive salaries, preferential industrial policies and huge consumer markets. By building up huge capacities, China outperformed many countries that were

30 The CEP certificate proves that the quality of the product being sold complies with the quality described in the relevant monograph of the European Pharmacopeia.

active ingredient suppliers in the global market. Investments in hard capabilities might be a necessary condition, but soft skills and knowledge are certainly needed to develop the industry. A quarter of global production is made in China, whose firms in 2021 brought 18 new active substances on the market (worldwide) (Fischer *et al.* 2023). Chinese manufacturers have a relatively small API portfolio but are continuously expanding (MundiCare 2020) and becoming competitive in producing new API associates with, among others, alimentary tract and metabolism, nervous system, respiratory system, musculoskeletal system and antiparasitic products. A highly dynamic and promising market, however, made China an attractive destination for global pharma players, although geopolitical tensions could challenge prospects.

China, however, has historically dominated the chemical API branch, becoming the world's second largest producer and exporter. Sectoral growth is driven by patent expiration, permitting companies to produce antibiotics, antipyretics, vitamins, and painkillers. To maintain its leadership, Chinese authorities turned to the biotech API branch, starting to seduce local and international entrepreneurships and firms focused on biosimilars. The initiative attracted the interest of Chemo, a firm of the Insud Group with more than 30 years of presence in China since 1987, and now with two plants in operation Chemway and GoldPharma. The group internationalization, however, would start fifteen years later, when Sigman decided to establish the GoldPharma regional consortium in China.

In a joint-venture agreement with Shanghai Fosun Pharma, Chemo invested $73 million in 2008 for a new research and development center, manufacturing plant and distribution center in Jinshan Industrial Zone at Shanghai dedicated to the production of "biosimilar generics". According to the agreement, Chemo pledged to provide the technology and know-how for the production of biosimilar[31] monoclonal antibodies (used among other things for

31 A biosimilar is a clone of a biological drug.

the treatment of cancer, infectious and inflammatory diseases) and is positioned as well as a strategic ally of the Asian giant for biotechnological developments. The funding used in cancer research for developing drugs will be directly injected into by Shanghai Chemo Wanbang Biopharma Co. Ltd., a joint venture involving Fosun and Chemo (Global Times 2010). Exeltis, on the other hand, has its own office in Shanghai, which imports medicines to the Chinese market.

2.4. Argentinean Firms Adventuring in China. Final Remarks

Not all Argentinean affiliates offer the same spillover to China (Lall and Narula 2004). When compared with Biogenesis – Bagó or Tenaris, Alfaro Abogados office generates few technological spillovers. Likewise, local authorities would be more interested in Satellogic commercial ambitions rather than the inauguration of a BNA representation office at Beijing. Henceforth, and besides the number of employees that foreigners could bring, what becomes strategic is the technological content.

Companies like Tenaris and Biosidus-Bagó were certainly shaped by the context in which they emerged, including benefited by the scientific and sectoral policies of the Argentine Government, which supplied crucial externalities for the construction of intangible assets by the firms (Campins and Pfeiffer 2017; Gutman and Lavarello 2014; Deciancio and Siegel 2022; Stubrin 2022).[32] It also explains INSUD's success, as its irruption is without a doubt associated to the historical relevance the pharmaceutical industry has in the country because of widespread scientifical knowledge in

32 Argentina has been a leading country in biotechnology, strongly dedicated to research and development, as witnessed by the presence of three Nobel Prize winners (Bernardo Houssay, 1947, Luis Federico Leloir, 1970, César Milstein in 1984). It also has a great capacity for private innovation, as the subsequent development of the pharmaceutical industry reveals.

biosimilar drug production among local laboratories, all allowing the company to adventure into the business and go global. Over a dozen local companies, the Insud group and Bago among them, are exporting biosimilars, primarily to other countries in the region and to Asia (Gutman and Lavarello 2017).

Both companies have profited from the national system of innovation and have created a R&D department that led to innovations and in-house patent, both involved in innovation with cooperation. They were also following the incremental Uppsala approach to internationalization, beginning the journey with exports, then going regional and finally global[33]. From a technological perspective, biopharmaceutical firms followed an industry-specific catching-up path.

Satellogic has also profited from public support, directly by INVAP, a state-owned company and satellite manufacturer with more than 2,000 employees that has built and launched multiple spacecraft. It employs more than 170 aeronautical engineers, AI experts and solution specialists, a true hi-tech firm. The company founded by Emiliano Kargieman became the first vertical integrated geospatial company, an industrial strategy which provides a massive cost advantage and shorter R&D cycles.[34] Satellogic Earth Observation Satellite Constellation can remap the planet at one meter of resolution every week, dramatically reducing the cost of high-frequency geospatial analytics. A new, disrupting start-up that in few years has constructed its own FSA.

33 In the case of Biosidus-Bagó, the description relates to Bagó. Internationalization, in this case, started at the beginning of the 1970s, when the family-owned firm opened a facility in Mexico (1972). Bolivia followed six years later. Regional expansion continued, with establishments opening in fifteen different countries of Latin America. Bagó international expansion continued in the new millennium, opening plants in Russia, Ukraine and Pakistan.

34 The company designs and built every component that goes into the satellites: cameras, on-board computers, power subsystems, sensors and actuators, optics, radios and propulsion system (for more information https://satellogic.com/technology/satellites/).

Argentinean financial and professional companies establishing in Beijing might eventually be able to obtain financial and intangible resources abroad, which subsequently would strengthen their domestic market position, even without (a priori) FSAs or CSA.

Investing abroad implies a deep challenge, as companies need to adapt to a different business culture which, in the case of China is certainly huge. Furthermore, the country is perceived as a single entity with cultural differences among regions being generally dismissed.

In the case of Tenaris, the following passage from López *et al.* (2022:172) is worth mentioning:

> "To deal with these issues, Tenaris opts for a strategy that consists of training senior staff extensively before sending them to Asian subsidiaries and stationing them there longer than is the case for staff in Western countries. This allows company officials to establish their own interpersonal relationships in Asia. As a result, there is little turnover in senior positions in Tenaris' Asian subsidiaries. Another strategy the company used initially to narrow the culture gap and thus speed up its deployment in the region was to assign bicultural staff (for instance, a Chinese Canadian director was assigned to the Chinese affiliate) who more easily adapted to the new environment and to doing business activities with local counterparts. The general feeling was that the company valued interpersonal relationships far more than formal contractual arrangements, which were nevertheless necessary.
>
> The company's strong interest in building a stable and trusting relationship with local agents was also related to its intentions in entering the Asian market —that is, not using its Asian plants just as a base for exporting to other regions."

This entails a gradual, lengthy deployment strategy so that the company will fully understand the host country's cultural specificities. Liu Jinghua Philix, who started working at Tenaris China as a sales engineer 17 years ago, is now the managing director for the country.

From a political perspective, relations with policy makers and government officials are crucial. Bilateral relations are also relevant, particularly for biotech firms like Biogenesis Bago,[35] as investments are made in sectors considered strategic by the Chinese government. Recall that both Tenaris and Biogenesis Bago[36] are entering a joint-venture agreement framework involving Chinese partners. According to Sebastián Perreta, Business Executive Director, who worked in the construction of Shaanxi lab:

> "China is the world's leading producer of pigs and has a very high consumption of pork, but that production has problems due to foot-and-mouth disease, which has even caused productivity problems. It was from this point that the need arose, in 2012, to add quality technology and, because of the worldwide recognition that Biogenesis has, they came looking for us",

He further added:

> [to be able] "to sell in China, you have to produce in China". "Having a Chinese partner opens doors for you and makes everything easier for you. If you do not have associates there, it is impossible".

Bilateral relations could also serve to solve problems for bringing new market opportunities, as observed after the ASF crisis affecting swine population in China as observed by Esteban Turic, CEO of Biogenesis Bagó. Consequently, Turic made initial contact with Chinese importers and the AAPP soon signed a memorandum of

35 "We would never have been able to achieve this result without the constant support of both governments. We believe that mutual interest is necessary for any cooperation in such distant areas of the planet. Proper planning is essential so that this type of long-range project is not left halfway and can crystallize", Esteban Turin, Director of Innovation at Biogénesis Bagó and the company's business in Asia, at the X Latin American and the Caribbean - China Business Forum, 14 - 15 October, Tangshan, Hebei, China.

36 Joint-ventures and cooperation agreements are part of Bagó internationalization experience, a strategy aimed at overcoming the uncertainties of entering international markets (Campins 2015)

understanding with the Chinese Association for the Promotion and Industrial Development (CAPID).

The entry of Argentinean firms is certainly not reduced to commodity producers but entails a group of firms working at the technology frontier as the previous cases demonstrated. Take the case of Hugo Sigman, Grupo Chema and President of the Argentinean Chamber of Biotechnology (ACB). At the First Forum of Agricultural Entrepreneurs, which took place at the G20 meetings in Hangzhou, China, 2016, he signalled the importance of ACB for Argentinean firms adventuring abroad, envisioning his mission as:

> "[to] seek to strengthen the leadership role of the country, promoting a global perspective that includes R & D to production, as well as the commercialization and export of biotechnological products with high added value".

A year later, Biogenesis – Bagó was opening its manufacturing facility at Yangling. The plant is part of a joint-venture agreement with Hile Biotechnology Company, a Chinese laboratory that makes high-tech vaccines for poultry and swine. At the inauguration, Hugo Sigman, shareholder of Biogenesis – Bagó and CEO of Grupo Insud, asserted:

> "The agreement is an example of what cooperation between companies that develop technology and innovation can achieve together in order to contribute to a better diet".

The entry of Biogenesis – Bagó in China has to do with technology transfer, a continuous process involving training a large part of the local personal operating the plant. By contributing to Chinese human capital formation, the Argentinean firm strengthens its cultural and institutional ties with the host country.

Likewise, Satellogic's entrance in China affects a much more sensitive sector. The company certainly qualifies as an "industry of the future", a knowledge-intensive firm certainly strategic to be placed in the realm of China's MIC 2025 plan. Satellogic's investment decision, however, is not exposing its strategic assets but exporting services with high value-added.

Geographically, Argentinean firms are largely concentrated in the east coast region (Shandong) and a couple of cities (Beijing and Shangai), with few exceptions.

To reduce cultural and institutional barriers, some companies opt for joint-venture agreements, but these schemes might also be used as foreigners are entering strategic sectors.

Whereas Beijing has established different policies and instruments to enhance local firms to go global, a hands-off policy prevails in Argentina, although the state has always promoted exports and some benefits could be granted to those aiming to open commercial offices abroad. Argentina - China bilateral relations, however, might generate a space for science and technology cooperation of utmost importance for Argentinean firms (Cesarín and Papini 2016). Created in 2008, the binational Centre for Food and Technology (CCAFST according to the Spanish acronyms), brings opportunities for association and financing, involving scientific researchers from both countries relevant for firms in the processing of bovine meat, animal proteins and vegetable.

Consider the following words, by the former Minister of Industry, Debora Georgi, under the government of Cristina Fernández de Kirchner, pronounced in the announcement ceremony by Hugo Sigman (Grupo Chema) and Chen Qiyu (FOSUM Pharma) regarding the construction of the Shanghai facility:

> "The agreement between Chemo and FOSUM Pharma is a concrete example of what the governments of Argentina and China intend to rethink and relaunch the bilateral relationship".

To further aggregate:

> "This project responds to the objective of our policies, since it means an export with a very high value added".

A dense web of political contacts is also highly valued by investors, in both countries and elsewhere. The proximity of Hugo Sigman with Argentinean and Spanish leaders is well known, as are their meetings are open and transparent (NUSO 2020).

Despite allowing the entrance of foreign investors, including the irruption of new, more transparent investment procedures and rules, in various industries the Chinese market remains partially or fully closed to foreign players, particularly in high-tech sectors. To enter into some other sectors, the government maintains joint-venture requirements. For firms from strategic sectors, it would certainly be underpinned by economic and national security issues. As the government desires to achieve global leadership in hi-tech sectors, joint-venture, alliances and similar agreements are used by the host country to advance technologically.

Although it might be beyond the scope of this paper to analyse whether (traditional) Argentinean firms with a presence in China would be able to adapt to this new scenario if forced to choose, some trends could be envisioned.

For those knowledge-intensive firms ambitioning to enter in the Chinese market, CEOs and managers should certainly be aware of China's alternative model of governance aimed to access and acquire foreign intellectual property (Branstetter 2018; Petricevic and Teece 2019). Managers should also be aware that deep market distortions might originate at sub-regional levels (region, municipalities), further eroding their innovative capabilities. Those entering China should also be considering geopolitical issues, as (emergent) tensions could block firm's operations in third countries (Luo 2022).

Launched in 2013 by Xi Jinping, the Belt and Road Initiative (BRI) is at the centre of China's foreign policy. Since its inception, the initiative sought to ameliorate infrastructure gaps and connect Asia with Europe. As the strategy expanded its geographical coverage and Latin American countries were invited to participate, the BRI has increasingly been under scrutiny by traditional partners. So far, the initiative obtained the adhesion of 20 Latin American countries, including Argentina, which on the 6th of February 2022 become an official member. Since 2020, Argentina is one of the 8 countries in the region incorporated into the Asian Infrastructure Bank (AIIB).

Infrastructure related investments are a crucial component and politically sensible sector as works is vital for economic growth and development. For Latin America, this is an opportunity to close its relatively large infrastructure gap. Although it does not count as FDI, Chinese transnational companies are also increasingly present in the region through construction contracts. If for Chinese International construction companies (CICCs) the initiative is perceived as an opportunity, for firms like Techint OBOR it might become a real threat (Stanley 2020). In a recent conference at the Faculty of Economics of the University of Buenos Aires (FCE - UBA), Paolo Rocca expressed:

> "Latin America experiences a process of de-industrialization. Economic re-primarization is guided by the emergence of the Chinese economy, eager for raw materials, and ambitious to conquer markets, especially with industrial products." (Ambito 2022).

Technology, on the other hand, associates with the Digital Silk Road (DSR): a program aimed at deepening international cooperation in the digital economy initiated in 2015. One of the main goals envisioned by the Chinese government is to establish a set of unified standards in 5G, artificial intelligence, satellite navigation, and other technical fields. President Xi Jinping conceives the [DSR] initiative as critical, and the arrival of new partners necessary for steering the beginning of a new economy.

Once again, Paolo Rocca affirmed:

> "My answer is decided. Latin America can redesign the value chain in countries that can provide solidity, security and a Western value chain" (Visión Desarrollista 2022).

He considers that the most relevant economies in Latin America, industrialized Argentina, Mexico and Brazil should:

> "Have an internal debate on the matter because today the BRICS are not a viable structure to interpret the world".

In addition, Paolo Rocca referred to the critical issue around 5G, where China is the leader and the United States wants the networks of its allies to be provided by Chinese companies,

> "We must not depend on China".

From a geopolitical perspective, in sum, Paolo Rocca asserted that relying on China generates large vulnerabilities for Argentina.

> "Our Group, which has steel in Europe, experienced the disruptions in the energy market from the invasion of Russia very closely. We learned something, but we should all learn, thinking about the next 5 or 10 years, where Western security, independence and integration will prevail. It is necessary to have a clear vision of the values in the design of the strategy towards the future."

What is surprising is the dual character of the group, which invests heavily in China while it fiercely prevents the arrival of Chinese (competitor) firms to Argentina. Certainly, Paolo Rocca is not alone, not in Argentina[37] nor among leaders of the region and beyond. A large group of industrialists, businessman and policy-makers in the West have become aware of the problem, asserting China's appetite for strategic assets. Political circles in the West are also reluctant due to the Xi Jinping landmark industrial strategy, Made in China 2025 policy, an initiative aimed at placing the country as a global powerhouse in high-tech industries, even though the initiative is inspired by Germany's Industry 4.0, and in line with previous approaches to economic development and

37 Hugo Sigman's (INSUD) presence in the above mentioned FCE – UBA conference might (or might not) reaffirm a new geopolitical vision arising from Argentinean leading businessman.

innovation. In a nutshell, what is under discussion is who will run the world: Geopolitics is back (Braw 2023) and it is influencing the corporate decisions of all types of global firms, not just those operating at the technological frontier.

Radical uncertainty and increasing complexity are also behind the pharmaceutical "reshoring" proposal made by a group of experts to the EU Parliament, with the purpose of improving the reliance in the supply chain and thus mitigating and preventing medicine shortage (Fisher *et al.* 2023). In a similar vein, the 2020 Pharmaceutical Strategy for Europe discusses reshoring to improve the supply chain resilience (European Commission, 2020). Finally, the European Parliament is urging the European Commission and Member States to introduce financial incentives, where appropriate, to preserve and expand the EU's pharmaceutical industrial base that would produce APIs. Only 33% of CEPs for APIs required in Europe are held by European manufacturers, more than 50% are held by Indian and Chinese manufacturers (MundiCare 2020). All described initiatives, in short, aim to explore potential measures to guarantee availability, henceforth exploring ways to move production back to Europe. Reports like this highlight the preoccupation among developed nations, whose response might influence the fate of the Argentinean pharmaceutical firms operating in China.

Political leaders in Argentina, however, still imagine a "perfect world". One group envisioning a market – led global insertion, another ambitioning the state leading national firms' internationalization process, both hoping to navigate the turbulent waters with no power attachment. Business leaders, to same extent, ambition a similar, not disruptive future. Techint as Insud, with their global presence, face a diversity of contexts. Would the present context push them (and the rest of Argentinean firms established in China), to rethink their strategies?

3. Conclusions

During the first wave of internationalization, emerging foreign direct investments (FDI) flows followed a South-South pattern. Argentinean firms were largely active in this stage, particularly investing in neighbour countries. In recent times, however, EMNEs internationalization has become more widespread. A distinctive phenomenon in this wave is that OFDIs from emerging markets are now also directed towards industrial countries – the traditional MNCs citadel. This is undoubtedly related to the emergence and increasing importance of high-tech firms from the south.

The decision to go global depends on many factors and is often induced by host country specific advantages. China has largely profited from its size, offering market access but imposing several conditions to those adventuring to enter. Mandatory joint venture association and technology transfer schemes were among those more representative, particularly at sectors classified as strategic whose definition periodically varied and evolved to include those technologically more advanced, opening the economy to those where local companies were now considered competitive. A planned strategy to catch up with the West, as followed by other Southeast Asian emerging economies in the past.

At the end of the day, the arrival of manufacturing and service firms allow China to climb the ladder. China is now a technological leader in many industries, but the frontier is always moving. Western economies' attitude towards China has changed, and a technological dispute brings geopolitical nationalism back.

A group of Argentinean firms operating at the technology frontier as knowledge intensive industries ventured into China. Some adopted a gradual approach, with all the recognized stages strategically picking their local partner in order to finally invest in the mainland. Others decided to adventure into China from the very start, as being global players permits them to do that.

The present chapter analysed the cases of Techint - Tenaris and Biogenesis – Bagó – Grupo Insud, among the largest Argentinean groups with a global presence. Both firms are playing globally, producing at a level that is in the technological frontier. Paolo Rocca and Hugo Sigman were both attracted by China from the very beginning of the market reform process. Starting with a commercial presence, years later their firms were investing in mainland China to fully engage with new projects, with both joining local partners.

During the past 30 years, multinational companies have enjoyed an increasingly open world. While subject to large obligations and duties, the Chinese governments eventually offered large incentives to MNCs. Argentinean companies adventuring in China confronted similar impositions and advantages but benefits largely outnumbered costs. Arriving in China was seen positively by home countries, particularly by Western authorities. Although it might be in the interest of the Argentinean government to further encourage local firms to operate at China, the globalization ideal is out of touch.

A series of disruptive events came to reshape the world and increase geopolitical tensions, a new business environment is forcing firms and policymakers to think about. new policies and re-design instruments. So far, countries might be forced to opt in one of the two leading geopolitical blocks: one led by the US, the other by China. Political alignment, though, might certainly influence MNCs corporate decisions, forcing them to choose whether to stay or to leave the country. This radical option would be constraining large MNCs with operations at both the US and Chinese markets. Geopolitical tensions are starting to disrupt value chains as MNCs intra-firm operations, particularly in some strategic industries.

Argentinean companies' engagement with local partners, the joint-venture framework, might prove resilient to geopolitical shocks. For those firms with global presence, tensions would force them to confront an option: stay in China and leave markets under the sphere of the US and its allies, or to leave and maintain operations at developed ("western") markets. In this case, the return of nationalism might eventually force Argentinean firms to sell their stake at the venture, leaving local partners the right to continue in business afterwards.

References

Aguilera, Ruth V., Ciravegna, Luciano, Cuervo-Cazurra, Álvaro, and González-Pérez, María Alejandra. 2018. "Multilatinas and the internationalization of Latin American firms". *Journal of World Business* 52(4), pp. 447-460.

Artopoulos, Alejandro. 2018. Sin recetas. La internacionalización de multinacionales de software argentinas (2002-2014). In, Barbero, María Inés and Cerutti, Mario (edits). *Dossier – Las nuevas multinacionales.* Anuario Centro de Estudios Económicos de la Empresa y el Desarrollo: Buenos Aires, pp. 135-186.

Basave Kunhardt, Jorge. 2016. "IED de las empresas multinacionales mexicanas y estrategias de "catch up" tecnológico". *Economía Informa* 399, pp. 3-15.

Battisti, Enrico, Miglietta, Nicola, Nirino, Niccoló and Villasalero Díaz, Manuel. 2020. "Value creation, innovation practice, and competitive advantage: Evidence from the FTSE MIB index". *European Journal of Innovation Management* 23(2), pp. 273-290.

Beugelsdijk, Sjoerd, Kostova, Tatiana, Kunst, Vincent E., Spadafora, Ettore and van Essen, Marc. 2018. "Cultural distance and firm internationalization: a meta-analytical review and theoretical implications". *Journal of Management* 44(1), pp. 89-130.

Bloomberg. 2019. "Tenaris S.A.: Tenaris and Severstal to form joint venture to build a welded pipe plant in West Siberia". *Bloomberg*, February 5.

Boehe, Dirk M. 2015. "The Internationalization of Service Firms from Emerging Economies: An Internalization Perspective". *Long Range Planning* 49(5), pp. 559-569.

Branstetter, Lee G. 2018. "China's Forced Technology Transfer Problem— And What to Do About It". *Peterson Institute for International Economics - Policy Brief* 18-13. xxx

Braw, Elizabeth. 2023. Corporations Can't Ignore Geopolitics Anymore: The global division into competing blocs comes at a high price for multinationals. Foreign Policy.

Buckley, Peter J. 2020. The theory and empirics of the structural reshaping of globalization. Journal of International Business Studies 51, 1580–1592

Campins, Mónica. 2015. Modes of Internationalization of Two Argentine Pharmaceutical Companies in Historical Perspective: The Cases of Bagó and Sidus.

Cantwell, John, Dunning, John H., & Lundan, Sarianna M. 2010. An evolutionary approach to understanding international business activity: The co-evolution of MNEs and the institutional environment. Journal of International Business Studies, 41(4): 567–586.

Capello, Roberta and Fratesi, Ugo. 2013. The Service Sector in the New Globalization Phase: Evidence from European Regions. Juan R. Cuadrado-Roura Editor "Service Industries and Regions: Growth, Location, and Regional Effects". Springer.

Casanova, Lourdes and Miroux, Anne. 2021. Emerging Market Multinationals (EMR) Report 2021: Building the Future on ESG Excellence. Cornell University - Emerging Market Institute

Cesarin, Sergio and Papini, Virginia. 2016. Saltando Periferias. Archivos del Presente. Año 21 (65).

Ministry of Commerce. 2022. Report on Foreign Investment in China 2022. Ministry of Commerce People´s Republic of China.

Chudnovsky, Daniel and López, Andrés. 2000. A third wave of FDI from developing countries: Latin American TNCs in the 1990s. Transnational Corporations. Vol 9 N 2: 31- 74.

Claessens, Stijn and Schmukler, Sergio. 2007: International Financial Integration Through Equity Markets: Firms from which Countries go Global?. IMF Working Paper, N° 138 International Monetary Fund Washington, D.C.

Damill, Mario; Frenkel, Roberto; and Rapetti, Martín. 2015. Macroeconomic Policy in Argentina During 2002–2013. Comparative Economic Studies 1-32.

Deciancio, Melisa and Siegel, Karen M. 2022. Creando condiciones para el desarrollo de la bioeconomía en la Argentina: El papel de las políticas estatales en biotecnología y biocombustibles (1990-2022). Revista Estado y Políticas Públicas Nº 19. octubre de 2022 - abril de 2023. ISSN 2310-550X, pp. 225-248

de Paula, Gerardo M. 2006. Maverick´s acquisition: Tenaris expands again. Steel Times International. Tomo 30 N 7.

Doidge, Craig; Karolyi, Andrew G.; and, Stulz, Rene M. 2001. Why are Foreign Firms Listed in the U.S. Worth More? National Bureau for Economic Research – NBER Working Paper No. 8538.

Dunning, John H. 1993. Multinational Enterprises and the Global Economy, Addison - Wesley.

Dunning, John H. and Lundan, Sarianna M. 2008, "Institutions and the OLI paradigm of the multinational enterprise", Asia Pacific Journal of Management, Vol. 25 No. 4, pp. 573-593,

Dussel Peters, Enrique. 2012. Mexican Firms Investing in China 2000–2011. Inter-American Development Bank, Integration and Trade Sector. Discussion Paper IDB DP 55.

Dussel Peters, Enrique; Armony, Ariel C.; and, Cui, Shoujun. 2018. Building Development for a New Era: China´s Infrastructure Projects in Latin America and the Caribbean. Published by the Asian Studies Center, Center for International Studies, University of Pittsburgh, and Red Academia de América Latina y el Caribe sobre China.

Dussel Peters, Enrique. 2019a. China´s Foreign Direct Investment and the Caribbean: Conditions and Challenges. Universidad Nacional Autónoma de México – Facultad de Economía.

-------------------. 2019b. China´s Financing in Latin America and the Caribbean. Universidad Nacional Autónoma de México – Facultad de Economía.

ECLAC – CEPALSTATS Bases de Datos y Publicaciones Estadísticas. (https://statistics.cepal.org/portal/cepalstat/dashboard.html?theme=2&lang=es)

Efrat, Kalanit; Gilboa, Shaked; and Yonatany, Moshe. 2016. When marketing and innovation interact: The case of born-global firms. International Business Review.

Estevadeordal, Antoni and Kahn, Theodore. 2012. Pathways to China: the story of Latin American firms in the Chinese market. Inter-American Development Bank

European Commission. 2020. Pharmaceutical Strategy for Europe. Communication from the Commission to the European Parliament, the Council, The European Economic and Social Committee, and the Committee of the Regions (available at https://eur-lex.europa.eu/legal-content/EN/TXT/PDF/?uri=CELEX:52020DC0761).

European Parliament. 2021. Shortage of medicines — how to address an emerging problem European Parliament resolution of 17 September 2020 on the shortage of medicines — how to address an emerging problem (2020/2071(INI)) (available at https://eur-lex.europa.eu/legal-content/EN/TXT/PDF/?uri=CELEX:52020IP0228).

Fischer, Stefan; Knoll, Verena; Alleweldt, Frank; and Vogler, Sabine. 2023. Potential measures to facilitate the productions of active pharmaceutical ingredients (APIs). European Parliament. Policy Department for Economic, Scientific and Quality of Life Policies Directorate-General for Internal Policies

Gammeltof, Peter and Cuervo-Cazurra, Alvaro. 2021. Enriching internationalization process theory: insights from the study of emerging market multinationals. Journal of International Management.

Garcia-Herrero, Alicia. 2022. China and the West: growing apart as geopolitical tensions grow. Bruegel – Blog post (https://www.bruegel.org/blog-post/china-and-west-growing-apart-geopolitical-tensions-grow).

Global Times. 2010. Shanghai Fosum on 500-billion-yuan deal with Grupo Chemo. (available at https://www.globaltimes.cn/content/552233.shtml).

Goldstein, Andrea and Toulan, Omar. 2007. "Multilatinas Go to China: Two Case Studies". In, Grosse, Robert and Luiz F. Mesquita. 2007. Can Latin American Firms Compete? Oxford University Press: Cambridge, pp. 269-292

Golub, Stephen S. 2009. Openness to Foreign Direct Investment in Services: An International Comparative Analysis. The World Economy.

Gutman, Graciela E. and Lavarello, Pablo J. 2014. Biopharmaceuticals and firm organization in Argentina. Opportunities and challenges.

Hennart, Jean-Francois.; Majocchi, Antonio; and, Hagen, Birgit. 2021. What's so special about born global, their entrepreneurs or their business model? Journal of International Business Studies 52:1665-1694.

Hoskisson, Robert E., Eden, Lorraine, Lau, Chung M. and Wright, Mike. 2000. Strategy in Emerging Economies, Vol. 43 No. 3, pp. 249-267.

Insud Pharma (https://www.insudpharma.com/en/)

Jackson, Gregory, & Deeg, Richard. 2008. Comparing capitalisms: Understanding institutional diversity and its implications for international business. Journal of International Business Studies, 39(4): 540–561.

Jones, Geoffrey. 2005. Multinationals and Global Capitalism: from the nineteenth to the twenty-first century. Oxford University Press.

Kirkman, Bradley L., Lowe, Kebin B. and Gibson, Cristina B. 2017. "A retrospective on Culture's Consequences: the 35- year journey", Journal of International Business Studies, Vol. 48 No. 1, pp. 12-29.

Knight, Gary A., & Cavusgil, S. Tamar. 2004. Innovation, organizational capabilities, and the born-global firm. Journal of International Business Studies, 35(2), 124-141

Kolovos, Alexandros. 2018. Managing Uncertainty from the Sky: Surveillance Through Three Generations of Commercial Earth Observation Satellites. Panagiotis Karampelas, Thirimachos Bourlai Editors "Surveillance in Action Technologies for Civilian, Military and Cyber Surveillance". Springer.

Kosacoff, Bernardo. 1999. Las Multinacionales Argentinas: Una nueva ola en los noventa. Comisión Económica para América

Latina y el Caribe – CEPAL, Oficina de Buenos Aires. Documento de Trabajo – DT 83.

Kostova, Tatiana, Beugelsdijk, Sjoerd, Scott, W.Richard, Kunst, Vincent E., Chua, Chei Hwee and van Essen, Marc. 2020. "The construct of institutional distance through the lens of different institutional perspectives: review, analysis, and recommendations", Journal of International Business Studies, Vol. 51 No. 4, pp. 467-497.

Kulu, Erik. 2021. Satellite Constellations - 2021 Industry Survey and Trends.

Lall, Sanjaya, & Narula, Rajneesh. 2004. FDI and its role in economic development: Do we need a new agenda? MERIT, Maastricht Economic Research Institute on Innovation and Technology. MERIT-Infonomics Research Memorandum Series No. 019 https://doi.org/10.26481/umamer.2004019

Lee, Yan Yin; Falahat, Mohammad; and Sia Bik-Kai. 2019. Impact of Digitalization on the Speed of Internationalization. International Business Research; Vol. 12, No. 4.

López, Andrés; Ramos, Daniela; and, Torre, Iván. 2012. Business models for trans-Latins: Latin American investments in Asia. In German King, José Carlos Mattos, Nanno Mulder, and Osvaldo Rosales editors "The changing nature of Asian-Latin American economic relations" Economic Commission for Latin America and the Caribbean (ECLAC). Santiago, Chile.

Lucke, Navina and Eichler, Stefan. 2016. "Foreign direct investment: the role of institutional and cultural determinants", Vol. 48 No. 11, pp. 935-956.

Luo, Yadong. 2021. New OLI advantages in digital globalization. International Business Review Volume 30, Issue 2.

——— 2022. Illusions of techno-nationalism. Journal of International Business Studies 53, 550–567.

Menza, Markus ; Kunisch, Sven; Birkinshaw, Julian; Collis, David J.; Fosse, Nicolai J.; Hoskisson, Robert E.; and Prescott, John E. 2021. Corporate Strategy and the Theory of the Firm in the Digital Age. Journal of Management Studies 58 (7) 1695 -

MundiCare. 2020. Where do our Active Pharmaceutical ingredients come from?. A World Map of API production – Final report.

Niosi, Jorge; Hanel, Petr; and Reid, Susan. 2012. The international diffusion of biotechnology: the arrival of developing countries. Journal of Evolutionary Economics.

Nueva Sociedad. 2020. El dueño de la vacuna - Hugo Sigman: de la izquierda a la farmacéutica. Revista Nueva Sociedad – NUSO,

Peng, Mike W., Wang, Denis Y.L. and Jiang, Yi. 2008. "An institution-based view of international business strategy", A Focus on Emerging Economies, Vol. 39 No. 5, pp. 920-936.

Pérez, Andrés M.; Ward, Michael P.; and Carpenter, Tim E. 2004. Control of a foot-and-mouth disease epidemic in Argentina. Preventive Veterinary Medicine. Volume 65, Issues 3-4 (217-226).

Petricevic, Olga and Teece, David J. (2019). The structural reshaping of globalization:

Implications for strategic sectors, profiting from innovation, and the multinational enterprise. Journal of International Business Studies. 2019. 50, 1487–1512

Ramamurti, Ravi. 2009. Why study emerging-market multinationals? In "Emerging Multinationals in Emerging Markets" edited by Ravi Ramamurti and Jitendra V. Singh, Cambridge University Press.

Rennie, Michael W. 1993. "Born global", The McKinsey Quarterly, No. 4, pp. 45-53.

Rugman, Alan M., Verbeke, Alain. 1992. A note on the transnational solution and the transaction cost theory of multinational strategic management. Journal of International Business Studies 23 (4), 761–771.

Rugman, Alan M., Verbeke, Alain. 2001. Subsidiary-specific advantages in multinational enterprises. Strategic Management Journal 22 (3), 237–250.

Rugman, Alan M., Girod, Stephane. 2003. Retail Multinationals and Globalization: The Evidence is Regional. European Management Journal Vol. 21, No. 1, pp. 24–37,

Rugman, Alan M., Verbeke, Alain. 2008. Internalization theory and its impact on the field of international business. In: Boddewyn,

J.J. (Ed.), International Business Scholarship: AIB Fellows on the First 50 Years and Beyond (Research in Global Strategic Management), Vol. 14. Emerald Group Publishing Limited, pp. 155–174.
Santiso, Javier (2008). La emergencia de las multilatinas. Revista de la CEPAL 95

Schoemaker, Paul J. H., Heaton, Shovi, & Teece, David J. 2018. Innovation, dynamic capabilities, and leadership. California Management Review, 61(1): 15–42.

Shim, Yongwoon, & Shin, Dong-Hee. 2016. Neo-techno nationalism: The case of China's handset industry. Telecommunications Policy, 40(2–3): 197–209.

Stanley, Leonardo E. 2013. Emerging Multinationals: Explaining Asian firms recent achievements in technologically leading industries (and why Latin America firms are lagging behind).

-------------- 2020. The infrastructure gap in Latin America and the arrival of Chinese infrastructure firms: special reference to the Argentinean case. In Soraya Caro Vargas editor "*Economic corridors in Asia: paradigm of integration? A reflection for Latin America*". Universidad del Externado de Colombia, Bogotá.

Stubrin, Liliana. 2022. Un análisis del crecimiento de la actividad biotecnológica en la Argentina en clave sistémica (1982-2022)

Techint. 2019. The Techint Group – 2021.

--------- 2019b. Tenaris unveils seamless pipe mill in Bay City, Texas

Teece, David J.; Pisano, Gary; and Shuen, Amy. 1997. Dynamic capabilities and strategic management. Strategic Management Journal, 18(7): 509–533.

Tenaris. 2021. Company Overview.

UNCTAD. 1993. Transnational Corporations from Developing Countries: Impact on Their Home Countries. United Nations Conference on Trade and Development – UNCTAD, Geneva.

Zheng, Bowen; Wang, Yarou; Kamal, Muhammad A.; and Ullah, Assad. 2020. The influence of cultural and institutional distance on China's OFDI efficiency: fresh evidence from stochastic frontier gravity model. International Journal of Emerging Markets

2.
BRAZIL'S OFDI TO CHINA

Celio Hiratuka

Introduction

As with several other Latin American countries, Brazil experienced an extraordinary increase in economic relations with China during the early 20th century. Academic researchers, think tanks, and the specialized media began to pay more attention to Brazilian and Chinese relations as they gained importance and complexity. While the number of studies on this subject has increased, the general contours of this relationship are becoming more solid.

The first decade of the 21st century was marked by the growth of bilateral relations, mainly in the commercial sphere. In the year 2000, Brazilian exports to China were around US$ 1 billion. China represented around 2 % of total exports and was the 12th most important destination market. In 2009, China became Brazil's main trading partner, surpassing traditional partners such as the United States and Argentina. That year, exports to China reached US$ 21 billion and represented 13 % of all Brazilian exports. In the following years, trade relations continued to grow and in 2020 China reached 32 % of Brazil's total exports. As a result of the reopening of trade with other partners after the pandemic, this share dropped to 27 % in 2022. China remains the Brazilian top export destination.

As for imports, a similar pattern can be observed. In 2022, China accounted for 22 % of Brazil's total imports.

Despite the emphasis placed on the growth in trade flows and the surplus in favor of Brazil as a result of relations with China, critics point out that the export basket is excessively concentrated in just a few items, while imports include many manufactured goods, including those that are more technology-intensive. In Brazil, since it has one of the largest domestic markets and the most diversified industrial structure in Latin America, this asymmetry in trade flows has also led to a debate about the impact of trade integration with China on long-term growth and the profile of sectoral specialization, which unfolded under terms such as Dutch disease, deindustrialization and natural resources curse (Borghi 2020; Jenkins 2015; Hiratuka and Sarti 2016).

Additionally, other dimensions have gained prominence in Brazil, increasing the visibility of Chinese products and businesses. Since 2010, Chinese investments have increased significantly in Brazil in several industries such as mining, energy, transport, manufacturing, and services (Cariello 2021; Hiratuka 2019; Kupfer *et al.* 2018; Shutte 2020). The Chinese presence has been highlighted for its unique characteristics, such as the high level of participation of state-owned companies leading this movement, as well as the support provided by its public development banks. (Hiratuka and Deos 2019). In addition, it is considered an important source of infrastructure contributions, especially since Brazil has a large gap in infrastructure (Hiratuka 2018; Rosito 2020; Ramos 2020; Schutte and Debone 2017). Furthermore, Chinese investments can be useful in leveraging new opportunities in more knowledge-intensive sectors related to the energy transition (Barbosa 2020; Hiratuka 2022). However, concerns have arisen over investments that reinforce commercial insertion focusing on commodities or that are aimed at large infrastructure projects to guarantee export flows, as they have the potential to impact the environment and society adversely, especially in sensitive areas such as the Amazon and Brazilian Cerrado (Studart and Myers 2021).

If regarding Brazil and China trade and Chinese foreign direct investments (FDI) in Brazil, quantitative and qualitative aspects, as well as surveys and analyses of relevant themes, have become increasingly important, the same cannot be said when it comes to Brazil's outward foreign direct investments (OFDI) in China. It is difficult to find systematic information about the size, characteristics, challenges, and opportunities of Brazilian companies expanding to China as well as studies on the topic.

By collecting and analyzing information from a variety of sources, including macroeconomic information, business information and case studies, this paper attempts to fill this gap. Besides this introduction, the article contains four other sections. In section 1, macroeconomic information is used to estimate foreign investment values, including some methodological warnings when analyzing Brazil's OFDI in China. Section 2 summarizes the literature and information gathered from business sources. Section 3 describes the experiences of three companies that have invested in China. They are different cases which shed light on different aspects related to the opportunities and obstacles related to the internationalization of Brazilian companies towards China. The last section closes the paper with conclusions and policy recommendations.

1. Brazil's OFDI in China: Analysis Based on Macroeconomic Data

Traditionally, Brazil has always been a major recipient of FDI. Brazil's industrialization during the post-war period relied heavily on foreign capital. Most capital-intensive industrial sectors, such as automotive and machinery and equipment, were dominated by companies from Europe and the United States.

A second wave of FDI occurred after the 1990s' trade and financial liberalization movement, diversifying investors and encompassing service sectors. The main change in the most recent period has been the increased participation of Chinese companies

(Cariello 2021; Hiratuka 2019; Schutte 2020). In 2010, based on foreign equity investments by the ultimate controlling country, China accounted for about 1 % and ranked 16th among the top investors. In 2021, it represented 5 % and was ranked 5th.

From the point of view of Brazil's OFDI, the movement has always been less intense. Brazilian companies began internationalizing in the 1970s focused on trade expansion, something that remained unchanged. During the 1980s, due to the debt crisis and severe downturn in the domestic market, some companies opened foreign branches. Companies in the civil construction sector, for example, due to the retraction of public investments, began their internationalization process by disputing projects in other countries in South America and Africa (Casanova and Kassun 2017).

Despite this initial movement, the opening of affiliates abroad has always been low and was concentrated until the 1990s in a few companies and sectors in the areas of service (engineering and civil construction and the financial sector) and production of commodities, configuring the defensive character of the internationalization strategy. There was an asymmetry resulting from the differences in competitiveness and technology and capital accumulation capacities of national and foreign companies.

The first decade of the 2000s witnessed slightly faster Brazilian economy growth. At the same time, a more intense movement towards Brazilian companies' internationalization was observed. This movement was associated with revenue growth, especially for commodity companies. However, cash reinforcement was additionally observed for companies focused on the domestic market due to significant growth in domestic demand. It should also be noted that the strong appreciation of the Brazilian currency occurred from 2003 onwards as a result of the commodity cycle and the increase in exports to China. Currency appreciation resulted in an increase in the purchasing power of assets by Brazilian companies. Also important was the resumption by the Brazilian government of policies to support the business system, with mechanisms explicitly aimed at supporting the financing of foreign investments, such as funding the subscription of bonds carried out by the BNDES (Casanova and Kassum 2017; Ricz and Szunomar 2019; Sarti and Hiratuka 2011).

Brazil's OFDI, however, lost momentum from 2012 onwards, showing marked volatility from then on. As can be seen in Table 1, considering the accumulated flows over 10 years, the value recorded as an OFDI flow by the Central Bank of Brazil went from US $7 billion between 1992 and 2001 to US $131 billion between 2002 and 2011. The ratio between FDI and OFDI went from 5% in the first period to 43% in the second. Between 2012 and 2021, the accumulated flow reached US $108 billion. In this last period, however, years of high outflows (as in 2017, which recorded a flow of US $21 billion) alternated with years of net capital repatriation (as in 2020, with a negative flow, that is, capital repatriation of nearly US $5 billion).

Table 1. Brazil: Accumulated Flows of OFDI and FDI (US $ million) (1992-2021)

Period	A-OFDI	B-FDI	A/B (%)
1992-2001	7,027	138,633	5%
2002-2011	131,332	306,367	43%
2012-2021	108,781	511,724	21%

Source: Own elaboration based on BCB (2022).

A large part of this volatility is related to the Brazilian economic crisis, which resulted in very low growth from 2012 onwards and a severe crisis between 2015 and 2016. On the one hand, the growth of the domestic market no longer served as a lever to increase the scale and project companies abroad. On the other hand, it reinforced the strategies of (few) companies that had already achieved a certain degree of internationalization and started operating on global markets and/or concentrating on commodities, aiming to strengthen its global position while reducing its domestic dependence. As the exchange rate devalued, assets abroad became relatively more expensive. Lastly, BNDEs significantly reduced their funding for internationalization. Recently, few new companies have emerged with outstanding performance on the global market.

But the volatility observed in the data is also a result of the increased presence of Special Purpose Entities (SPE) formation abroad, becoming critical agents in determining OFDI flows. SPEs are defined by the Brazilian Central Bank (BCB) as institutional entities with 0 to 5 employees, with no or little physical presence and no or little physical production in the economy in which they are constituted. By establishing SPEs in specific jurisdictions in tax havens, owners seek to secure access to capital markets or sophisticated financial services, reduce regulatory and tax burdens, and ensure confidentiality. These SPEs are usually used to channel resources between different countries, organizing so-called "pass-through" funds. These are funds received from abroad by a resident company and then forwarded to another economy (Banco Central do Brasil 2022). Due to their configuration, they make it difficult to identify the origin and final destination of the investment and have little or no influence on the economies ofthe intermediate part of the route, generally offshore centers such as the Cayman Islands.

In Brazil, the Central Bank estimates that SPEs represent 64 % of companies with capital registrations abroad and 86 % of the value of direct investment companies abroad (Banco Central do Brasil 2022). The expressive number of SPEs abroad makes it more difficult to establish a direct relationship between FDI statistics and the internationalization movement of companies.

In addition to being linked to greater volatility of flows and causing the boundary between direct and portfolio investment to become more blurred, it also makes it more difficult to identify the final geographic destination of investments and the sectors invested in from traditional sources of information compiled by official institutions. As an example, Brazil's OFDI stock statistics for 2022 showed the Netherlands, Cayman Islands, British Virgin Islands, and Bahamas as the top countries.

In light of these caveats, the following information presents some basic information on OFDI flows and stocks from Brazil to China. Graph 1 shows data on Brazil's OFDI in China based on statistics from the Brazilian Central Bank (BCB) and the National Bureau of Statistics of China (NBSC). From the graph, it is evident that there is a discrepancy between the two sources, especially in the first period, where China registers much higher number of direct investments received from Brazil than Brazil registers as outflows. Based on the cumulative data between 2003 and 2012, Bacen data totaled US $139 million, while NBSC data totaled US $408 million. Between 2013 and 2022, the discrepancy is smaller, and the trend is more similar, although there are still significant differences. Brazil's statistics for this second decade total US $299 million, whereas China's total is US $300 million.

Figure 1. OFDI Flows from Brazil to China (US millions) (2003-2022)

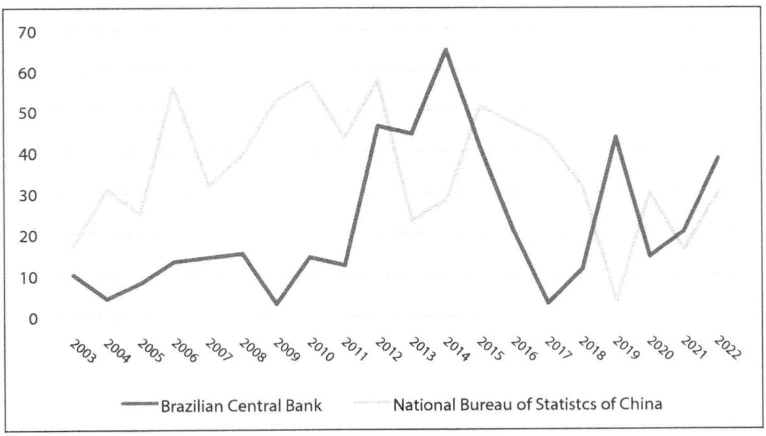

Source: own elaboration based on BCB (2022) and National Bureau of Statistics of China (2022).

Considering the information on investment stock, Figure 2 shows available information on Brazil's investment stock in China from 2008 onwards. An upward trend is observed until 2018, when it reaches US $350 million, followed by a fall important in 2019. New increases were observed in 2020 and 2021. At the end of 2021, the stock registered was US $273 million. Although significantly higher than what was seen at the beginning of the series, what stands out are the relatively low values, which is also consistent with the low volume observed from the flows. Also noteworthy is the small share of China within the total Brazilian OFDI stock, which never reached much higher above 0.1 % of the total.

Figure 2. Brazil: OFDI Stock in China (US$ millions) (2008-2021)

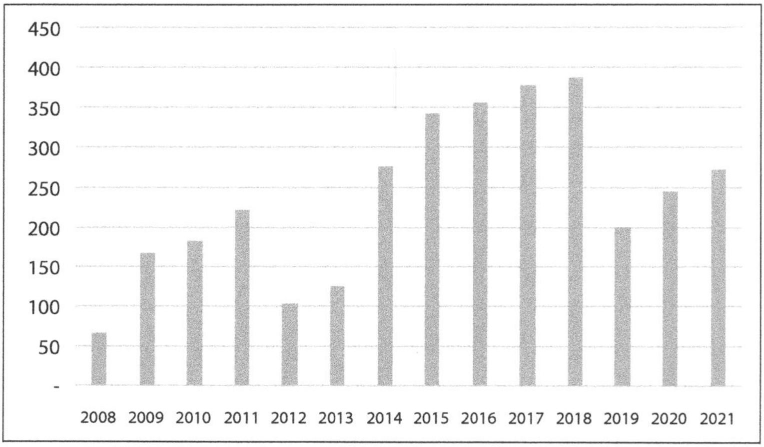

Source: own elaboration based on BCB (2022).

As with other destinations, it is possible that part of the investments in China were channeled indirectly through SPE in offshore centers. This methodological limitation cannot be overcome from aggregated data, so far. These difficulties increase the importance of working with alternative information, such as databases that organize business data.

2. Brazil's OFDI in China: Analysis Based on Microeconomic Data

One of the most used databases to map crossborder investments flow is the fDI Markets. Unctad, in its World Investment Report, uses this information in addition to macroeconomic and Balance of Payments data.

One can access fDI Markets to find out about companies' investments based on their country of origin, destination, and industry sector. It is worth mentioning that, unlike the information from the official statistical bodies, which record foreign exchange flows, investments here are organized from the perspective of the investing company and the country where the investment will be made. In other words, just because an investment was announced with a certain amount of Brazilians in China does not translate to an exchange flow in the same manner. For example, the resources may have been obtained with financing from China itself. Also, a given investment amount may correspond to actual disbursements over a period of several years, or it may be cancelled in the future. There may be an overestimation of the recorded values in this case.

Despite these limitations, the data provides additional information to our subject. fDI Markets estimates Brazilian companies invested US $2.8 billion between 2003 and 2022 in 57 projects in China. Using a breakdown by decade of the entire period, it becomes apparent that the number of highlighted investment projects in the first decade was higher even though the values were very similar. In the first period (2003-2012), 38 projects were registered with an accumulated value of just over US $1.4 billion. In the second period (2013-2022), 19 projects were registered with a value of just under US $1.4 billion.

This value is significantly higher than the official information shown in the previous section. Moreover, a higher estimate can also be made in terms of its relative contribution to the total. Between 2003 and 2022, Brazilian projects with China as a destination represented 4.4 % of the total number of projects and 3.3 % of the total value.

A relatively dispersed distribution is observed by sector, with the financial services and metals and mineral sector each featuring 8 projects, followed by the consumer products and automotive components. In terms of value, however, there is more concentration, with the Automotive OEM sector the most significant, followed by financial service and metals and minerals.

Table 2. Brazil: Company Investments in China. Breakdown by Sector (US$ million) (accumulated during 2003 and 2022)

Sector	Value	Share in Value	Projects	Share in Projects
Automotive OEM	626	22.1	2	3.5
Financial services	494	17.4	8	14.0
Metals and Minerals	385	13.6	8	14.0
Electronic components	233	8.2	2	3.5
Transportation & Warehousing	230	8.1	4	7.0
Consumer products	195	6.9	6	10.5
Aerospace	183	6.5	2	3.5
Textiles	156	5.5	5	8.8
Automotive components	108	3.8	6	10.5
Food & Beverages	65	2.3	2	3.5
Business services	48	1.7	3	5.3
Chemicals	40	1.4	1	1.8
Software & IT services	38	1.4	3	5.3
Communications	17	0.6	2	3.5
Coal, oil & gas	7	0.2	1	1.8
Consumer electronics	4	0.1	1	1.8
Non- automotive OEM transport	3	0.1	1	1.8
Total	2,831	100	57	100

Source: FDI Markets.

Manufacturing has been the predominant corporate function in China: 57 % of the value of projects and 35 % of the projects were turned to manufacturing activity, which indicates that a significant part of Brazil's investments in China sought favorable production conditions for industrial production, which can either be sold domestically or exported to other countries. Although less important, investments aimed at setting up a sales and marketing structure accounted for about 25 % of the total projects. This indicates the importance of investments aimed at accessing the growing Chinese market with the development of local commercial support.

Table 3. Brazil: Company Investments in China. Breakdown by Corporate Function (US$ million) (accumulated during 2003-2022)

	Value	Share in Value	Projects	Share in Projects
Manufacturing	1,620	57.2	20	35.1
Business Services	541	19.1	11	19.3
Retail	272	9.6	7	12.3
Sales, Marketing & Support	199	7.0	14	24.6
Logistics, Distribution & Transportation	125	4.4	3	5.3
Headquarters	75	2.7	2	3.5
	2,832	100.0	57	100.0

Source: FDI Markets.

Jiangsu province ranks first in value, with 35 % of the total. In number of projects, the municipality of Shanghai stands out, with 26 %. Hong Kong, Beijing and Guangdong also appear as important areas in a number of projects.

Table 4. Brazil: Company Investments in China. Breakdown by Province (US$ million) (accumulated during 2003-2022)

	Value	Share in Value	Projects	Share in Projects
Jiangsu	1.006	35.5	8	14.0
Shanghai Municipality	722	25.5	15	26.3
Hong Kong	214	7.6	8	14.0
Heilongjiang	165	5.8	1	1.8
Guangdong	164	5.8	5	8.8
Beijing Municipality	160	5.6	7	12.3
Not Specified	123	4.3	6	10.5
Zhejiang	76	2.7	3	5.3
Hebei	64	2.3	1	1.8
Henan	64	2.3	1	1.8
Tianjin Municipality	51	1.8	1	1.8
Chongqing Municipality	22	0.8	1	1.8
Total	2,832	100.0	57	100.0

Source: FDI Markets.

Finally, another set of information concerns surveys that sought to raise, through business information from different sources, the number and profile of Brazilian companies operating in China.

The most complete survey was carried out by the Brazil China Business Council (CEBC) in 2012. In general, the survey emphasized that the internationalization movement and increased investment by Brazilian companies abroad that occurred in the first decade of the 21st century had also been directed towards China, albeit in small amounts. Brazilian companies operating in China totaled 57, operating in a variety of sectors. Among the companies categorized by their main activity, 51 % were in the service sector, 28 % were in the manufacturing sector, and 12 % were in the natural resources sector.

Even though service sector companies accounted for the majority of companies, they usually had smaller operations, concentrating on segments such as legal advice, consulting, trading, and financial services. Meanwhile, manufacturing companies, such as Marcopolo, WEG, Embraco, and Embraer were generally larger companies. A noteworthy aspect of these companies is that, in addition to dominating the domestic market, they also stood out as examples of industrial companies with a strong international presence because of their accumulated technological and productive capabilities, which made them highly competitive firms. Natural resource companies, like Vale and Petrobras, sought mainly to establish logistics and distribution channels to strengthen their global exports.

Table 5. Brazil: Companies in China by Sector of the Headquarter (2012)

Business Sector	Companies	%
manufacturing	16	28
services	29	51
Natural resources	12	21
Total	57	100

Source: CEBC (2012).

A total of 40% of the companies in the sample operated as representative offices, followed by 39% of companies operating as service delivery offices. There were only eight companies in China that performed manufacturing activities, or activities aimed at industrial production. In other words, despite the 16 companies classified in the manufacturing sector, only 8 had a production facility in China. The remaining manufacturing companies had representative offices to support exports or sourcing from Chinese suppliers. The sample also included 4 Brazilian restaurants on the Chinese market.

Table 6. Brazil: Companies in China. Activities of the subsidiary in China (2012)

	Companies	%
Representation office	23	40
Service delivery office	22	39
Production unit	8	14
Restaurant	4	7
Total	57	100

Source: CEBC (2012).

The CEBC study found that the first wave of Brazilian companies entering China faced several obstacles, including:

a) Because of the peculiarities of the Chinese business environment, Brazil is physically and primarily culturally distant from the Asian country. From a different perspective, Silva (2020) highlighted the difficulties of adapting to expatriates from Brazilian companies in China due to these differences in habits and culture and the lack of prior preparation to deal with these differences.
b) The lack of understanding and knowledge about how to enter China and deal with the various instances of the Chinese government, as well as the restrictions of the Chinese government for projects in regulated sectors.

c) The misalignment between the strategic objectives of Brazilian companies and Chinese partners when joint ventures were established.
d) The non-recognition of international standards adopted by the Chinese legal system, especially regarding intellectual property.
e) Difficulties in establishing a network of reliable suppliers, the inadequate qualification of labor, the lack of training of suppliers, and the difficulties in establishing Chinese sales channels.

Brazilian companies did not expand to a relevant set of new companies after this first movement into China, based on the latest information available. It appears that Brazilian investments in China have not experienced a similar growth and diversification as Chinese investments in Brazil since 2010. According to Fleury (2021), there were 30 companies operating in China in 2019, with 45 subsidiaries. Although difficult to compare, as it is based on surveys with non-standard methodologies, the comparison with the information obtained by the CEBC in 2012, coupled with the data analyzed from the fDI market, at least shows that the number of Brazilian firms present in China did not significantly increase.

Table 7. Brazil: Companies in China (2019)

Sector	Companies	Number of subsidiaries
Natural resources/ agribusiness	4	7
manufacturing	16	28
services	10	10
Total	30	45

Source: FGV/CEI, according to Fleury (2021).

While there was a reduction in the number of Brazilian companies involved in the Chinese market compared to the CEBC survey carried out in 2012, Fleury (2021) points to continuity and evolution in Brazilian companies' engagement with the Chinese market.

Companies that had already been mentioned in the CEBEC analysis were again mentioned in Fleury's analysis.

WEG, for example, which at the time of the CEBEC survey had only one company, now has four plants in China (see the following section). Another industrial company that expanded was the Randon Group, which in addition to already having a manufacturing unit in the country, increased its production capacity in 2020. In addition to industrial companies, there are also outstanding cases of consumer companies, such as Natura (cosmetics), Arezzo (shoes) and Miolo (wines), and service companies such as Stefanini (software) expanding operations and looking to break into the China market. These initiatives allowed these companies to better understand Chinese companies' business models and learn about the Chinese consumer.

According to the author, Brazilian companies with operations in China have revealed continuous learning in how to conduct business, adapting to the country's government policies, developing new strategies and products, and improving the art of relationships. This gain in experience has even been reflected in the repatriation of knowledge, providing enhanced competitiveness for these organizations.

The information analyzed in this section made it possible to verify a slightly broader picture regarding Brazilian OFDI in China than that allowed only by macroeconomic information. Although there is a lack of information and studies, an impressionist portrait could be constructed allowing us to see a very limited movement of OFDI from Brazil to China, dominated by a few companies. There appears to have been the strongest movement in the first decade of the 21st century, while the second decade was characterized more by adaptation, consolidation, and expansion for companies that had entered the previous decade, thus overcoming the difficulties highlighted in CEBEC (2012). A few large Brazilian companies have joined the restricted list of companies with direct operations in China.

3. Case Studies

This section presents 3 case studies of Brazilian companies that performed OFDI in China. A combination of information from different sources was used to describe these three experiences: a bibliographic review of books and academic journals, a research of business-specific journalistic media materials, and interviews with business executives, sector experts and government officials.

3.1 WEG

WEG is a Brazilian electrical and electronic equipment company, which operates globally and its main business segments are Industrial Electronic Equipment, Electric Motors, Industrial Automation, Equipment for Energy Generation and Transmission and Paints and Varnishes.

Currently the company has 52 industrial plants in 15 countries around the world, employing around 39,000 people globally. These numbers make WEG one of the most global Brazilian companies. The company's revenue in 2022 reached BRL 19.9 billion (about US $5.8 billion), with about 50 % coming from sales outside Brazil (WEG 2023).

Founded in 1961, the company exported electric motors mainly to South America from the 1970s. Throughout the 1980s, the company expanded its production capacity in Brazil and diversified its activities. Abroad, the company increased its network of commercial representatives, at the same time expanding its participation in international fairs. But it was during the 1990s that the company accelerated its international expansion, creating a branch to handle this expansion called WEG Exportadora. Its function was to coordinate the installation of branches to develop sales, logistics and services abroad.

Several branches were established since then, starting in the United States in 1991, and later reaching Belgium, Japan, Argentina, Germany, UK, and Mexico, among other countries. The main consequence of this expansion was the decrease in dependence on distributors and the growth of direct sales to large customers. Because of the unique nature of large and special products, WEG was required to participate directly without the use of intermediaries. From the point of view of product mix, the company already had a wide range of electrical system components, such as motors, generators, control and protection equipment. By the end of the 1990s, the company was already exporting to more than 55 countries and the foreign market represented around 30 % of sales (Melo 2013; Marson and Costa 2105).

The year 2000 marked the beginning of a new phase with the acquisition of production plants abroad, starting with Argentina and then Mexico. In 2002 the company acquired another factory in Portugal. In 2004, the company entered China. Commercial presence was preceded by exports, initially to Taiwan, Hong Kong, and eventually to mainland China. Contacts with Chinese representatives in the Asian region served as the first approach to the Chinese market and its strong expansion. Producing in China was part of WEG's strategy to expand its global business, using China to reach both the Chinese market and the Asian market (Floriani *et al.* 2009; Schiavini *et al.* 2011).

Based on a search for investment opportunities in different regions, supported by a consulting company that presented several options, the company chose the municipality of Nantong in Jiangsu province. The Provincial Government offered WEG the purchase of a local state-owned company, including all its assets. The Nantong factory, dedicated to electric motor manufacture, had a constructed area of about 30,000 m^2 and land of approximately 67,000m^2 with 350 employees (Floriani *et al.* 2011). The fact that the investment was directed towards a sector with no restrictions on foreign capital entry allowed the acquisition of 100 % of the equity capital.

The adaptation period was relatively long and the company started operating under the WEG brand only 2 years after acquisition. The main difficulty encountered in adapting the company to the local market was the cultural issue. The company handled this difficulty by hiring Chinese-Brazilian employees to send to the operation in China, who, in addition to being fluent in Portuguese, Chinese and English, had contact with both cultures. For other expatriates from Brazil, it offered training on cultural differences between the two countries. In addition, I brought employees to Brazil for long training periods (6 months) in areas such as engineering, human resources and controlling. According to an interview given by WEG's superintendent director in 2012, understanding the importance of Guanxi for establishing trust relationships in business was fundamental to leveraging the company's strategy. In the same interview, concerns about strong local competition and the possibility of copying products manufactured by the company by Chinese firms was mentioned. However, the strong customization capability protected WEG against these threats (CEBC 2012).

Based on local production, WEG's perspective was not only to produce for the growing domestic market in China, but also to establish a base for supplying the Asian market. Over time, the facilities were modernized and production capacity increased. As a result of local production, the company's operational and commercial logistics also improved and its competitiveness in the region increased. In 2022, the plant had the capacity to produce more than 60,000 engines/year and employs 653 people.

By taking advantage of the reduction in asset prices abroad caused by the global crisis between 2009 and 2011, the company accelerated its international expansion, opening production plants in Mexico and India and purchasing companies in South Africa, Argentina, Denmark, Austria, and the United States. By 2010, 7 % of sales came from outside Brazil, and this share grew rapidly over the course of the decade, as the company became truly global from a production perspective.

In 2014 the company made a second investment in China, with the acquisition of two companies in Changzhou, also in Jiangsu province. The Chinese manufacturer of electric motors for washing machines and dryers Sinya Electromotor Co. Ltd and component maker Changzhou Machine Master (CMM) Co. Ltd. SINYA was founded in 2005 and was producing electric motors for washing machines and other "white line" appliances, developing advanced technology products for the main world manufacturers. The factory had an area of 28,550 square meters, with a new factory unit with an area of 68,760 square meters under construction at the time of purchase. The SINYA Group's turnover in 2012 was approximately US $88 million. CMM was manufacturing transmissions and mechanical components for the "white line" solutions sold by the SINYA Group and had revenues of approximately US $17 million in 2012 (WEG 2014).

A year later, WEG started the construction of its third and largest industrial plant, in Rugao, also in Jiangsu province. The announced investment value was US $135 million and the factory became WEG's largest production unit in China. Inaugurated in 2016, the production plant had a constructed area of 35,000 square meters and 350 employees. In 2022, the factory had 880 employees and had expanded to verticalize production, occupying an area of 55,000 square meters and with a capacity to produce 600,000 engines/year.

Finally, in 2018 the company started investing in its fourth factory in China, also in Changzhou. Focused on the production of industrial automation equipment and the manufacture of Drivers and Controls, the investment meant the expansion of the product portfolio in the country and the continuity of the bet on increasing the presence in one of the largest and most dynamic markets for industrial equipment in the world.

The factory opened in 2019 and has a built area of 27,500 square meters. The production capacity is 25 thousand Automation Drives/year. The production plant had around 120 employees in 2022.

The company's global reach is shown in Figure 3. About 27 % of revenues come from products produced and sold abroad. The Asian market, where China is the main production base, represents around 5 % of the total sales destination. Considering all the plants in China, WEG employed around 1,930 people, which represented around 5 % of the company's total number of employees in 2022.

Figure 3. WEG's Operation Revenue (BRL million) (1996-2022)

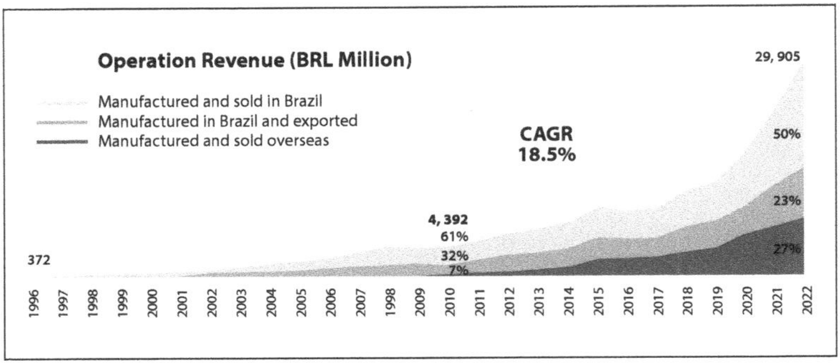

Source: WEG (2022).

A significant point to be made is that the company has been operating in China for the past few years in one of its main business areas, which is the manufacture of motors and electrical equipment, with no restrictions on its entry due to Chinese foreign investment laws. The company instead relied on a variety of local incentives to attract investors. As a result, it was able to buy all the capital of the Chinese companies it acquired upon entering China. Due to the absence of a local partner, the company had to redouble its efforts to adapt to local business cultures and markets. As a result of the long apprenticeship, WEG was able to expand into Greenfield investments, including subsidiaries controlled 100 % by the company. As a protection against copying and strong competition in the Chinese market, WEG operates with a strong vertical integration strategy while providing customized products for large customers.

WEG's trajectory in China has been successful, and the company's presence in a rapidly changing and increasingly competitive market has contributed to the company's global continuous improvement strategy. In contrast to the period of installation in China, when labor and materials costs were important reasons for the investment, the company observes that currently the main advantages of being in the Chinese market are the prospect of market growth and the ability to leverage sales to the entire Asian market at present, as well as monitoring the rapid changes in the Chinese economy and the possibility of learning to raising productivity.

3.2 Embraer

Embraer was founded in 1969, as a state-owned company linked to the Brazilian State's project (at the time under military dictatorship) to promote air force sovereignty and modernization, articulated with the need for regional integration and industrial development. The idea was to make production feasible based on technological knowledge organized at the Technological Center of Aeronautics (CTA) and the Technological Institute of Aeronautics (ITA) in previous decades. The first product launched by the company was a twin-engine turboprop for 15 to 21 passengers designed by CTA.

Over the following years, the company gained expertise in the development of key technologies, focusing on design, manufacturing, systems integration and final assembly of aircraft. The strong support of the Brazilian State was also fundamental to the evolution of the company and the entire aeronautical industry in the country (Caliari and Ferreira 2022). Aside from concentrating scientific, technological and financial support on Embraer, the state has been an important demand during the company's consolidation period.

The 1980s were marked by an increase in the company's internationalization, which led to important sales in the international market and the establishment of a support structure for sales and technical assistance abroad. As a result, technical assistance and maintenance centers were established in countries such as the United States, France, and Portugal. In addition to diversifying its products, the company established important international technological partnerships that allowed it to establish itself as a leading company in the small aircraft market segment.

The company's financial results were adversely impacted by a combination of factors, such as pressure for market liberalization and privatizations. For example, BNDES financing for sales abroad proved difficult. The privatization of the company in 1994 allowed the return of the company's capitalization, the modernization of its management and the resumption of important projects, such as the ERJ 145 project, gestated during the company's state-owned period, but completed after the privatization process. It was a 50-seat jet, which stood out for its low operating costs compared to its competitors. The aircraft family derived from the ERJ 145 consolidated Embraer as a leading company in the regional jet sector.

Between 1996 and 2000, the number of aircraft delivered to the world market and the number of employees practically doubled as the company accelerated its expansion trajectory.

In this context of strong international expansion, the promising Chinese market entered Embraer's radar. In 2000 the company opened its commercial representative office in Beijing in 2000. Then it established one distribution center in Beijing, jointly with China Aviation Supplies Import and Export Corp. The occupied area was 750m^2, and had the capacity to store more than 6,000 spare parts. It was connected to other storage centers in Brazil and around the world. At the same time, it began sales in the country, with the delivery of 5 ERJ 145 jets in 2002.

At the end of the same year, Embraer announced the signing of a contract for the construction of its first aircraft production unit outside Brazil. This was done through the Harbin Embraer Aircraft Industry Co. Ltd, a joint venture with Harbin Aircraft Industry Group Co. Ltd and Hafei Aviation Industry Co. Ltd., companies controlled by China Aviation Industry Corporation II (AVIC II). It would be responsible for production, assembly, sales and after-sales support activities for the ERJ 135/140/145 family aircraft. The contract enables the production under license of all versions of the regional jet family to be sold in Chinese territory. The total capital investment in the joint venture was US $25 million, used mainly to set up a new production facility, with an area of 24,000 m^2 in Harbin, in the north of China.

If, on Embraer's side, the objective was to penetrate one of the markets with the highest growth in regional aviation, from the Chinese perspective there was the strategy of acquiring production capacity in a strategic sector. Since the 1980s, China has sought to advance in this capacity, through a joint venture between Shanghai Aviation Industrial Corp. (SAIC) and McDonnell Douglas to assemble the MD82 medium-range aircraft. Between 1986 and 1994, thirty-five MD 80 series jets were assembled in China, including five exported back to the United States. There was a plan to assemble the larger MD 90 aircraft but McDonald Douglas' merger with Boeing ended that production line (McIntyre and Hoadley 2021).

In 1999, China Aviation Industry Corporation, a state-owned holding company created to organize investments in the Chinese aviation sector, was split into two units, seeking to strengthen the sector's competitiveness. AVIC I had assets related to large aircraft, while AVIC II should focus on smaller aircraft.

The joint-venture, therefore, would combine Embraer's interests in expanding into the Chinese market, with AVIC II's need to absorb productive and technological capacity for production on the local market.

Despite the partnership resulting in effective production, with Chinese aviation companies already placing orders in 2004, significant changes in the following years made the Join-Venture's continuity unfeasible.

In the first place, Embraer already was preparing in the early 2000s for the launch of its new family of aircraft, called E-Jets (ERJ 170/190/195) with capacities from 70 to 110 seats. The company's expectation was that once the ERJ 145 family jets had already been produced, the company could begin moving towards the production and sale of its upcoming family of aircraft.

However, on the Chinese side, in 2008 AVIC I and II were merged again. At the same time as a spin-off of AVIC, China Commercial Aircraft Co. (COMAC) was established. COMAC was born to be a worldwide competitive commercial aircraft company. The company bets on two main products in order to accomplish this. The ARJ-21, and the C919. The ARJ-21, whose aircraft design for up to 90 seats was being developed since the early 2000s by AVIC I, was transferred to COMAC. In 2009 it started to make test flights and was certified by the Chinese civil aviation authority in 2014. In 2015 it made its first sale in the Chinese market to Chengdu Airlines (Reuters, 2015).

COMAC, therefore, represented in practice a direct competitor to Embraer, disputing the preference for Chinese airlines in the purchase process. Having produced and delivered more than 40 aircraft in China by 2016, Embraer ended the Joint-Venture in 2016.

Embraer's case illustrates the challenges of competition in a market where China has clearly demonstrated its ambition to become a leading global manufacturer. A joint venture strategy to produce locally in return for market access was blocked by the ambition of the Chinese government to create its own players.

Following the closure of Embraer's operations in China, especially after Airbus acquired Bombardier's regional aircraft division, Embraer faced tough times. This threat led the Brazilian company to enter into an agreement with Boeing, where the civil aviation division became a part of the American company. Boeing pulled out of the deal as a result of the pandemic and the 737 Max airjet crisis.

Embraer is currently betting on its new line of E-2 aircraft, which is capable of carrying up to 150 passengers. In the next ten years, the company expects a demand of 5,500 units in this market, with Asia expected to account for about a third of the total, with China accounting for the largest share. Considering that it is situated between ARJ-21 and C919 capacity ranges, the company expects to be able to sell again to China in the near future. New contracts were expected to be announced during President Lula's visit to China in April 2023, but the expectation has not materialized until the time this paper is being finished.

3.3 Suzano

Suzano is a pulp and paper company and one of the largest producers in the world. Founded in 1924 as a paper distributor, in 1939 it started producing paper and soon after World War II it integrated pulp production. Throughout the 1960s, starting with eucalyptus pulp production, it became one of the most prominent producers in Brazil. After a diversification process throughout the 1980s and 1990s, the company focused on the Pulp and Paper area, incorporating other national producers, and consolidated itself as one of the largest pulp producers in the world. Of its total revenue, which reached BRL 49 billion in 2022 (about US $9.5 billion), 83 % came from sales abroad, although the company has practically all of its production activity installed in Brazil (Suzano 2023).

The company's competitive advantage comes from its capabilities in technology and forestry innovation, allowing it to achieve high productivity per area planted with eucalyptus, reducing raw material costs. As a result of the need for better forest management through biotechnology, Suzano acquired FuturaGene in 2010, a company based in Israel specializing in biotechnology research and development for forestry and biofuels. Among FuturaGeneo's research activities are the creation of new eucalyptus varieties, which utilize state-of-the-art technologies like genetic recombination and bioinformatics. With this operation, Suzano reinforced its commitment to the development of sustainable technologies with a strong environmental orientation to meet the growing demands for higher productivity and quality of eucalyptus fibers, as well as better use of natural resources, such as land, water, and carbon absorption.

As the world's largest eucalyptus producer, FutureGene operated mainly in Brazil, but also in China, the country's second largest producer. FutureGene's operations in China were characterized by strong interaction with Chinese Universities and Research Centers. For example, by agreements with Beijing Forestry University to develop advanced plantation forestry for cheaper bioenergy, and with Guangxi Academy of Sciences to develop sustainable bio-fuel processes for yield-enhancing eucalyptus.

One year after being bought by Suzano, FuturaGene established an R&D center in Shanghai, which centralized research activities and coordinated field operations on trial farms. Shanghai was chosen because of its close proximity to the local research system and strategic location in a country where sustainability was gaining importance (China Daily, 2011).

One of the examples of the application of the technology used by FuturaGene in China was a project in Minqin, Gansu province, to combat desertification, through the selection, analysis and planting of trees that thrive in desert conditions, and the development of management practices and appropriate management to integrate environmental, social, and economic aspects. In addition to combating desertification, the project had the objective of improving soil quality and reducing CO_2 levels in the atmosphere through a partnership with Gansu Desert Control Research Institute and Shanghai Advanced Research Institute (SARI) of the Chinese Academy of Sciences). As a result, rural people were provided with a sustainable source of biomass as well as improved livelihoods (New Generation Plantations 2015).

Although FuturaGene operated with management autonomy in regard to its main pulp and paper activities, its operations provided a bridge to the Chinese market's potential, not only in terms of pulp and paper consumption, but also other segments related to sustainability and climate change resilience.

At the same time, Suzano, in its recent strategy, has begun to emphasize more and more its advantages associated with sustainable production, highlighting carbon capture and sustainable management of its 2.6 million hectares of planted areas. The company has also tried to diversify its portfolio by developing innovative products, including wood-based products to replace chemical products in textiles and building materials, and establishing a venture capture arm to take advantage of bioeconomy business.

In this context, in 2022, Suzano announced the construction of an innovation center in China, with investments of US $10 million. Located in the Science City of Zhangjiang, in Shanghai, Suzano China Innovability Hub will seek to prospect and serve customers in view of the growing needs for cellulose and new biobased and sustainable materials. The center will be dedicated to developing new bio-based materials and applications, as well as to cooperating with partners in China and overseas to drive sustainable development through innovation.

The Innovability Hub will consist of an advanced laboratory, an interactive experience center and various collaboration spaces. Not only will the Hub cater to local customers' changing needs on existing products and applications, but it will also serve as a development base for new bio-based materials and applications, which will be derived from Suzano's scientifically cultivated and managed eucalyptus farms–a renewable and natural resource.

The Innovability Hub also aims to learn Chinese innovation initiatives that may be applied to Suzano's businesses and adapted across other regions. In addition to strengthening relationships with its stakeholders in China, Suzano expects its new facility to attract attention from further afield across the globe by promoting knowledge and sharing experiences.

Suzano's strategy in establishing this unit in China, therefore, has a dual objective: first, to prospect a market where initiatives are booming for sustainable solutions. A second objective is to establish connections with the Chinese innovation system, which is extremely dynamic as well as highly capable of leveraging the development of green products and solutions. To facilitate innovative bioeconomy businesses in the local market, Suzano signed cooperation agreements with several institutions and universities in China during the inauguration of the Hub and launched an open call for start-ups in China.

Having just been inaugurated, it is not yet possible to verify the consequences of this initiative, but this is a case worth following up, as it signals a promising direction for Brazil-China relations.

4. Conclusions and Policy Recommendations

Unlike trade relations or Chinese investments in Brazil, Brazil's OFDI in China has not been extensively studied. The analyses carried out throughout this chapter highlighted that, despite the methodological difficulties, it is possible to state that Brazilian OFDI in China is small and dominated by a relatively limited number of large global companies. Despite the existence of smaller companies, especially in diversified service segments, gathering information about their activities is more difficult.

In quantitative terms, the Brazilian OFDI stock in China, measured by official statistics, represented only 0.1 % of the Brazilian total in 2021. Considering information from the FDI Markets database, China accounted for 4.4 % of all projects and 3.3 % of Brazilian investments abroad between 2003 and 2022. Information obtained from a survey of companies also indicated a relatively restricted number of companies operating in China, largely established during the period of increased internationalization of Brazilian companies in the first decade of this century. It appears that the second decade was a decade of consolidation and expansion of previously established companies, with little new entry.

The difficulties of increasing investments in China remain the complexity of the Chinese market, including cultural distance. This is combined with regulatory issues that require a lot of learning and continuous monitoring, in addition to extreme competition on the local market. These characteristics require skills, capacity for long-term planning and a volume of investment that is generally available to few Brazilian companies. The case studies confirm this perception.

In areas considered strategic and where the Chinese Government is interested in developing its own companies, entry is quite difficult, as shown by the case of Embraer. The speed of change in the Chinese economy also represents a major challenge, since a sector where investment is sought at a given moment may become restricted over time, in accordance with the evolution of China's development strategy.

WEG and Suzano experiences show that operating in China requires a long-term effort, in order to ensure effective learning of market conditions and ways of doing business in China. From its first investment through the acquisition of a local company, WEG made a greenfield investment more than 10 years later, when its expertise on local conditions had already been established. Furthermore, it shows how important it is to operate in China to achieve a global strategy, both due to its size and to its favorable conditions for reaching the entire Asian region. Since then, the cost of labor in China, once a factor of location advantage, has been replaced by effects in terms of learning and management methods that can increase productivity for the company globally.

A gradual involvement is also evident in Suzano's case, which began in 2010 and only accelerated in 2022, when its Shanghai Inovabilty Hub was set up. Even though the Suzano case is very recent, it indicates an involvement via OFDI that suggests a new direction for the company, as it is framed within a global strategy for strengthening environmentally sustainable businesses. The presence in China, in this case, seems important not only for market opportunities, but also for the chance to interact with the innovation ecosystem in a field where China has important innovative capabilities, and which is at the heart of the long-term strategy of the country.

As far as policy propositions are concerned, they can be divided into two groups. At a more general level, it is possible to point out the very low level of Brazilian OFDI destined for China. Even recognizing the factors that are commonly listed as obstacles to Brazilian companies entering China, it would be important to expand measures that could mitigate these obstacles.

The expansion of support structures for companies looking to expand their investments in China, especially smaller ones, is one of these measures. Due to the weight of trade relations and Chinese investments in Brazil, bodies responsible for this action, such as the Brazilian Export Promotion Agency and embassies and consulates in China, often focus their support activities and human resources in that direction. Nevertheless, it would be important to extend support for investments in China, as well as to spread information regarding regulations, incentives, restrictions, and investment opportunities in China, in order to break this cumulative causation circle. Due to the particularities of the Chinese market, its complexity and the speed of change, this is an effort that requires constant updating.

At a more strategic level, the Brazilian OFDI in China can encourage the advancement of bilateral relations beyond the one in which they were consolidated over the last few years, that is, exports concentrated in a few commodities in exchange for imports of a diversified set of manufactured goods. Brazil's new government, which took office in 2023, is concerned about reactivating industrial development through the incorporation of more innovations and sustainability.

It would be important to focus on areas where investment can boost mutual knowledge and capabilities. Suzano is an example of an investment of this type that can expand bilateral ties in new directions. To move forward in segments that are more intensive in knowledge, technology, and sustainability, it would be necessary to conduct a more in-depth analysis of sectors and companies where there is potential for complementarity between public and private interests in both countries.

A high-level instrument, such as the Sino-Brazilian Commission of High-Level Concertation and Cooperation (Cosban), which is headed by vice-presidents of the two countries, can be an important tool for identifying and promoting these partnership opportunities.

References

Banco Central do Brasil. 2022. Relatório de Investimento Direto. Brasília: Banco Central do Brasil.

Batista Barbosa, Pedro Henrique. 2020. "New Kids on The Block: China's Arrival in Brazil's Electric Sector". *GCI Working Paper* 012 (Global Development Policy Center), pp. 1-68.

Borghi, Roberto. A. Z. 2020. "China's Trade Specialization pattern with Latin America and African Economies: Revisiting the Core-Periphery dichotomy". *Revista Tempo do Mundo* 24, pp. 27-52.

BusinessWire. 2022. "Suzano breaks ground on its Innovability Hub development in China". *BusinessWire*, November 29.
Caliari, Thiago and Ferreira, Marcos J. B. 2022. "The historical evolution of the Brazilian aeronautical sector: a combined approach based on mission-oriented innovation policy (MOIP) and sectoral innovation system (SIS)". *Economics of Innovation and New Technology*, v. 1, pp. 1-18.
Cariello. Tulio. 2021. *Investimentos Chineses no Brasil: Histórico, Tendências e Desafios Globais (2007–2020).* CECB: São Paulo.
Casanova, Lourdes and Kassun, Julian. 2017. "Are Brazilian multinationals competitive enough?" In, Andonova, Veneta and Losada-Otáloro, Mauricio. *Multilatinas Strategies for Internationalisation.* Cambridge: Cambridge University Press, pp. 252–274.
CEBC (Conselho Empresarial Brasil-China). 2012. *Empresas Brasileiras na China: presença e experiências*. Rio de Janeiro: CEBC.
Crane, Keith, Luoto Jill E., Harold, Scoth W., Yang, David, Berkowitz, Samuel K. and Wang, Xiao. 2014. *The Effectiveness of China's Industrial Policies in Commercial Aviation Manufacturing*. Santa Monica, CA: RAND Corporation.
ECLAC (Economic Commission for Latin America and the Caribbean). 2015. Latin America and the Caribbean and China: towards a new era of economic cooperation. ECLAC: Santiago de Chile.
FDI Markets. https://www.fdimarkets.com/
Fleury, Maria. T. 2021. "A presença de multinacionais Brasileiras em território Chinês." *GVExecutivo* 20(2), April/June, pp. 37-40.
Floriani, Eliete, Borini, Felipe M. and Fleury, M. T. 2009. "O processo deinternacionalização como elemento gerador de capacidades dinâmicas: o coas da WEG na Argentina e na China." *Revista Brasileira de Gestão de Negócios* 11 (33): 367-382.
Hiratuka, Celio. 2018. "Chinese infrastructure projects in Brazil: Two Case Studies". In: Dussel Peters, Enrique, Armony, Ariel and Cui, Shoujun (edits). *Building Development for a New Era: China's Infrastructure Projects in Latin American and the Caribbean.* University of Pittsburgh/Academic Network of

Latin America and the Caribbean on China: Pittsburgh, pp. 122-143.

Hiratuka, Celio. 2019. "Chinese OFDI in Brazil." In, Dussel Peters, Enrique (edit.). *China's Foreign Direct Investment in Latin America and the Caribbean. Conditions and challenges.* Red ALC-China: Mexico, pp. 167-188.

Hiratuka, Celio and Deos, Simone S. 2019. "Chinese financing in Brazil (2000-2018)." In, Dussel Peters, Enrique (edit.). *China's Financing in Latin America and the Caribbean. Red ALC-China: Mexico, pp. 209-234.*

Hiratuka, Celio and Sarti, Fernando. 2011. "Investimento Direto e Internacionalização de Empresas Brasileiras no período recente". *Texto para Discussão* (IPEA) 1610, pp. 1-56.

Jenkins, Rhys. 2012. "Latin America and China: a new dependency?" *Third World Quarterly*, vol. 33, no. 7, p. 1337-1358, 2012.

Jenkins, Rhys. 2015. "Is Chinese competition causing deindustrialization in Brazil?". *Latin American Perspectives* 42(6), pp. 42-63.

Kupfer, David and Rocha, Felipe. F. 2018. "Directions of Chinese Investment in Brazil 2010-2016: National Strategy or Search for Opportunities." In, Jaguaribe, A. (org.). *Direction of Chinese global investments: implications for Brazil.* FUNAG: Brasilia, pp 215-266.

McIntyre, John R. and Hoadley, James R. 2021. "Chinese Commercial Aircraft Manufacturing Policy: The View from the Commanding Heights". In, Spigarelli, Francesca and McIntyre, John R. *The New Chinese Dream.* Palgrave Macmillan Cham: London, pp. 105-119.

Melo, Germana T. 2013. "Como, por que e para onde vamos? O caso de internacionalização da Weg." *XXXVII ANPAD*. Rio de Janeiro, September 7-13.

Moura Junior, André J. D. 2020. *Algoz ou herói: a participação do Estado brasileiro na internacionalização da Embraer S.A (1994-2018)* (1994-2018). Doctoral Thesis. *UNB*.

National Bureau of Statistics of China. 2022. *China Statistical Yearbook 2022.* NBS: Beijing.

New Generation Plantations. 2015. *Suzano Trees in the Gansu Desert.* China. At: https://www2.newgenerationplantations.org/blog-post/trees-in-the-desert-gansu-province/.

Ramos, Danielly, Lessa, Antonio Carlos and Urrejola, Laura. 2020. "One Step Closer: The Politics and the Economics of China's Strategy in Brazil and the Case of the Electric Power Sector." In, Bernal-Meza and Raul, Xing, Li. *China–Latin America Relations in the 21st Century.* Palgrave Macmillan: London.

Reuters. 2015. "China's COMAC delivers first ARJ21 jet plane to domestic airline". *Reuters,* November 28.

Ricz, Judith and Szunomár, Ágnes 2019. "Driving forces behind the international expansion strategies of non-European EMNEs – a comparative analysis of the Chinese and Brazilian cases". *Köz-Gazdaság - Review of Economic Theory and Policy,* 14(3), pp. 168-189.

Rosito, Tatiana. 2020. *Bases for a long-term strategy by Brazil towards China.* BCBC: Rio de Janeiro.

Schiavini, Janaina M. Scherer, Flávia L., de Moura, Gilnei L. and Minello, Italo F. 2011. "Os desafios do processo de expatriação no cenário sino-brasileiro. O caso da WEG S.A na China." *Revista Eletrônica de Negócios Internacionais (Internext) 6(2),* pp. 22-47

Shutte, Giogio R. and Debone, Victor S. 2017. "The expansion of Chinese direct investments. The case of the Brazilian energy sector". *Conjuntura Austral* 8(44), pp. 90-113.

Shutte, Giorgio R. 2020. *Oasis Para o Capital: Solo Fertil Para a Corrida de Ouro.* Apris Editora: Curitiba.

Studart, Rogerio and Myers, Margaret. 2021. *Reimagining China-Brazil Relations Under the BRI: The Climate Imperative.* (2021). CFR/CEBRI: New York.

WEG. 2022. WEG *Investor Presentation.* At: https://ri.weg.net/publicacoes-e-comunicados/apresentacoes-e-documentos/.

3. CARIBBEAN OFDI TO CHINA

Jevon Minto, Chevano Baker and Noel Young

Introduction

Chinese investments in Latin America and the Caribbean (LAC) have received significant attention in recent years. While studies have extensively explored Chinese outward foreign direct investment (OFDI) in the region, the focus on LAC investment flows to China has been relatively limited. This discrepancy becomes particularly pronounced when examining the Caribbean sub-region, which, unlike its Latin American counterparts, lacks indigenous firms or home-grown domestic enterprises that have directly invested in China. However, what sets the Caribbean apart is its distinct role as an offshore financial center (OFC), attracting multinational corporations (MNCs) from other regions to utilize its offshore financial destinations, like Bermuda or the Cayman Islands, as gateways for establishing their presence in China. Several scholars have delved into the determinants of OFDI from LAC to China, highlighting the positive correlation between the strong macroeconomic performance of the home country and increased overseas investments by LAC enterprises. Market-seeking MNCs, such as Grupo Bimbo, a prominent food conglomerate from Mexico, have been identified as key drivers of Mexican OFDI in China (see chapter 6 of Dussel Peters in this book). These corporations leverage their comparative advantages, including ownership experience and innovation, to enter and compete in foreign markets that share characteristics similar to their domestic environments.

However, what often goes unnoticed in studies on foreign investment in and out of the region is the role and significance of OFCs. While the Caribbean may not have a significant number of homegrown investments and MNCs operating in China, OFCs in the region serve as major sources of capital outflows to China. This reinforces the Caribbean's position as a bastion of OFCs within the international financial architecture. Notably, during the post-2008 subprime mortgage crisis, the importance of OFCs became evident as resilient emerging markets like China sought efficient capital allocation, confidence-boosting institutional regulations, and cost-effective investment processes to sustain their demand. Contrary to popular belief, OFCs are not solely havens for tax avoidance. Instead, they play significant roles in international finance by offering niche services facilitated by favorable legislative frameworks and highly-skilled professionals. These services encompass various areas such as collective investment schemes, international banking, insurance, structured finance, and foreign direct investment (FDI). Moreover, the interconnectedness of OFCs with other international financial centers such as London, Switzerland, and Hong Kong adds to their significance. This interconnectedness helps explain the dominance of Caribbean states like the British Virgin Islands (BVI) and the Cayman Islands in the overall flow of LAC OFDI. In fact, approximately 30 % of total FDI flows originate from tax havens, with Bermuda listed among the 30 countries acting as the origin or destination for the world's largest FDI stocks.

Understanding the complex dynamics between the Caribbean, China, and the broader LAC region requires a comprehensive examination that considers the unique role of OFCs. By shedding light on the interplay between OFCs, MNCs, and investment flows, this study offers a deeper understanding of the Caribbean's position within the global investment landscape and its impact on China-LAC relations. The research sets out to investigate the patterns and trends of Caribbean OFDI in China. To achieve this, a mixed-methods approach was employed, combining quantitative data analysis with qualitative insights from relevant sources. The primary data analysis in this study relied on the fDi Markets database of LAC OFDI to China between 2003 and 2021.[1] However, it is important to note that the most recent transactions from Caribbean countries occurred in 2019. The study also draws on data from the LAC-China Network's Chinese OFDI Monitor in LAC (*Monitor*), the National Bureau of Statistics of China, the United Nations Conference on Trade and Development (UNCTAD), U.S. Securities and Exchange Commission (SEC) 10-Q filings, and Bermuda's Registrar of Companies, among others. The quantitative data gathered was analyzed using descriptive statistics to identify patterns and trends in Caribbean OFDI to China, including distribution across sectors and countries.

We complemented the quantitative data with qualitative information gathered from diverse sources such as company websites, press releases, news articles, and SEC 10-Q filings. These sources were used to develop in-depth case studies of select MNCs, enabling a deeper understanding of the motivations, strategies, and impacts associated with their investments. The integration of quantitative and qualitative data analysis enables a comprehensive examination of Caribbean OFDI in China as it combines statistical trends with contextual insights. The study employs the eclectic paradigm as a theoretical framework to analyze the Caribbean OFDI in China conducted by MNCs. In general, the examined strategic investments and activities of these MNCs demonstrate a strong orientation to leverage location-specific advantages to pursue market-seeking investments while also following a horizontal FDI strategy. This approach differs from that of Latin American firms, which mainly depend on ownership advantages such as innovative distribution systems and technological innovations to attain successful investments in China. The research findings will contribute to a deeper understanding of the dynamics and

1 fDi Markets is an extensive database provided by the Financial Times that monitors global crossborder investments in all countries and sectors, providing real time data on investment projects, capital investment, and job creation.

implications of Caribbean investments in the region and the significant role that OFCs play. Further, it will inform policymakers, business communities, and other stakeholders involved in LAC-China economic relations of the multifaceted and evolving nature of the partnership.

The rest of the paper is organized as follows. The subsequent section explores the political economy of China-Caribbean relations, with a specific focus on FDI and other forms of investment. The third section explores the interconnectedness between China, the Caribbean, and OFCs, highlighting the mutual economic benefits. Section 4 presents the theoretical framework employed in the study. Section 5 features case studies of two OFCs, the Cayman Islands and Bermuda, with a focus on two companies from each jurisdiction. Specifically, Herbalife and Cedrus Investments are examined for the Cayman Islands, while XL Catlin (Catlin Group) and Accenture are analyzed for Bermuda Finally, Section 6 concludes the paper and discusses the policy implications for the broader biregional partnership.

1. The Political Economy of China-Caribbean Relations

The LAC region has remained relatively resilient and attractive as a destination for OFDI, with an increase in investments from US$ 16.7 billion in 2020 to US$ 26.2 billion in 2021.[2] This accounted for 15% of China's annual OFDI in 2021, compared to 11% in 2020, as reported in the China Statistical Yearbook by the National Bureau of Statistics of China (2022). Notably, this trend stands out when compared to Chinese OFDI patterns in other regions, such as Europe and North America (Figure 1). In Europe, Chinese OFDI decreased from US$ 12.7 billion in 2020 to US$ 10.9 billion in 2021, representing 8% of Chinese OFDI in 2020 and 6% in

2 Notably, these figures include China's OFDI to two financial centers, the Cayman Islands and the British Virgin Islands.

2021. Meanwhile, Chinese OFDI in North America slightly increased from US$ 6.3 billion in 2020 to US$ 6.6 billion in 2021, accounting for 4 % of Chinese OFDI in both periods.

Figure 1. China's OFDI by Region (2010-2021)

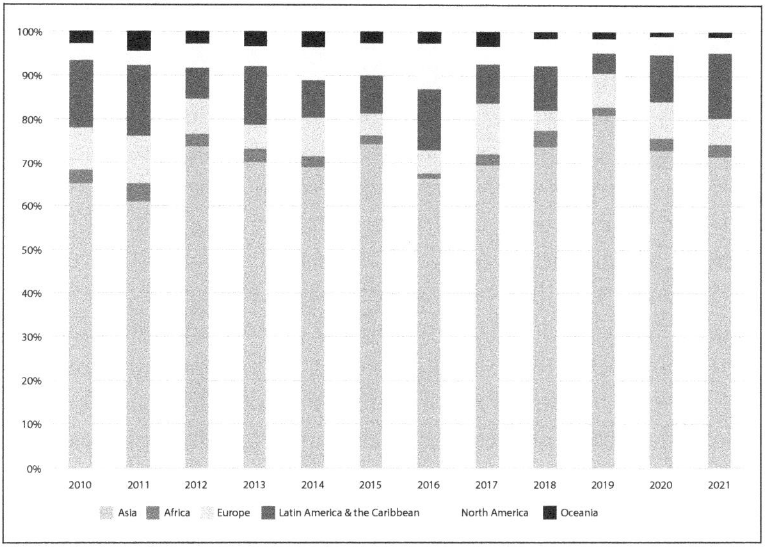

Source: own elaboration based on National Bureau of Statistics of China (2011-2022).

Based on data from the *Monitor*,[3] the total number of Chinese OFDI transactions in LAC during 2022 was 37, amounting to a total value of US$ 12,024 million. This figure represented a decline of -6.7 % compared to the previous year. The *Monitor's* data

3 The data provided by the Monitor differs from other sources, such as MOFCOM and UNCTAD, primarily due to methodological issues in recording OFDI. Dussel Peters (2019) argues that these issues include distinguishing between announced and completed transactions and differentiating between OFDI and other financial activities like loans and infrastructure projects. Red ALC-China has made a valuable contribution to addressing these issues by providing a better understanding of the use of loans for Chinese OFDI in the Caribbean. The Monitor employs a rigorous verification process utilizing multiple sources such as fDi Markets, Thomson-Reuters, Bloomberg, Capital IQ, the China Global Investment Tracker (CGIT), and investment announcements reported by the trade press. This comprehensive approach enables a firm-level analysis of Chinese OFDI in LAC.

highlights that Chinese OFDI in LAC reached its peak in 2010, contributing to 13.61 % of the region's FDI. It subsequently held the second position in 2019, with a share of 11.70 %, but experienced a decline due to the impact of the COVID-19 pandemic. However, in 2022, there was a rebound, with Chinese OFDI accounting for 7.63 % of the regional FDI (Dussel Peters 2023). In the Caribbean sub-region, Chinese OFDI for 2020–2022 involved seven transactions with a total value of $ 3,221 million, resulting in the creation of 4,594 jobs. Regardless of the specific statistics examined, the political economy of China-Caribbean relations is intriguing and warrants further analysis, considering the interaction between China's strategic interests and the region's receptivity through government policies and other economic initiatives.

Securing FDI has been adopted as a strategic objective for countries aiming to achieve economic growth and development. Since the 1960s, most Caribbean countries have pursued an open-door policy to attract FDI into import-substituting industries. Bilateral investment treaties (BIT), primarily with European and North American nations, have been a key strategy for the Caribbean to attract FDI. However, several countries have signed BITs with China to create a more favorable investment climate and reduce investment risk: Jamaica in 1994, Barbados in 1998, and Trinidad and Tobago in 2002. Jamaica, Barbados, and Trinidad and Tobago signed a Double Taxation Agreement (DTA) with China in 1996, 2000, and 2003, respectively, which provides for lower transactional taxes (Bernal, 2016). Beyond these instruments, Caribbean countries provide financial incentives for FDI, including relief on income taxes, dividends, and property taxes; reduction in duties on imported materials required in new investment; specific training grants or R&D subsidies; exemption from exchange controls; and accelerated depreciation allowances, among others (De Groot and Ludeña 2014). These abundant incentives often come with loose eligibility requirements, and tax holidays are offered for export-focused investment even in extractive industries. For example, in 2016, Jiquan Iron and Steel Company (JISCO), a Chinese state-owned company, acquired Jamaica's largest bauxite refinery from UC Rusal, a Russian firm, for $ 300 million. While JISCO was subject to income tax, the mining company obtained a waiver from the Jamaican government of the bauxite production levy for five years (Jamaica Gleaner, 2018). The decision to acquire the plant exemplified China's strategic efforts to secure and access key commodities in order to meet surging demand for the domestic market (Minto 2019).

Caribbean countries have also participated in trade fairs and investment conferences and used investment promotion agencies to promote their countries as investment destinations. Barbados, for example, has announced plans to re-establish an investment office in Beijing (Austin, 2019). There are also policies that ease migration restrictions for foreign investors; for instance, regulations in Belize, Curaçao, and Sint Maarten. Additionally, countries such as Saint Kitts and Nevis, Dominica, and Antigua and Barbuda offer Citizenship by Investment (CBI) programs through which foreign investors can obtain citizenship thanks to investment (De Groot and Ludeña 2014). These instruments open the discussion for analyzing Caribbean OFDI outflows, as ratified BITs result in higher average increases in FDI stocks compared to FDI stocks of country pairs not having ratified a treaty (Lejour and Salfi 2015).

The Caribbean region shares common interests and objectives with China's development strategy. This alignment, as we witnessed in the last two decades, led to an expansion of Beijing's political, economic, and diplomatic engagement with the region, strategically aimed at enhancing its soft power influence. China's pursuit of internationalization, accelerated via the Belt and Road Initiative (BRI) and assertion of the "One China Policy", influences its trade policies governing capital allocation, aid, and OFDI flows to diplomatic allies who recognize the People's Republic of China (PRC). This explains its economic engagement with the eleven Caribbean states with diplomatic ties to Beijing: Antigua and Barbuda, Barbados, Cuba, the Commonwealth of Dominica, the Dominican Republic, Guyana, Jamaica, Trinidad and Tobago, Suriname, The Bahamas, and Grenada (Foreign Affairs 2022). All except the Bahamas have signed onto the BRI. Moreover, PRC-backed Confucius institutes have been established in all the countries with diplomatic ties except the Commonwealth of Dominica and the Dominican Republic. China's diplomatic strategy goes hand in hand with the historic trend of loan commitments to government and state-run agencies in nine Caribbean Community (CARICOM)[4] member states from a group of 20 between 2000 and 2018. A disaggregated analysis of the concentration of loans and financing reveals significant allocation to infrastructure projects, accounting for 55 % of Chinese financing to CARICOM between 2000 and 2018, followed by mining, energy, and tourism (Minto 2019). According to an earlier study by Minto (2019), governments and state-run businesses in nine CARICOM countries received loan commitments from China's two main policy banks, the China Development Bank and the Export-Import Bank of China (Exim), totaling US$ 8.9 billion and covering forty projects up to 2018. Beyond 2018, there was a "precipitous decline" in loans to the region, similar to a wider trend observed across the wider LAC region. A recent report from the Inter-American Dialogue and the Global Development Policy Center at Boston University attributes this to "pandemic-related challenges" and a general "reconsideration of the functions and focus" of these banks by Chinese authorities (Myers and Ray 2023:1).

Beyond loan commitments and disbursements, Chinese low-interest loans for infrastructure development have long been considered an attractive solution for Caribbean states grappling with significant debt burdens and sluggish economic growth. These states often face limited fiscal space for capital expenditures. Chinese loan policies strategically prioritize transportation infrastructure projects such as expanding airports like Nassau Airport, resurfacing roads such as the Paramaribo Road project in Suriname, and constructing Jamaica's North-South Highway. These loans also extend support to tourism, energy, and telecommunications infrastructure initiatives in the region. Overall, China's investment in infrastructure projects such as ports, highways, and

4 CARICOM is the socio-economic bloc of nations in or near the Caribbean Sea.

airports is consistent with the BRI, which aims to improve infrastructure connectivity and promote trade and investment between China and other countries. In recent years, China's Digital Silk Road (DSR)—widely regarded as the world's biggest technology infrastructure project—has been a fundamental pillar of the BRI, and the Asian country has used public-private partnerships to finance telecommunications infrastructure projects in the region. For instance, in Guyana, the implementation of the national broadband strategy and the development of smart city surveillance cameras, an additional data center, and improvements to the government's network capacity are being funded by a loan of US$ 36.5 million from the China Exim Bank (Thomas, 2020).

China's role in global OFDI has significantly grown over the years, with its share increasing from less than 1% in 1991 to 19.69% in 2020 (Dussel Peters 2023). However, China has not only been active in OFDI but has also been aggressive and successful in attracting FDI itself. In fact, the UNCTAD's 2022 World Development Report ranks China as the world's second-leading destination for FDI and the first in Asia. According to the report, FDI inflows into China increased by 5.74% in 2020 to US$ 149.34 billion, up from US$ 141.22 billion in 2019, before a further increase to US$ 180.95 billion in 2021 (Figure 2). UNCTAD attributes successful pandemic containment measures and rapid recovery for this ranking. China has implemented various policies to attract FDI, including aggressively shaping a suite of foreign investment laws and regulations with, for example, stipulations for special economic zones and other related preferential policies, with a focus on attracting export-oriented FDI (Long 2005). Many MNCs have invested in China as a result of the preferential treatment accorded to foreign-invested enterprises (FIEs) over domestic firms (Long 2005). In 2018, China —the world's largest economy since 2013— also implemented new incentives, including methods to improve the delivery of key foreign investment projects, streamline customs clearance, lower import tariffs, and enhance FDI regulatory tools by building an online filing system (Chipman Koty 2018). China's central and local governments have continued with massive tax incentives and preferential subsidies in 2022 to foster a competitive business environment, expand market access, and spur foreign investment (Donovan 2018).

China's investment policies generally encourage foreign participation in manufacturing, high-technology services, service sectors, new materials or equipment production, renewable energy, recycling, and environmental protection (Zhang 2020). Conversely, there are limitations on investments in strategic sectors where China aims to develop domestic firms into globally competitive MNCs, as well as in sectors historically dominated by state monopolies (China Briefing, 2022). Speculative investments involving money, real estate, or assets are also discouraged. Data from the National Bureau of Statistics of China suggest that the manufacturing sector receives the majority of FDI, followed by real estate and then business services (Figure 3). China's FDI policy has played a crucial role in the country's economic development and export success (Haberly and Wojcik 2013). Indeed, throughout the last two decades, the total import and export value of FIEs has consistently accounted for over 40 % of China's exports. FDI has also

Figure 2. China's FDI (1990-2021)

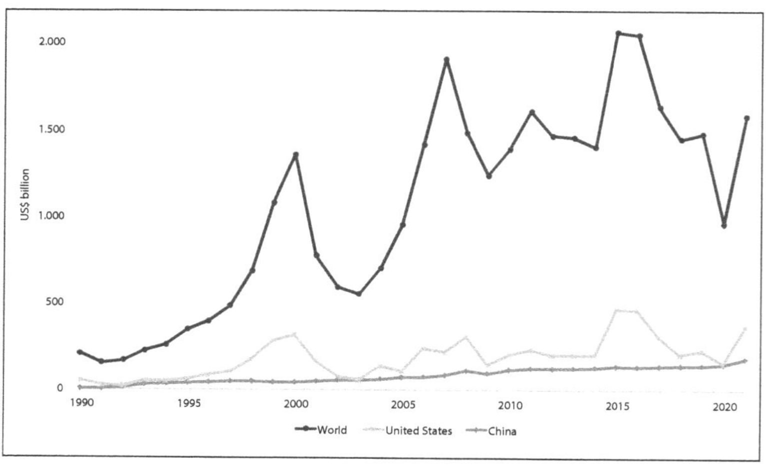

Source: own elaboration based on UNCTAD (2022).

improved China's technological capability, established R&D centers, and generated technological spillover effects (Geng 2004).

Figure 3. Share of China's FDI by Major Sectors (2010 and 2020)

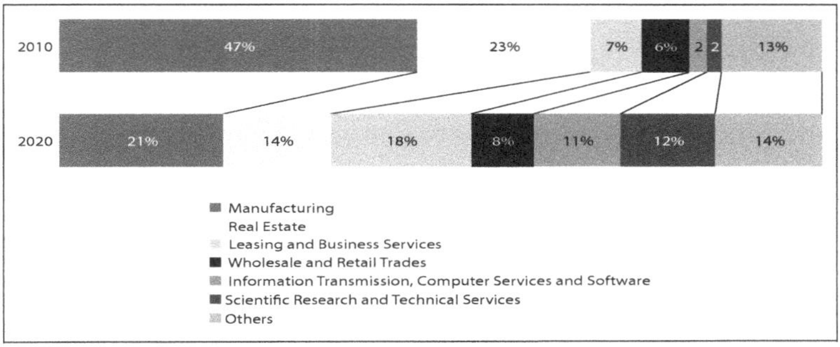

Source: own elaboration based on National Bureau of Statistics of China (2011, 2021).

2. Caribbean's Offshore Financial Centers and OFDI to China

While there is a growing body of literature examining the flow, concentration, and nature of Chinese OFDI to the LAC region, few studies have traced LAC investment flows to China. In the case of the Caribbean, this is even more pronounced, unlike in the wider region, where scholars have examined the behavior of OFDI flowing from Mexico, Argentina, and Chile (Kunhardt 2013). In assessing the determinants of OFDI from LAC to China, Correa da Cunha *et al.* (2022) conclude that a strong macroeconomic performance in the home country is positively associated with increased overseas investments by LAC firms, suggesting that LAC firms are more likely to expand their investments overseas when domestic market conditions are favorable. In analyzing Mexican OFDI in China, Kunhardt (2013) comes to the conclusion that market-seeking MNCs, like the food conglomerate Grupo Bimbo, use their comparative advantages to enter and compete in foreign markets, like China, that are similar to their domestic environments.

What is often unaccounted for in studies relating to foreign investment in and out of the region is the role and significance of OFCs. Although there are very few Caribbean homegrown investments and MNCs in China, relative to the larger LAC countries, OFCSs are sources of significant capital outflows from the region to China, reinforcing the region's role as a bastion of OFCs. The role of OFCs within the international financial architecture is significant. Using the period of the post-2008 subprime mortgage crisis to demonstrate their significance, Morris (2011) explains that amidst the wipeout of wealth caused by the crisis, resilient emerging markets like China required efficient capital allocation, confidence-inspiring institutional regulations, and cost-effective investment processes to service and sustain their demand. Outside of crises and refuting assertions that OFCs are havens mostly for avoiding taxes, Lane and Milesi-Ferretti (2010) also posit that OFCs play significant roles in international finance, providing niche services augured by comparative advantages like favorable legislative frameworks for the incorporation of financial entities and the existence of highly skilled professionals for services such as collective investment schemes, international banking, insurance, structured finance, and FDI. Lane and Milesi-Ferretti (2010) further argue that, though OFCs are almost always solely intermediaries for capital flow, their interconnectedness with advanced economies is of great significance. Approximately 30 % of global FDI flows are attributed to tax havens, and Bermuda is among the 30 countries identified as either the source or destination of the largest FDI stocks worldwide (Haberly and Wójcik 2013).

Vlcek (2010) challenges the assumption that OFCs' role in China's FDI is solely for tax minimization purposes and suggests alternative explanations such as reducing transaction costs and accessing investment capital. This alludes to the motivations and determinants of foreign investment to and from China, which have also evolved with the PRC's internationalization. A key determinant is the political divide between the Chinese Communist Party (CCP) and Taiwan, which has seen Taiwanese investors utilize OFCs to circumvent sanctions and restrictions, with many starting

Hong Kong initially and then transitioning to Caribbean OFCs post-reintegration (Chen 2014). CCP policies to entice FDI have also proven significant. Given China's provision of preferential policies to attract FDI, such as tax advantages, fiscal incentives, and property rights protection, round-tripping has been seen as a useful mechanism for companies, many of whom are wary of restrictive domestic regulations and loose and ad hoc enforcement of laws. Given the gap that prevails due to the lack of studies on the phenomenon of OFDI flow between China and the Caribbean, resulting in the scarcity of updated information evaluating any possible evolutions in the determinants of the flow, this research is of utmost importance.

The historical origins of OFCs shed light on the connection between the flow of FDI between China and the Caribbean. British and Canadian investors are credited with the creation of the first Caribbean OFC in the Bahamas in 1936 (Suss *et al.* 2002), which saw an expansion in the 1960s to the Cayman Islands, BVI, and Anguilla. The expansion of OFCs is attributed to the United Kingdom (UK) because it was seeking to engender economic development in its colonies, given their low-cost, high-profitability nature. Hong Kong would follow this development pattern until its reversion to Chinese jurisdiction in 1997, which would prove significant in establishing the relationship between the former colony and Caribbean OFCs. Vlcek (2010) posits that ties between the Caribbean and Hong Kong were further entrenched following the announcement of the latter's planned reversion to China, leading to the flight of firms that relocated their corporate registration to OFCs like the BVI, Bermuda, and the Cayman Islands so that there would be less exposure to possible nationalization and expropriation by the CCP. Though there may have been an initial rationale for the flow of FDI between the territories, it also brought China into contact with the realm of offshore finance. As a result of China's integration into the global economy, culminating in its ascension to the World Trade Organization, the CCP aggressively promulgated a legal framework and regulations to govern and entice foreign investment. As a result, Chinese companies witnessed a staggering 92 % increase in offshore mergers and acquisition investments in 2003 compared to the previous year. Furthermore, between 2002 and 2006, this growth expanded to surpass an impressive US$ 15 billion (Long 2005).

The presence and relevance of Caribbean OFCs during that early expansion were extremely visible yet inexplicably ignored, as highlighted by the growth in OFDI to the Cayman Islands, which in 2003 accounted for 28.3 % of aggregate Chinese OFDI, increasing to US$ 7.83 billion (44 %) by 2006 (Sutherland *et al.* 2012). As China emerged and integrated into the global economy at the turn of the twenty-first century, the Cayman Islands and the BVI became top sources of FDI for China. These two territories accounted for over 80 % of the capital that left China as investments and returned as FDI between 2003 and 2006 (OECD 2008). Haberly and Wójcik (2013) also asserted that the Cayman Islands and the BVI are important sources for an estimated 15 % to 50 % of FDI to China, which first leaves the country as capital and returns in FDI form. This practice has been termed "round-tripping". Some of the incentives that have been identified for round-tripping include tax advantages, property rights protection, exchange rate expectations, and, importantly, the competitiveness of Hong Kong as an international financial center that allows for cross-border transactions (Geng 2004). This is particularly significant as observed by Vlcek (2013), who asserts that OFDI to China is to some degree domestic capital re-routed through OFCs so as to disguise its domestic origins, returning to the Mainland as FDI, in order to secure the advantages afforded by such classification. "Round-tripping" as Vlcek (2013) posits, calls into question conclusions on the measurement of gross OFDI to China, arguing that it is not possible to arrive at sound conclusions on foreign investments to China, considering the challenges in separating the foreign and domestic beneficial interests behind them. Vlcek (2010) also explores the relationship governing direct investment flow between China and OFCs, highlighting that in 2008, among the top ten FDI sources for China, five were OFCs, with the BVI and the Cayman Islands ranking second and fifth, respectively, only behind Hong Kong as the leading OFC source. Further, the BVI emerged as the second-largest investor in China between 2006 and 2012 and ranked fifth for OFDI in 2012 (Donovan 2018). This trend continued into 2014, as highlighted by Chen (2018), with both the BVI and the Cayman Islands remaining in the top ten, with the latter dropping to eighth. The BVI, which recorded US$ 16 billion in 2008, saw outflows to China rise to US$ 141.8 billion by the end of 2014. During the same period, the Cayman Islands experienced a significant rise in investments, with the amount increasing from US$ 3.2 billion to US$ 28.7 billion. The vast investment flows between those two territories and China have elevated LAC's share of investment in Mainland China above that of North America and Europe (Breslin 2004). This observation is supported by Dussel Peters (2019), who reported the data recorded by the *Monitor* in 2019. It is important to note that when excluding the BVI and Cayman Islands from the analysis, Chinese OFDI is reduced to US$ 9,034 (or 13.65% of total OFDI to LAC) for the 2010–2015 period. This emphasizes the importance of investigating OFDI flows, particularly from Caribbean OFCs, to China.

At first glance, it would appear that the role of Caribbean OFCs is solely for round-tripping purposes, but the data points to another factor, which is the focus of this study: MNCs incorporated in or operating in OFCs seeking market access to China. The locational choices of these MNCs play an important role in the significant OFDI from these Caribbean OFCs. The Cayman Islands, with its dominant position as a domicile for over 75% of global hedge funds with over US$ 1 trillion in assets under management, offers a competitive advantage relative to its rivals (Sutherland *et al.*, 2010). Its niche financial services appeal to Chinese entities seeking to access financial markets via IPO listings on the US or Hong Kong stock exchanges. The proximity to major Western financial institutions and access to comparatively more efficient and developed financial markets also make it an attractive destination for Chinese investment. Similarly, the BVI, for which Hong Kong and mainland China-based companies account for 40% of the over US$ 1.5 trillion in assets that are mediated through the jurisdiction, has positioned itself as a successful facilitator of cross-border business with a familiar English common law-based legal system (Donovan 2018). Chinese companies, faced with legal and political barriers restricting cross-border transactions and global capital accumulation of investments in certain markets, find value in using shell companies based in the BVI and the Cayman Islands to attract foreign investment while complying with Chinese protectionist laws, especially in strategic sectors such as the technology industry, which restricts foreign ownership of equity (Belsie 2023). The strategies implemented by the BVI, in particular, such as allowing Chinese character names on company certificates, have been well received by Chinese businesses, signaling a welcoming attitude and acceptance of Chinese culture. These factors may play a significant role in shaping Caribbean OFDI to China, and it is crucial to evaluate their influence and explore new rationales for this phenomenon.

3. Explaining the Driving Factors of Caribbean OFDI in China

In contrast to other Latin American nations, the Caribbean lacks indigenous companies that have made direct investments in China. However, the sub-region exhibits a distinctive characteristic where MNCs from other locations utilize the Caribbean's position as a cross-border financial center to establish their presence in China. These corporations typically incorporate themselves in prominent offshore financial destinations like Bermuda, the BVI, or the Cayman Islands. In turn, this process drives a multifaceted yet complex relationship among the interested parties and ultimately facilitates economic growth and development for smaller jurisdictions. In this regard, OFCs act as conduits for capital flows and investments, enabling these territories to access essential resources that would otherwise be inaccessible. Vlcek (2010) contends that this enables the offshore realm to play a vital role in bolstering China's economic advancement. Further, given China's position as a prominent global economic force, it needs a diverse array of financial intermediary services to facilitate its trade and investment endeavors. The OFCs, renowned for their expertise in banking, wealth management, and corporate finance, are well-equipped to offer these services in a cost-effective and efficient manner. As a result, the interconnection between China, the Caribbean, and the OFCs yields mutual benefits, fostering economic development and promoting prosperity.

Examining the motivations of FDI through the eclectic paradigm, also referred to as the OLI framework, developed by Dunning (1980), we can further understand the underlying drivers of this complex situation and the multifaceted relationship between China, the Caribbean, and the OFCs. The framework consists of three main factors that influence a firm's decision to invest in foreign markets: (i) ownership advantages, (ii) location-specific advantages, and (iii) internalization advantages. *Ownership advantages* refer to the unique advantages that a firm possesses, such as specialized knowledge, managerial skills, or proprietary technology. These advantages allow the firm to compete effectively in foreign markets and gain a competitive edge over local firms. Firms may choose to invest in foreign countries to expand their business globally. Secondly, *location-specific advantages* are advantages that are specific to a particular foreign country or region. They can include access to natural resources, skilled labor, favorable regulatory conditions, infrastructure, or a large market. Investing in a specific location can provide significant benefits to the firm, such as cost savings, market access, or the ability to cater to local consumer preferences. Finally, *internalization advantages* refer to the benefits a firm gains by owning and controlling foreign operations rather than relying on licensing or exporting. Internalization allows the firm to better exploit its ownership and location advantages and maintain greater control over its operations. By directly investing in foreign markets, a firm can protect its intellectual property, maintain quality standards, and have closer proximity to customers, thereby enhancing its competitiveness.

Along with the eclectic paradigm, which primarily seeks to examine both patterns and reasons for FDI, Dunning (1993) outlines four investor-specific motivations that can explain the swell of outbound FDI from the Caribbean to China through OFCs: natural resource-seeking, market-seeking, strategic asset-seeking, and efficiency-seeking. Natural resource-seeking investments are motivated by the desire to access and exploit natural resources such as minerals, oil, gas, and agricultural products in foreign countries to secure and gain a competitive advantage in their industries. Market-seeking investments are motivated by an interest in serving domestic or regional markets when firms identify untapped consumer demand or a growing market. These types of investments are usually correlated to the size of the foreign economy and its growth potential. By establishing a presence in these markets, firms can expand their customer base, increase sales, and achieve economies of scale. With strategic asset-seeking investments, investors seek to acquire strategic assets that will enhance their competitive position in a given market. These strategic assets can include well-known brands, talented human capital, established distribution networks, patents, or technological capabilities. Investors may pursue mergers and acquisitions to gain access to these assets and strengthen their market position. Firms engage in efficiency-seeking investments when they invest in foreign countries to benefit from factors that enable them to compete more effectively in international markets. This can include accessing lower-cost inputs such as labor, raw materials, or production facilities. By rationalizing their global activities and leveraging cost advantages, firms can improve efficiency and reduce production costs.

Understanding the difference between horizontal and vertical FDI can also help us understand the different strategies used by MNCs when investing in foreign markets. Horizontal FDI involves investments by a company in a similar operation or business as its existing one (Aizenman and Marion 2004). These investments are primarily market-seeking, involving the establishment of new production facilities or the acquisition of existing companies in foreign markets to meet local demand, enter new markets, or compete with local rivals. Horizontal FDI allows a firm to leverage its expertise and technological capabilities without the risk of them being taken over by external entities, which is a greater possibility when supply chains are involved (Carril-Caccia and Pavlova 2018). On the other hand, vertical FDI refers to investments that seek to optimize the supply and value chain and therefore fragment the production process internationally. As vertical FDI is primarily efficiency-seeking, multinationals strategically locate different stages of production or sourcing activities in different countries to achieve cost savings, enhance efficiency, or gain access to specialized capabilities. Multinationals leverage the unique characteristics of the different countries, and their headquarters and subsidiaries engage in specific economic activities with trade links connecting the different production sites through imports and exports (Hanson, Mataloni Jr. and Slaughter 2005). By optimizing their supply and/or value chains, firms can improve their overall competitiveness and better meet customer needs. Essentially, horizontal FDI seeks to expand market presence by replicating the same line of business in foreign markets, whereas vertical FDI seeks to extend control over various stages of the production process.

These different motivations for FDI highlight the diverse reasons why investors choose to expand their operations into foreign markets. A combination of ownership advantages, location-specific advantages, internalization benefits, or particular objectives like accessing resources, markets, strategic assets, increasing efficiency, or optimizing the supply and/or value chain could be the driving force behind foreign investment decisions.

4. Descriptive Analysis of Caribbean Investments in China: Two OFCs' Case Studies

The economic ties between China and the Caribbean have witnessed substantial growth and expansion, as reflected in the capital investments for the period spanning 2003–2022. According to our analysis based on cross-border transactions recorded by fDi Markets, Caribbean countries have invested a total of US$ 1,698.7 million and generated 9,062 jobs in China from 2003 to 2019.[5] The years 2006 and 2014 stood out with the highest number of jobs created, 3,489 and 1,681, respectively, while capital investments peaked in 2009 and 2018 at US$ 233.7 million and US$ 224.2 million, respectively (Figure 4). The contributing countries include the Bahamas, Bermuda, the Cayman Islands, Cuba, and Saint

Figure 4: Caribbean OFDI to China by Year (2003 - 2019)

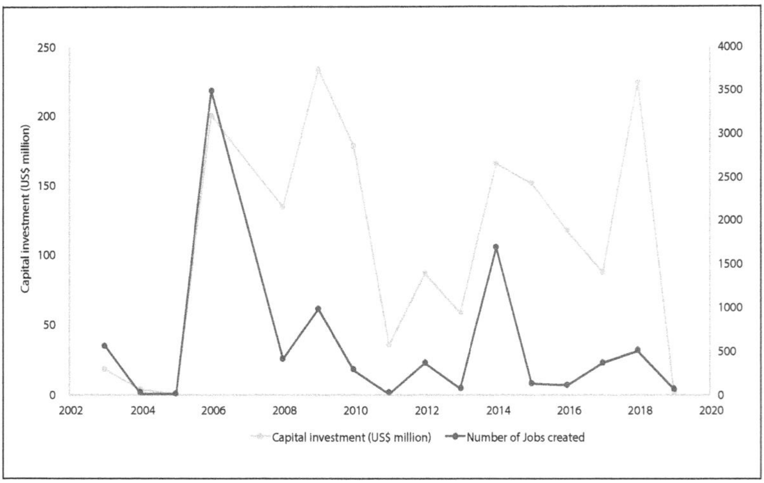

Source: own elaboration based on data from fDi Markets.

5 The data used for the analysis is updated to 2022, but the most recent transactions from Caribbean countries in the dataset occurred in 2019.

Figure 5. Caribbean OFDI to China by Country (2003 - 2019)

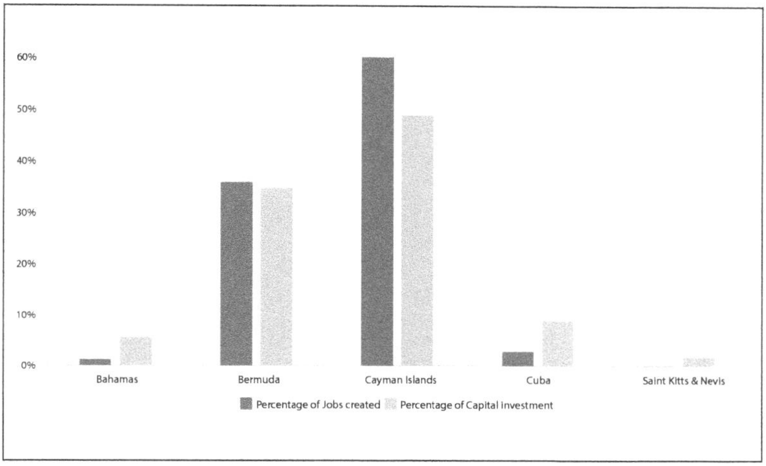

Source: own elaboration based on data from fDi Markets.

Kitts and Nevis. The Cayman Islands and Bermuda —two OFCs— accounted for the majority of investments, representing 49 % and 35 % of the capital investments, respectively, and 60 % and 36 % of the jobs created (Figure 5). As such, the two case studies will focus on the Cayman Islands and Bermuda, examining the factors that led firms in these countries to invest in China, their challenges, and their investments' impact on both countries.

In terms of destination cities, Hong Kong and Shanghai received the highest capital investments at 29.5 % and 23.4 %, respectively (Figure 6). However, when it comes to job creation, Nanjing took the lead with 14.6 % of the jobs created. Earlier research by Luo *et al.* (2008) indicated that two key factors, namely industry agglomeration and policy incentives, play a crucial role in determining the location of OFDI in China. The investments cover a range of sectors, including automotive components, automotive OEM, biotechnology, business services, consumer products, financial services, hotels and tourism, pharmaceuticals, plastics, semiconductors, software and IT services, textiles, and transportation and warehousing. Among these sectors, financial services accounted for most of the capital investment at 49.9 %, while consumer

Figure 6. Caribbean OFDI to China by Destination City (2003 – 2019)

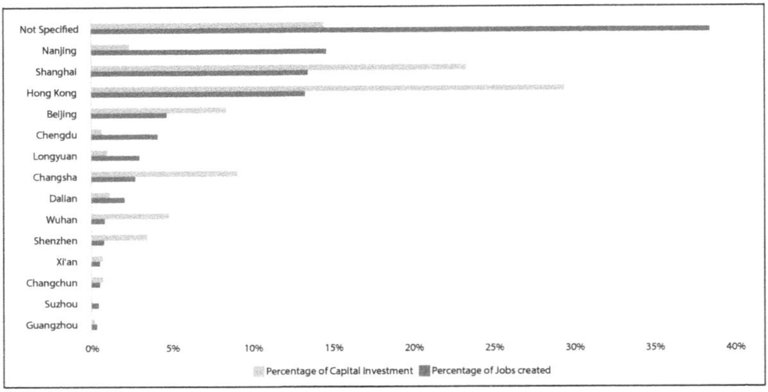

Source: own elaboration based on data from fDi Markets.

Figure 7. Caribbean OFDI to China by Sector (2003 – 2019)

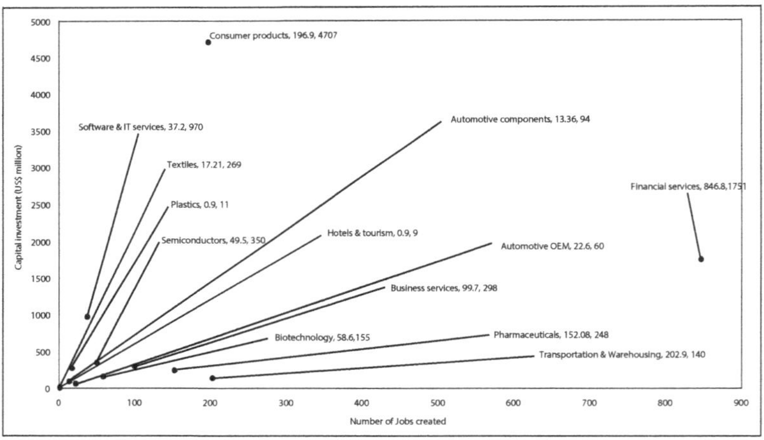

Note: The number of jobs created is represented on the x-axis (horizontal), while the capital investment in terms of US dollars is represented on the y-axis (vertical). For a particular point on the figure, e.g., (consumer products, 196.7, 4,707), the interpretation is that the amount of OFDI is US$ 196.7 million in capital investment with a corresponding 4,707 jobs.

Source: own elaboration based on data from fDi Markets.

products contributed to 51.9 % of the jobs created (Figure 7). In terms of market activity, business services showed a notably higher capital investment, while manufacturing accounted for the highest job creation. This finding aligns with research indicating that MNCs tend to invest in export-oriented and labor-intensive sectors with high productivity levels (He 2008; Lin and Kuan 2011).

The motivations for firms from the Cayman Islands and Bermuda to invest in China are multi-faceted and include factors such as access to new markets, cost advantages, potential for growth, government incentives, and favorable policies. For example, China has a large consumer market, which can be attractive for firms looking to expand their customer base. Additionally, China's lower labor and production costs can provide a cost advantage for firms that invest in the country. China also offers government incentives and favorable policies to foreign investors, such as tax exemptions, subsidies, and simplified approval procedures, which can make investing in the country more attractive. It is also likely that the specific motivations for each firm will vary depending on their business objectives, size, industry, and targeted cities.

4.1 Case Study 1: Cayman Islands' OFDI in China

The Cayman Islands, a British Overseas Territory located in the western Caribbean Sea, became an associate member of CARICOM in 2002. However, the UK largely manages the territory's foreign relations. The Cayman Islands is renowned for being an OFC and is considered one of the top ten financial centers globally. Its status as a tax-neutral jurisdiction, favorable regulatory environment, and strategic location contribute to its success. The territory has a stable and business-friendly environment and is home to international businesses, investors, and high-net-worth individuals. Despite having a small population of around 78,000 and a GDP of US$ 5.9 billion, the territory's economy heavily relies on the financial and insurance services sector, accounting for approximately 33.4% of the country's GDP in 2021 (World Bank 2022).

While the Cayman Islands is traditionally known as an FDI recipient, the country has also emerged as the largest sender of

OFDI from the Caribbean to China, with $ 830.7 million in capital investment and 5,442 jobs created across various cities, including Beijing, Changsha, Chengdu, Hong Kong, Nanjing, Shanghai, and Shenzhen (Figure 8). Hong Kong topped the list in terms of capital investment with $ 207.3 million, which accounted for 25 % of the total. Nanjing was the leader in job creation, accounting for 1,327 jobs, equivalent to 24 % of the total. The investments were made in various sectors, such as automotive, business services, consumer products, financial services, plastics, software and IT services, and transportation and warehousing. Financial services made up 44 % of the total investment, followed by transportation and warehousing and consumer products with 24 % each. Consumer products contributed the most to job creation, accounting for 86 % of the total, while all other sectors, except for financial services with 6 %, each contributed less than 5 % of the total jobs created. Overall, for the sectors, the capital investment and the jobs created appear to be highly correlated.

Several companies, including Aviation Management Services (Cayman), BitMart, Block.one, Campbells, Cedrus Investments, China Chaintek United, CML Offshore Recruitment, DMS Governance,

Figure 8. Cayman Islands OFDI to China by Sector (2003 - 2019)

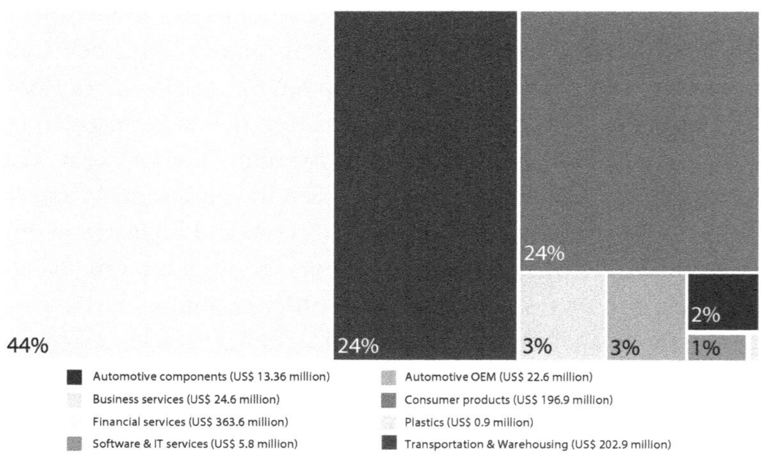

Source: own elaboration based on data from fDi Markets.

Gemilang International, Herbalife, MaplesFS (Maples Finance), Paradigm Industries, Thorp Alberga, Walkers, and Yangzhou Jinsei Wheel Manufacture, have invested in China from as early as 2005 up to 2019. However, this case study will focus on two companies, Herbalife Nutrition Ltd. and Cedrus Investments. Herbalife has created the highest number of jobs, while Cedrus Investments has made the highest capital investment, making them both significant contributors to the overall stock of OFDI flow from the Cayman Islands to China.

4.1.1 Cedrus Investments

Cedrus Investments, a global boutique investment firm based in the Cayman Islands, made an important move in October 2010 by opening its Hong Kong office, marking its expansion into Asia (Cedrus Investments 2010). Founded in 1997, Cedrus specializes in private wealth management, asset management, and financial advisory services and strategically chose the Cayman Islands as its headquarters to serve its institutional, corporate, and private clients on a global level. During the announcement of the Hong Kong office opening, Rani Jarkas, the Chairman of Cedrus Investments, emphasized that the office would bring unique investment opportunities to Greater China and Hong Kong (Cedrus 2010). Jarkas also highlighted the company's global network, expertise, and organizational structure, which includes the Arabian Gulf region, as key factors that would create real value. At the time of this expansion into China, capital markets were struggling due to weak growth in the West and low bond yields, forcing investors to look for better opportunities elsewhere. Hence, investing in China became increasingly attractive (Cedrus 2010).

Following its successful expansion into Hong Kong, Cedrus Investments further expanded its presence in the region by opening offices in Shanghai and Beijing shortly after (Cedrus Investments 2015). In May 2018, the company announced that the local government had approved the establishment of an office in Shenzhen

(Cedrus Investments 2018). At the time, Shenzhen was one of China's fastest-growing cities in terms of GDP and was considered an emerging megacity with a vigorous market dynamic, particularly in the fields of life sciences and high-tech innovation, which are areas of active investment for Cedrus. The strategic location of Shenzhen near the Pearl River Delta and its proximity to Hong Kong, one of the world's leading financial centers, made the city even more attractive. By expanding its business in Shenzhen, Cedrus Investments aimed to strengthen its commitment to serving clients in a more comprehensive and specialized way, leveraging its decade-long experience as a partner and advisor to firms in facilitating both their inbound and outbound investments in the Greater China region (Cedrus Investments 2018).

Cedrus Investments, on its website, has outlined five key goals as part of its strategic plan to expand its operations in China (Cedrus Investments 2023):

1. Introduce innovative, value-added investment products to the local investment community;
2. Share the firm's experience in the technology and finance industries;
3. Serve as a bridge between our clients in China and the Western world, as well as between leading foreign institutional investors and the Asian markets;
4. Identify promising investment opportunities in China that allow both our global clients and locals to capitalize on the growth in this very important market; and
5. Become the leading adviser on cross-border investment opportunities.

In addition to its China strategic plan, Cedrus Investments has a global market-entry strategy that involves integrating into local communities. This is achieved by assembling teams of highly regarded local professionals who understand the language, culture, and specific needs of clients' valuable relationships within the business community. In this regard, the company has supported initiatives that align with the interests of the local investor community in Greater China and Hong Kong. Notable events include its annual global investor conference and life sciences luncheons (Cedrus Investments 2011, 2016). Cedrus has also sponsored events, and its senior executives have delivered keynote speeches at prominent gatherings such as the China Mining Congress and Expo and the Chengdu Municipal People's Government Global Innovation and Entrepreneurship Fair (Cedrus Investments 2012, 2014, 2017). These engagements have provided the company with opportunities to connect with government officials and stakeholders, facilitating cross-border collaborations and discussions on industry trends and opportunities related to China's pursuit of innovation across diverse sectors.

Cedrus has built reputable local teams in China by integrating its local resources with extensive international experience and global networks. The company has established valuable partnerships with local entities and has solidified itself as a trusted advisor and facilitator of cross-border businesses and capital flows between China and countries abroad, with a focus on fast-growing markets such as major Belt and Road countries (Cedrus Investments 2023). Additionally, Cedrus sees itself as a bridge for companies seeking to leverage the opportunities offered by the BRI. The company claims to have strong global capabilities and offers unique value to companies and institutions seeking access to the highly sought-after Chinese and broader Asian markets.

Cedrus Investments' activities in China over the years highlight the significance of Hong Kong as a global financial center, its connection to the Cayman Islands, and its combined role in enabling investment to and from the Caribbean. The company's press release upon the launch of its Shenzhen office in 2020 emphasized that the firm was headquartered in Hong Kong (Cedrus Investments 2020). Hong Kong, a major financial hub with many financial institutions, is in the center of Asia and benefits from close financial connections with mainland China as well as extensive networks around the world. In addition to its sound legal system, Hong Kong offers a competitive tax system, free movement of capital, a diverse selection of financial products, and an abundant supply of financial talent within the region. While Cedrus still maintains an office in the Cayman Islands, the company's website now indicates that it is strategically headquartered in Switzerland and Hong Kong to serve its diverse international client base (Cedrus Investments 2023). The addition of Switzerland is interesting, as Switzerland is an internationally recognized financial hub and a leading provider of global financial services, including wealth management and sustainable finance. The European country has gained popularity among companies in the pharmaceutical, biotechnology, and medical technology sectors, and Cedrus' positioning in the country reflects its commitment to serving clients in China and Asian markets. More broadly, the Cayman Islands is increasingly competing with global financial centers like Singapore and Hong Kong as the preferred destination for Asia's hedge funds and wealthy individuals to store their assets. Recently, these two Asian countries have introduced new fund structures, offering low-tax vehicles and government subsidies for setup expenses (Wiggins *et al.* 2023). In a bid to counter this competition, the Cayman Islands is considering opening an office in either country to assist investors in setting up and managing funds within the Caribbean jurisdiction (Wiggins *et al.* 2023). This move would be the Cayman Islands' first presence in Asia, highlighting not only the economic significance of the region but also its connection to other global financial centers.

Cedrus Investments' motives for expanding into China closely align with the ownership advantage factor of Dunning's eclectic paradigm. The company leverages its specialized knowledge, managerial skills, and global network to compete effectively and create value in the Chinese market. The company's focus on innovative investment products, sharing industry experience, and acting as a bridge between Chinese and Western clients further highlights its ownership advantages. While Cedrus also benefits from location-specific advantages such as the growing Chinese market and access to skilled labor, the ownership advantages primarily drive Cedrus' decision to invest in China. Cedrus Investments' expansion into China is best classified as a market-seeking investment. This motivation is evidenced by the company's decision to establish a stronger presence in key Chinese cities, which was primarily driven by its objective to capitalize on the growing market and seize the opportunities presented by the Chinese economy. Cedrus Investments' expansion into China suggests a horizontal FDI strategy as it involves establishing a similar line of business focused on providing innovative investment products that add value to the local investment community.

4.1.2. Herbalife

Herbalife Nutrition Ltd. is a worldwide multi-level marketing corporation specializing in the development and sale of dietary supplements. Founded in 1980, the company employs nearly 10,000 individuals worldwide and operates via a network of about 4.5 million members and independent distributors in 95 countries (Herbalife 2023). The company is incorporated in the Cayman Islands and maintains its corporate headquarters in Los Angeles, California. Herbalife has manufacturing facilities in the United States, China, and Canada, and some of its products are produced by third-party suppliers around the globe.

As per Herbalife's 2023 SEC filings, the company operates uniquely in China through a group of subsidiaries under regulations related to direct selling and pyramid promotional schemes, which require the company to use a different business model specifically for China. Since multi-level marketing is not allowed in China, Herbalife applies for licenses to establish direct-selling enterprises. The Chinese business model also involves the sale of products through independent service providers and sales representatives and the use of company-operated retail stores and platforms. Chinese regulations also prohibit non-Chinese nationals from engaging in direct selling. In areas where Herbalife lacks a direct selling license, customers are served through company-operated retail stores. Sales representatives are rewarded with scaled rebates based on product volume and transition to independent service providers when they meet certain volume thresholds and performance requirements. These independent service providers are eligible to receive compensation from Herbalife Nutrition for marketing and support services but must comply with all applicable Chinese laws and company rules. Given the restrictions on direct selling, full-time employed sales representatives in China receive wages, bonuses, and benefits as opposed to distributor earnings, allowances, and royalty overrides.

In 2006, Herbalife recognized the growth potential of the Chinese direct-selling market and invested heavily to capitalize on the opportunity (Herbalife 2007). The company formed a management team with expertise in direct selling, established a Shanghai headquarters, expanded manufacturing capacity in Suzhou, and opened retail locations while registering additional products. By the end of 2008, Herbalife had labor contracts with approximately 48,000 sales representatives, net sales of US$ 145.0 million, and 84 stores across 30 provinces with six direct selling licenses in China (Herbalife 2009) (Table 1). In 2010, the company initiated the construction of a new botanical extract facility in Changsha with the support of the Hunan provincial and Changsha city governments (Herbalife 2010). This facility sources botanicals from regional farms, carries out extraction processes, and supplies raw materials to Herbalife's manufacturing facilities or third-party manufacturers globally. By December 31, 2010, Herbalife had labor contracts with around 49,000 sales representatives, 16 direct-selling licenses, and operated 71 retail stores across 30 provinces, generating net sales of US$ 184.4 million (Herbalife 2011).

To cater to the growing demand in its Chinese market, Herbalife Ltd. established a new manufacturing facility located at the Jiangning High-tech Industry Park in Nanjing, China, in 2014 (Herbalife 2014). Richard Goudis, who was the CEO of Herbalife at the time, stressed the importance of having a robust infrastructure that can meet current and future demand. At the end of 2014, the company operated 66 retail stores in 29 provinces, 25 of which were licensed for direct selling, and reported net sales of

Table 1. Herbalife's China operations (2006 — 2022)

Year	Number of stores	Number of Provinces with Herbalife presence	Net sales (US$ million)
2006	42	21	32.1
2008	84	30	145
2010	71	30	184.4
2014	66	29	664.3
2019	—	—	752
2020	—	—	809.6
2021	—	—	629.5
2022	—	—	391

Notes: — means no data available.

Source: own elaboration based on Herbalife's SEC 10-Q filings from 2006 to 2022.

US $664.3 million in China (Herbalife 2015). As online ordering became more prevalent, the demand for company-operated retail stores declined. Therefore, Herbalife shifted its focus to expanding its e-commerce platform, conducting sales promotions, and launching social media-driven marketing campaigns.

With the opening of a new training center in Chengdu with a capacity of 600 people, Herbalife Nutrition increased its presence in China in 2019. The Chengdu Training Center, established in the Xicun Lifestyle Center, is used for educating and training customers and distributors about nutrition and healthy meal preparation (Herbalife 2019). John DeSimone, then a co-president and chief strategic officer of Herbalife Nutrition, pointed to the pivotal role that the training centers would play in the company's efforts to positively impact the community through good nutrition and education. Net sales in China amounted to US$ 752.0 million in 2019 (Herbalife 2020). But by the end of December 2022, the company's net sales in China had fallen to US $391 million, despite efforts to strengthen Herbalife's operations in China through improved digital capabilities and expanded offerings (Herbalife 2023). This decline was attributed to an unfavorable sales mix, adverse foreign currency exchange rates, and COVID-19 infection surges.

Over the years, Herbalife operations in China have benefited from government policies, including a tax holiday from 2008 to 2012, during which the company enjoyed a zero-tax rate in China in 2008 and 2009, followed by a graduated tax rate ranging from 11 % in 2010 to a maximum of 25 % in 2011 and 2012 (Herbalife 2011). Herbalife has also received several grants from provincial governments in China to encourage local investment and operations. These grants amounted to approximately $ 14.5 million, US $ 31.5 million, US $ 29.8 million, and US $ 50.8 million in 2020, 2019, 2018, and 2017, respectively (Herbalife 2020, 2021).

Herbalife encountered regulatory and legal risks in China, which had an impact on its operations. In 2019, the Chinese government conducted a 100-day review to investigate illegal promotion and sales of health products, resulting in negative media attention for the entire health industry. This review had a detrimental effect on Herbalife's operations as its members reduced their business activities and sales meetings (Herbalife 2021). In 2020, Herbalife reached a US $ 123.1 million settlement with the US Department of Justice, including a criminal fine of US $ 55.74 million and disgorgement and interest amounting to US $ 67.31 million (SEC 2020). The charges alleged that between 2007 and 2016, the company bribed Chinese officials to obtain direct selling licenses, minimize government scrutiny, and suppress negative media attention. Additionally, Herbalife settled corruption charges and agreed to pay $ 20 million to the SEC for misleading investors regarding its Chinese business in U.S. regulatory filings over a six-year period (SEC 2019). While Herbalife claimed that its China business model differed from other countries, the SEC found that it employed a similar compensation model in China as it did elsewhere. Without admitting or denying the SEC's findings, Herbalife consented to the SEC's order, which determined that the company violated certain anti-fraud and federal securities laws on reporting provisions.

Herbalife's operations in China leverage location-specific advantages, including the size of the market, growth potential, and government support. Their strategic investments and adaptations to local regulations demonstrate their focus on capitalizing on the unique advantages and conditions offered by the Chinese market. These activities, with their focus on market-seeking motivation, aim to expand their market presence and meet consumer demand through establishing subsidiaries, expanding manufacturing capacity, opening retail locations, and facilitating e-commerce to serve the Chinese market. These activities aimed at market expansion in the Chinese domestic market primarily align with the characteristics of horizontal FDI. While Herbalife engages in some vertical integration for raw materials, its primary focus remains on market entry and complying with market-specific regulations.

4.2 Case Study 2: Bermuda's OFDI in China

Bermuda, an overseas territory of the UK located in the North Atlantic Ocean, has a population of approximately 60,000 people. Despite not being geographically part of the Caribbean region, Bermuda joined CARICOM in July 2003 as an associate member, primarily driven by historical ties and the desire to strengthen cultural links with the region. Even though Bermuda is a small island, it is a well-established offshore financial center with minimal standards of business regulations and laws, as well as no direct taxation on personal or corporate income, capital gains, VAT, sales, or wealth tax. This absence of corporate income tax has made Bermuda an attractive destination for international companies seeking to minimize their tax obligations. For instance, in 2017, Google employed a strategy that shifted US $23 billion to Bermuda, enabling the company to reduce its foreign tax liabilities, as revealed in documents filed with the Dutch Chamber of Commerce (Reuters 2019).

Despite several international companies operating physical businesses in Bermuda, most of them are exempt companies incorporated in Bermuda but do not have a physical office there. An exempted company is one that is "exempted" from the Bermuda Companies Act of 1981 requirements for local companies, particularly the requirement that Bermudians must own and control at least 60 % of a company's equity (Attride-Stirling & Wolonieck 2008). According to the latest data from the Registrar of Companies in Bermuda, there are 12,571 international companies registered in Bermuda, and 78 % of the total number of companies registered are exempted international companies (Table 2).

Table 2. Businesses Registered in Bermuda (2012 — 2020)

	New Registrations						Number on Register at Year-end						
	Exempted	Exempted partnership	Exempted LLC	Non-Resident	Total International	Total New Registrations	Exempted	Exempted partnership	Exempted LLC	Non-Resident	Non-Resident Insurance	Total International	Total Number on Register
2012	743	68	0	44	855	969	11,540	941	0	508	12	13,001	16,212
2013	888	77	0	36	1,001	1,143	11,352	980	0	521	10	12,863	15,988
2014	888	65	0	69	1,022	1,178	11,403	985	0	569	8	12,965	16,187
2015	752	96	0	48	896	1,084	11,548	1,022	0	595	8	13,173	16,480
2016	665	109	0	28	802	1,024	11,188	1,056	3	585	8	12,840	16,204
2017	626	95	19	44	784	942	11,210	1,098	21	609	8	12,946	16,329
2018	603	183	15	26	827	1,010	11,087	1,243	34	546	8	12,918	16,363
2019	544	125	8	4	681	846	10,725	1,239	39	497	8	12,508	15,907
2020	535	134	37	27	733	880	10,680	1,311	75	497	8	12,571	16,091

Source: own elaboration from Bermuda's Registrar of Companies (2022).

According to our data analysis, Bermuda is the second-largest sender of OFDI to China in terms of capital investment and the number of jobs created between 2013 and 2022. With 22 investments, capital investment from Bermuda to China amounts to US $591 billion, and a total of 3250 jobs have been created in several cities. Shanghai and Hong Kong received the majority of the investments, 33 % and 39 %, respectively, in terms of capital investment and 33 % and 28 %, respectively, in terms of jobs created (Figure 9). The only other city with double-digit percentages is Beijing, with both capital investment and jobs created at 10 %. Cities such as Changchun, Chengdu, Dalian, Guangzhou, Suzhou, and Xi'an all received investments amounting to less than 10 % of the total. The data also shows that the investments were made in various sectors, including biotechnology, business services, financial services, semiconductors, software and IT services, and textiles. Among the top sectors for capital investment are financial services (61 %), business services (13 %), and biotechnology (10 %), while the top sectors in terms of jobs created are financial services (27 %), software and IT services (27 %), and semiconductors (11 %).

The amount of capital investment appears to be highly determined by the number of jobs created. Zoning in on the financial services sector shows that it is the overall leading sector for FDI from Bermuda to China, with capital investments of US $359.2 billion and 1,320 jobs created, representing 61 % and 41 % of the totals, respectively. Capital investment in software and IT services totaled 31.4 billion, representing 5 % of the total capital investment and 27 % of the total jobs created. Between 2005 and 2018, several companies, including Accenture, ALC Health, Allied World Assurance Holdings, Apex Group (Apex Fund Services), Appleby, Catlin Insurance Company, CG Technologies, Genpact (GECIS), Ironshore Insurance, Lazard Asset Management, Marvell Technology, Roivant Sciences, and XL Catlin (Catlin Group), have been involved in operations in China. However, for the purpose of this case study, our focus will be on XL Catlin (Catlin Group) and Herbalife, as they are interesting examples of companies that have made substantial investments and created jobs in China. These two firms have also worked closely with Chinese government officials and organizations to conduct business operations there.

4.2.1 XL Catlin (Catlin Group)

The Catlin Group Limited, founded in 1984 by Stephen Catlin, was an underwriting agency at Lloyd's of London. In 1999, the company established a holding company in Bermuda, initially named Catlin Westgen Holding Limited but later changed to Catlin Group Limited. With this tactical move, Catlin became the first among the more traditional Lloyd's of London managing agents in creating a Bermuda-based holding company. Subsequently, other competitors, such as Omega Underwriting and Hiscox, followed suit (Daley 2006). As a specialty insurance and reinsurance firm headquartered in Bermuda, Catlin organized its operations into six underwriting hubs located across the globe, including in Bermuda, London/UK, Europe, the United States, Canada, and Asia-Pacific, and it maintained a worldwide presence with over 55 offices. Following XL Group plc's acquisition of Catlin Group Limited in May 2015, the insurance and reinsurance subsidiaries of XL Group Ltd. adopted the global brand XL Catlin (XL Group Plc 2015).

In April 2012, the insurance and reinsurance company made the largest capital investment in China, with a value of $61.4 million and 339 jobs created. Having received approval from the China Insurance Regulatory Commission, Catlin established a wholly-owned representative office in Beijing, which operated as part of Catlin's Singapore-headquartered Asia-Pacific underwriting hub (Catlin Group Limited 2012). The primary rationale for the Beijing representative office was to enhance collaboration with relevant Chinese government departments and insurance industry organizations, as well as conduct market research on insurance and reinsurance in China. Prior to the investment, Catlin entered into a strategic partnership with China Reinsurance Corporation (China Re) in November 2011 (PWC 2012). China Re, which is jointly owned by the Ministry of Finance of China and Central Huijin Investment Corporation, established a special purpose syndicate at Lloyd's that provides whole-account quota share reinsurance coverage for Catlin Syndicate (Syndicate 2003). The partnership was driven by the desire to facilitate knowledge transfer for Catlin, particularly in understanding the insurance and reinsurance practices and market developments in China, which was critical for satisfying the needs of the complex growth market (Kent, 2011). In addition, the partnership allowed for the secondment of China Re's employees to Catlin, which speaks to the mutually beneficial arrangement. Dr. Li Peiyu, the then chairman of China Re Group, said: "As the biggest reinsurance company in China, China Re's strategy is to grow both in the home market and abroad and to have a greater involvement in international markets. This new venture will not only help us to gain a better knowledge of Lloyd's and benefit from its worldwide network, but it will also increase China Re's experience of international reinsurance operations and management and help build a foundation for China Re to grow into an important player in the world reinsurance market" (Kent, 2011).

Figure 9. Bermuda OFDI to China by Sector (2003 - 2019)

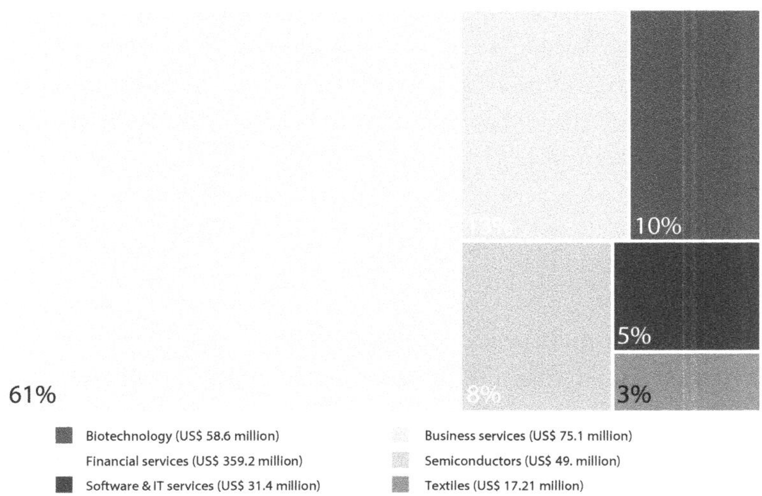

Source: own elaboration based on data from fDi Markets.

The then Chief Executive of Catlin Group Limited, Stephen Catlin, said that China offered great opportunities to international insurers and reinsurers. Furthermore, the then Head of Treaty, Agnes

Chang, pointed out that "China is strategically important to Catlin, not only for sheer business potential but also as a great source of diversification in terms of geography and product mix" (Catlin Group Limited, 2012). At the time, China's growth prospects were promising, and the insurance market was the world's sixth largest. Overall, Catlin Group Limited's significant investment in China was important not only for developing knowledge of the insurance market but also for seizing potential market opportunities.

Through its investment in China, Catlin Group Limited leveraged location-specific advantages by establishing a representative office in Beijing and forming a strategic partnership with China Reinsurance Corporation. This allowed them to access government departments and industry organizations and conduct market research, which offers opportunities to gain valuable knowledge of the Chinese insurance industry and tailor their products to local conditions. Catlin's motivations were market-seeking, as the company recognized China as a strategically important market with significant business potential. While the specific type of FDI, vertical or horizontal, is not explicitly mentioned, it can be inferred that Catlin's investment aligns more closely with horizontal FDI as they sought to replicate their core business and serve the domestic market in China.

4.2.2. Accenture

Accenture, a management consulting and technology services company, is an example of how international companies have used Bermuda to facilitate OFDI in China. Originally a division of Arthur Andersen focused on business and technology consulting in the early 1950s, Accenture broke ties with Arthur Andersen after an arbitration settlement in 2000 and listed on the New York Stock Exchange as a publicly traded company in 2001 (Martin 2000; CNN 2001). While Accenture positioned itself as a global company without a central headquarters, capable of conducting business anywhere and in any language with its workforce of

75,000 employees operating across 46 countries, its SEC filings identified it as a Bermuda-based holding company (Manor *et al.* 2001). Bermuda's tax laws allow companies incorporated in the country to defer US taxation on foreign income indefinitely and to earn interest, dividends, and capital gains from investments in the US without paying taxes. In 2002, when the Congressional General Accounting Office (GAO) examined federal contractors incorporated in a tax haven, Accenture was identified as one of the four publicly traded federal contractors identified (New York Times 2002; GAO 2002). Although reports suggested that Accenture's decision to incorporate in Bermuda was motivated by U.S. tax avoidance strategies, the company asserted that it was not originally a US-based company before its incorporation in Bermuda. The GAO also characterized Accenture not as a U.S.-based company but as "a series of related partnerships and corporations under the control of its partners through the mechanism of contracts with a Swiss coordinating entity" (GAO 2002). A company official in 2001 cited Bermuda's favorable business environment and well-settled corporate law as factors that attract large companies to the territory (Manor *et al.* 2001).

Between March 2003 and February 2009, Accenture made a significant investment of 31.4 billion in China, which resulted in the creation of 893 jobs, the highest number of jobs created by a single Bermudian company according to our data analysis. These five transactions were for projects in the software and IT services sector in several Chinese cities, including Dalian, Shanghai, Guangzhou, and Chengdu.

In March 2003, Accenture announced a capital investment of 3.7 billion in China for a global delivery center in Dalian, aimed at enhancing the company's capabilities in providing technology services, particularly in the Chinese and Japanese markets (Accenture 2003/a). The center, which focused on business processes, outsourcing solutions, software engineering, systems integration, and application development and maintenance, became part of Accenture's global network, allowing them to support client operations that required expertise in Chinese and Japanese language skills. This investment was seen as a strategic move by the company despite global economic conditions, including the SARS outbreak and sluggish growth in Asian economies (Accenture 2003/b). According to Joe Forehand, Accenture chairman and CEO, "The launch of Accenture's center in Dalian is an important step in our strategy to develop a competitively differentiated global sourcing approach that allows us to deploy professionals with knowledge, skills, and experience wherever and whenever our clients need them" (Accenture 2003/a). Chi-Wei Wang, the Accenture executive who oversaw the Dalian center at the time of the investment, remarked: "Dalian's well-developed communications infrastructure, stable commercial environment, and highly skilled technology workforce will allow Accenture to expand our ability to deliver a wider array of industry-leading services to clients, primarily in Asia-Pacific" (Accenture 2003/a).

Following the investment in Dalian, Accenture invested in Guangzhou, establishing an office there that would serve multinationals and local enterprises in South China (Accenture 2004). This strategic move was driven by the desire to leverage Guangzhou's highly skilled workforce and enhance Accenture's capabilities. By capitalizing on the economic vibrancy of one of China's dynamic areas, Accenture sought to maximize market opportunities and strengthen its business prospects. The client base in the region includes the state government, large local enterprises, regional companies, and multinational corporations spanning various industries. Gong Li, Accenture's Chairman for China at the time, stated that "the Guangzhou office reflects our deep commitment to China, which continues to be an important market for Accenture" (Accenture 2003). Recognizing the economic integration between Hong Kong and Southern China, Accenture's Hong Kong office was positioned to provide talent and industry expertise to support the Guangzhou office in the effort to assist firms in the South China market in achieving greater innovation and high performance.

Accenture's investment in China has proven fruitful over time. In 2005, the company secured a significant opportunity to collaborate with SAP and lead the technology transformation for China Minsheng Banking Corporation (CMBC), the first privately owned nationwide commercial bank in China (Accenture 2005). Han Wei Xi, then general manager for IT at CMBC, cited Accenture's strong reputation, extensive experience, risk management capabilities, and track record of successful long-term partnerships as the reasons for choosing the company. Accenture's 2006 annual report highlighted the continuous expansion of its presence in China, with approximately 2,500 professionals in Greater China by the end of the fiscal year (Accenture 2006). This growth signifies the company's success in forging new client relationships in China with firms such as Allianz China, Beijing Mobile, China National Offshore Oil Corp., Diageo Shanghai, Lenovo, and TCL. In its SEC filings for 2008, Accenture reported that it continued to boost recruitment in key locations of its global delivery network in China (Accenture 2008). In addition, its business in China, combined with its operations in Japan and Singapore, played a significant role in driving revenue growth in the Asia-Pacific region. In fiscal 2008, the company recorded net revenues of US $2,115 million, representing a 26 % annual increase (Accenture, 2009). This result indicates the positive impact of Accenture's investments in China on the country's economy and employment landscape.

In 2009, Accenture decided to relocate its headquarters to Ireland as a response to the U.S. government's plans to enact tax regulations (O'Hora 2009). Other significant MNCs, such as Warner Chilcott Ltd., also made the decision to move to Ireland during this time. Unlike Bermuda, Ireland had tax treaties with the U.S., which was a crucial factor in reducing concerns about tax avoidance that had been associated with Accenture since its incorporation in Bermuda in 2001. In addressing the move to Ireland, Accenture stated that it did not anticipate any significant changes in its financial performance or tax treatment, but it believed that Ireland would offer economic advantages (Reuters 2009). William Green, the company's chairman at the time, highlighted that Ireland's membership in the European Union provided access to a sophisticated and well-established legal, corporate, and regulatory framework (Reuters 2009). Additionally, Ireland's longstanding trade agreements, commercial relationships, and tax treaties with countries across the globe where Accenture operates were cited as reasons for choosing Ireland, echoing similar justifications given for incorporating in Bermuda years earlier.

Accenture's investments in China can be best explained by the ownership advantage factor. The company's specialized knowledge, managerial skills, and expertise in business and technology consulting gave it a competitive edge. This led to its strategic investment in China, expanding its global business, and establishing a global delivery center in Dalian. By leveraging its ownership advantages, Accenture's investments in Guangzhou and its growing presence in China further showcased its commitment to leveraging local workforces and enhancing capabilities. Accenture also benefits from location-specific advantages in China. By investing in specific locations such as Dalian and Guangzhou, Accenture gains access to a skilled technology workforce, well-developed infrastructure, and market opportunities. These advantages enhance their capabilities and client relationships and enable them to cater to various industries.

The company's China investments were market-seeking, driven by the desire to tap into the growing domestic and regional markets. The establishment of a global delivery center in Dalian and subsequent investments in Guangzhou aimed at expanding their customer base, increasing sales, and benefiting from the untapped consumer demand and economic growth potential in China. Partnerships with prominent Chinese companies further demonstrate their focus on market opportunities and meeting consumer demand. Alongside the market-seeking motivation, Accenture's investments in China were efficiency-seeking, aimed at strategically optimizing its supply chain and enhancing its competitiveness in international markets. Establishing the Dailan global delivery center highlights its pursuit of efficiency gains in terms of accessing lower-cost, such as labor and leveraging the skilled technology workforce in the region. Overall, Accenture's investments showcase a combination of horizontal and vertical FDI.

The company's establishment of a global delivery center in Dalian, which focused on application development, software engineering, systems integration, and business process outsourcing solutions, can be considered an example of horizontal FDI as these services focused on market presence and replication. On the other hand, Accenture's investments in different cities, including Guangzhou, indicate elements of vertical FDI, aiming to optimize the supply chain and gain access to specialized capabilities.

5. Conclusions and Policy Proposals

This paper highlights the significant role of OFCs in facilitating the flow of FDI between China and the Caribbean region. The interdependent relationship between China, the Caribbean, and OFCs contributes to economic development and job creation while underscoring the complex and diverse nature of the bi-regional partnership. Until now, little research had delved into OFDI originating in the Caribbean and destined for the Chinese market. However, clear evidence now indicates that the FDI relationship between China and the Caribbean is bi-directional, accomplishing the twin goals of facilitating trade and investment endeavors. According to our calculations based on data, Caribbean countries have invested a total of US$ 1,698.7 million and generated 9062 jobs in China from 2003 to 2019. The years 2006 and 2014 stood out with the highest number of jobs created, 3,489 and 1,681, respectively, while capital investments peaked in 2009 and 2018 at US$ 233.7 million and US$ 224.2 million, respectively. The contributing countries include the Bahamas, Bermuda, the Cayman Islands, Cuba, and Saint Kitts and Nevis. The Cayman Islands and Bermuda accounted for the majority of investments, representing 49 % and 35 % of the capital investments, respectively, and 60 % and 36 % of the jobs created, respectively. This justified our decision to use these OFCs as a case study, examining the factors that led firms in these countries to invest in China, their challenges, and the impact of their investments on both countries.

The motivations for firms from the Cayman Islands and Bermuda to invest in China are multifaceted and include factors such as access to new markets, cost advantages, potential for growth, government incentives, and favorable policies. The expansion of firms such as Herbalife, Cedrus Investments, Accenture, and the Catlin Group out of Caribbean OFCs into China demonstrates the importance and significance of location-specific and ownership advantages augmented by internalization advantages, as outlined by the eclectic paradigm discussed in this study. This differs from Chinese OFDI to the Latin American and Caribbean (LAC) region, where investments are more strategic asset-seeking in nature, targeting projects in the transportation, extractive metals, tourism, energy, and agriculture sectors.

Overall, the strategic investments and activities of these multinational corporations (MNCs) indicate a strong orientation to leverage location-specific advantages for market-seeking and motivated investments while pursuing a horizontal FDI strategy. For example, Accenture leveraged Caribbean OFCs to invest in China, utilizing location-specific advantages as well as ownership and endowment advantages such as specialized knowledge, managerial skills, and expertise in business and technology. The Catlin Group strategically invested in China to take advantage of location-specific benefits, establishing an office in Beijing and forming a strategic partnership with China Reinsurance Corporation to access government departments and industry organizations and conduct market research. Cedrus Investments' expansion into China is driven by ownership advantages and location-specific advantages, leveraging specialized knowledge, managerial skills, and a global network to provide value-added investment products. Herbalife's operations in China also benefit from location-specific advantages such as market size, growth potential, and government support. All of these firm investments mainly align with market-seeking motivations and predominantly reflect the characteristics of horizontal FDI.

The strong orientation of multinational corporations (MNCs) towards leveraging location-specific advantages for market-seeking, motivated investments suggests that MNCs from the Caribbean are actively targeting foreign markets, such as China, to expand their customer base and increase sales. Latin American firms, in contrast, primarily leverage ownership advantages like innovative distribution systems and technological innovations to achieve successful investments in China. The prevalent use of a horizontal FDI strategy indicates their intention to replicate their existing business operations in foreign markets to meet local demand and compete with local rivals. The findings imply that other firms from the respective countries and the wider LAC region can benefit from observing and learning from the strategic investments and activities of these MNCs in China. By understanding how these firms leverage location-specific advantages and adopt market-seeking and horizontal FDI strategies, as discussed in this study, local firms can enhance their own capabilities and expand into international markets. For instance, adherence and adaptations to local regulations were critical factors for companies in highly regulated industries like Herbalife to capitalize on the unique advantages and conditions offered by the Chinese market.

We suggest broader policy proposals with implications for the governments and local firms in OFCs and other Caribbean countries, with the aim of them drawing insights from the experiences of MNCs in OFCs. As mentioned earlier, the majority of Caribbean OFDI to China originates from MNCs, which are strategically located in the Caribbean and may move their operations or incorporation elsewhere abruptly. Notwithstanding, indigenous Caribbean firms seeking to invest in China can learn from their activities, and policy can support or enable them to do so. For instance, Caribbean governments can promote knowledge exchange between MNCs with successful investments in China and local firms through partnerships, joint ventures, or mentorship programs, which can facilitate the transfer of expertise, best practices, and market insights to local firms seeking to invest in China. In addition, governments can enhance institutional support, such as through investment promotion agencies or trade organizations, to provide guidance, information, and resources to firms interested in investing in China. This can include assistance in market research, legal frameworks, regulatory compliance, and accessing financial incentives or grants. Regionally, the governments can foster international networks for firms from the respective countries to connect with potential Chinese partners, investors, and customers through trade missions, business forums, and industry-specific events. Companies such as Accenture and Cedrus highlight the importance of leveraging ownership advantages. As such, investments should be made in education and training programs that equip local firms with the necessary skills and knowledge to navigate the Chinese market successfully. This can include language proficiency, cultural understanding, market entry strategies, negotiation skills, and knowledge of local business practices. This is also consistent with the widespread view of the role of FDI in the transfer of knowledge. In fact, the case studies also emphasize the knowledge generation practices used by the MNCs studied to participate and integrate within China through attending trade conferences, partnerships, and other collaborations. Finally, bilateral agreements between the respective countries and China should be strengthened to promote investor protection, facilitate trade flows, and provide a favorable business environment for companies seeking to invest in China. Along those same lines, bilateral agreements and regulatory cooperation for cross-border financial services can help strengthen financial integration between China and Caribbean OFCs.

To enhance China's attractiveness for OFDI from MNCs based in Caribbean OFCs and, more generally, Caribbean firms, several policy proposals can be implemented. It is important for China to recognize the distinctive characteristics of the Caribbean OFDI compared to Latin America, with the former primarily leveraging location-specific advantages and the latter utilizing ownership advantages. Considering the OFDI orientation of Caribbean MNCs, China should streamline investment procedures by simplifying administrative processes and reducing bureaucratic hurdles to facilitate smoother market entry and operations for foreign investors. Strengthening legal frameworks and enforcement mechanisms is crucial to enhancing investor protection, in conjunction with safeguarding intellectual property, enforcing contracts, and providing transparent and fair dispute resolution mechanisms so as to instill investor confidence. Moreover, improving transparency in policymaking processes and providing clear guidelines and regulations for foreign investors would reduce regulatory uncertainties, enhance predictability, and increase China's appeal as an OFDI destination. Additionally, promoting industry collaboration and partnerships between local industries and foreign investors can facilitate knowledge and technology transfers and skill development, fostering mutually beneficial relationships. These policy proposals can help China create an enabling environment that leverages China's location-specific advantages and supports the market-seeking motivations of Caribbean firms. By implementing these measures, China can position itself as an attractive destination for Caribbean OFDI and further strengthen its economic ties with the region.

References

Accenture Ltd. 2003. *Quarterly report pursuant to section 13 or 15(d) of the Securities Exchange Act of 1934.* SEC: Washington, D.C.

Accenture. 2003. "Accenture Expands Global Delivery Center Network with New Facility in China." *Accenture Newsroom*, March 13.

Accenture. 2004. "Accenture Establishes Guangzhou Office to Maximize Opportunities in South China." *Accenture Newsroom*, November 8.

Accenture. 2005. "China Minsheng Banking Corporation Selects Accenture and SAP to Lead Technology Transformation." *Accenture Newsroom*, November 28.

Accenture. 2006. *High performance business: We Know What it Takes. Annual Report 2006.* Accenture: Bermudas.

Accenture. 2008. *Annual report pursuant to section 13 or 15(d) of the Securities Exchange Act of 1934.* SEC: Washington, D.C.

Accenture. 2009. *Annual report pursuant to section 13 or 15(d) of the Securities Exchange Act of 1934.* SEC: Washington, D.C.

Aizenman, Joshua and Marion, Nancy. "The merits of horizontal versus vertical FDI in the presence of uncertainty." *Journal of International Economics*, vol. 62, no. 1, 2004, pp. 125-148.

Attride-Stirling & Wolonieck. 2008. *Memorandum on Incorporation of an Exempted Company.* ASW: Bermuda.

Austin, Sharon. 2019. "Government to re-establish investment office in Beijing." *GIS*, 17 September.

Belsie, Laurent. 2023. "Chinese firms access foreign capital in International Tax Havens." *National Bureau of Economic Research*, March 3.

Bernal, Richard. 2016. *Chinese Foreign Direct Investment in the Caribbean. Potential and Prospects.* IADB: Washington, D.C.

BIQ. 2012. *Bermuda Insurance Quarterly*, January.

Breslin, Shaun. 2004. *Foreign Direct Investment in China: What the Figures Don't Tell Us.* University of Warwick: UK

CNN. 2001."Accenture IPO gains in first trades. *CNNMoney*, July 19.

Carril-Caccia, Federico and Pavlova, Elena. 2018. "Foreign direct investment and its drivers: a global and EU perspective." *Economic Bulletin Articles*, vol. 4.

CATLIN. 2012. "Catlin Group Limited Annual Report and Accounts 2012." CATLIN: Bermuda.

CATLIN. 2017. "Catlin Group Limited." *Opencorporates.com*, at: https://opencorporates.com/companies/bm/26680.

CARICOM. 2002. "Cayman Islands newest associate member of CARICOM." CARICOM, May 16.

CEDRUS. 2017. "Cedrus Investments Head of Life Sciences Ms. Kimberly Nearing Presented at the Chengdu Global Innovation and Entrepreneurship Fair." *Cedrus Investments*, October 23.

CEDRUS. 2012. "Cedrus Investments Hosts 2012 Annual Dinner in Hong Kong." *Cedrus Investments*, May 21.

CEDRUS. 2012. "Cedrus investments hosts life sciences luncheon in Shanghai." *Cedrus Investments*, November 1.

CEDRUS. 2010. "Cedrus Investments Launches In Hong Kong as First Step in Asia Expansion." *Cedrus Investments*, October 5.

CEDRUS. 2014. "Cedrus Investments Sponsors The Mines & Money Tianjin Program at the China Mining Congress and Expo." *Cedrus Investments*, October 16.

CEDRUS. 2020. "Cedrus Investments Successfully Launched a New Office in Shenzhen China." *Cedrus Investments*, March 23.

CEDRUS. 2015. "Cedrus Investments Will Open Shanghai Office - Third Office in Greater China Region." *Cedrus Investments*, April 21.

CEDRUS. 2023. "Cedrus Investments. Greater China." At: Investmehttps://cedrusinvestments.com/en/greater-china/.

CEDRUS. 2012. "Cedrus Investments' Annual Global Investor Conference to Be Held in Hong Kong on May 16 – 17, 2012." *Cedrus Investments*, November 2.

CEDRUS. 2018. "Cedrus Investments Will Launch a New Office in Shenzhen." *Cedrus Investments*, May 9.

Chen, Chin-Jou Jay. 2014. "Taiwanese Business in China: Encountering and Coping with Risks." Asian Studies 60, pp. 31-47.

Chen, Chunlai. 2018. "The Liberalisation of FDI Policies and the Impacts of FDI on China's Economic Development." In, Garnaut, Ross, Song, Ligang and Cai, Fang Cai (edits.). *China's 40 Years of Reform and Development: 1978-2018*. ANU Press: Acton, pp. 600-617.

China Briefing. 2022. "China's 2022 Negative List for Market Access: Here Are the Key Changes." *China Briefing*, April 13.

National Bureau of Statistics. 2011. *China Statistical Yearbook*, 2011. NBS: Beijing.

National Bureau of Statistics. 2021. *China Statistical Yearbook*, 2011. NBS: Beijing.

National Bureau of Statistics. 2012. *China Statistical Yearbook*, 2011. NBS: Beijing.

Chipman Koty, Alexander. 2018. "China's FDI Policy: Wider Market Access, New Incentives Announced." *China Briefing News*, October 15.

Correa da Cunha, Henrique, Singh, Vikkram and Xie, Shengkun. 2022. "The Determinants of Outward Foreign Direct Investment from Latin America and the Caribbean: An Integrated Entropy-Based TOPSIS Multiple Regression Analysis Framework." *Journal of Risk and Financial Management 15*(3).

Daley, James. 2006. "Business analysis: Lloyd's under pressure as Bermuda Exodus gathers." *The Independent*, September 19.

De Groot, Olaf and Ludeña, Miguel Pérez. 2014. "Foreign Direct Investment in the Caribbean: Trends, Determinants and Policies." Studies and Perspectives Series - The Caribbean 35, pp. 1-49.

Donovan, Elise. 2018. "Going for Global Growth: Why China Chooses the BVI." *IFC Review*, June 29.

Donovan, Elise. 2018. "Knowing on which side the BVI's bread is buttered: Government of the Virgin Islands." Government of the Virgin Islands, June 23.

Dussel Peters, Enrique. 2019. "China's OFDI in Latin America and the Caribbean (2000-2018)". In, Dussel Peters, Enrique. *China's Foreign Direct Investment in Latin America and the Caribbean. Conditions and challenges.* Red ALC-China, UDUAL and UNAM/Cechimex: Mexico, pp.105-120.

Dussel Peters, Enrique. 2019. *Monitor of Chinese OFDI in Latin America and the Caribbean 2019.* Red ALC-China: Mexico.

Dussel Peters, Enrique. 2023. *Monitor of Chinese OFDI in Latin America and the Caribbean 2023.* Red ALC-China: Mexico.

FDI Markets. 2023. FDI *Markets: The in-Depth Crossborder Investment Monitor from the Financial Times.* fDi Markets: London.

Geng, Xiao. 2004. "Round-Tripping Foreign Direct Investment in the People's Republic of China." *ADBI Research Policy Brief* 10, pp. 1-7,

Haberly, Daniel and Wójcik, Dariusz. 2013. "Tax Havens and the Production of Offshore FDI: An Empirical Analysis." *SSRN Electronic Journal*, pp. 1-24.

Hanson, Gordon H., Mataloni Jr, Raymond J. and Slaughter, Matthew J. 2005. "Vertical Production Networks in Multinational Firms." *The Review of Economics and Statistics* 87(4), pp. 664-678.

He, Canfei. 2008. "Foreign Manufacturing Investment in China: The Role of Industrial Agglomeration and Industrial Linkages." *China & World Economy* 16(1), pp. 82–99.

Herbalife Nutrition Ltd. 2006. *ANNUAL REPORT UNDER SECTION 13 OR 15(d) OF THE SECURITIES EXCHANGE ACT OF 1934*. SEC: Washington, D.C.

Herbalife Nutrition Ltd. 2008. *ANNUAL REPORT PURSUANT TO SECTION 13 OR 15(d) OF THE SECURITIES EXCHANGE ACT OF 1934*. SEC: Washington, D.C.

Herbalife Nutrition Ltd. 2010. *ANNUAL REPORT PURSUANT TO SECTION 13 OR 15(d) OF THE SECURITIES EXCHANGE ACT OF 1934*. SEC: Washington, D.C.

Herbalife Nutrition Ltd. 2010. "Herbalife breaks ground for extraction facility in China." *Herbalife Press Releases*, October 12.

Herbalife Nutrition Ltd. 2014. *ANNUAL REPORT PURSUANT TO SECTION 13 OR 15(d) OF THE SECURITIES EXCHANGE ACT OF 1934*. SEC: Washington, D.C.

Herbalife Nutrition Ltd. 2014. "Herbalife plans expansion of manufacturing capabilities in China." *Herbalife Press Releases*, July 31.

Herbalife Nutrition Ltd. 2019/a. *ANNUAL REPORT PURSUANT TO SECTION 13 OR 15(d) OF THE SECURITIES EXCHANGE ACT OF 1934*. SEC: Washington, D.C.

Herbalife Nutrition Ltd. 2019/b. "Herbalife Nutrition announces four new training centers throughout China." *Herbalife Press Releases*, December 4.

Herbalife Nutrition Ltd. 2019/c. "Herbalife to Pay $ 20 Million for Misleading Investors." SEC *Press Release*, September 27.

Herbalife Nutrition Ltd. 2020. *ANNUAL REPORT PURSUANT TO SECTION 13 OR 15(d) OF THE SECURITIES EXCHANGE ACT OF 1934*. SEC: Washington, D.C.

Herbalife Nutrition Ltd. 2022. *ANNUAL REPORT PURSUANT TO SECTION 13 OR 15(d) OF THE SECURITIES EXCHANGE ACT OF 1934*. SEC: Washington, D.C.

Kent, Jonathan. 2011. "Catlin teams up with China re in Lloyd's deal." *The Royal Gazette | Bermuda News*, November 21.

Kunhardt, Jorge B. 2013. "Mexican OFDI in China—Ownership Advantages to Gain New Markets: Two Case Studies." *China-USA Business Review* 12(12), pp. 241–253.

Lane, Philip R. and Milesi-Ferretti, Gian Maria. 2010. "Cross-Border Investment in Small International Financial Centers." *IMF Working Paper* 10/38.

Lejour, Arjan and Salfi, Maria. 2015. "The Regional Impact of Bilateral Investment Treaties on Foreign Direct Investment." *CPB Discussion Paper* 298.

Lin, Mi and Yum K. Kwan. 2011. "Sectoral Location of FDI in China." *The World Economy* 34(7), pp. 1181–1198.

Long, Guoqiang. 2005. "China's Policies on FDI: Review and Evaluation." In, Moran, Theodore H., Graham, Edward M. and Blomstrom, Magnus (edits). Does Foreign Direct Investment Promote Development? PIIE: Washington, D.C., pp. 315-336.

Luo, Laijun, Brennan, Louis, Liu, Chang and Luo, Yuze. 2008. "Factors Influencing FDI Location Choice in China's Inland Areas." *China & World Economy* 16(2), pp. 93–108.

Manor, Robert and Delroy Alexander. 2021. "Island Life Appeals to Accenture." *Chicago Tribune*, August 20.

Minto, Jevon. 2019. "Examining the Lending Practices of Chinese Policy Banks in the Caribbean (2000-2018)." In, Dussel Peters, Enrique (edit). *China´s Financing in Latin America and the Caribbean.* Red ALC-China, UDUAL and UNAM/Cechimex, pp. 153-176.

Morris, Gilbert. 2011. "The Significance of IFCS in the Global Financial System." *IFC Review*, November 1.

Myers, Margaret and Ray, Rebecca. 2022. *At a Crossroads: Chinese Development Finance to Latin America and the Caribbean.* Boston University Global Development Policy Center: Boston.

National Bureau of Statistics. 2011. *China Statistical Yearbook*, 2011. NBS: Beijing.

National Bureau of Statistics. 2021. *China Statistical Yearbook*, 2011. NBS: Beijing.

National Bureau of Statistics. 2012. *China Statistical Yearbook*, 2011. NBS: Beijing.

O'Hora, Ailish. 2009. "Accenture moves its HQ to Ireland as US targets tax havens." Independent.ie, May 27.

Red ALC-China. 2022/a. "Monitor OFDI China en ALC. Estadísticas. Islas Caimán". Red ALC-China: Mexico.

Red ALC-China. 2022/b. "Monitor OFDI China en ALC. Estadísticas. Islas Vírgenes Británicas". Red ALC-China: Mexico.

Reuters Staff. 2009. "Refile-update 3-accenture to shift incorporation to Ireland." *Reuters*, May 27.

Reuters. 2019. "*Google shifted $23bn to tax haven Bermuda in 2017, filing shows*". Reuters, December 5.

Ruehl, Mercedes. 2023. "Cayman Islands Fights Attempts by Singapore and Hong Kong to Lure Asia's Wealthy." *Financial Times*, May 25.

Selburn, C. "Fig 16: Industry share to Cayman Islands GDP at constant basic prices". Economic and Statistics Office: Cayman Islands.

Suss, Esther, Williams, Oral and Mendis, Chandima. 2002. "Caribbean Offshore Financial Center: Past, Present, and Possibilities." *IMF Working Paper* WP/02/88, pp. 1-34.

Sutherland, Dylan, El-Gohari, Ahmad, Buckley, Peter and Voss, Hinrich. 2010. "The Role of Caribbean Tax Havens and Offshore Financial Centers in Chinese Outward Foreign Direct Investment." Paper presented at 2nd Conference on Emerging Market Multinationals, Copenhagen Business School.

Sutherland, Dylan, Matthews, Ben and El-Gohari, Ahmad. 2012. "An Exploration of How Chinese Companies Use Tax Havens and Offshore Financial Centres". In, Fu, Xiaolan (edit.). *China´s Role in Global Economic Recovery*. Routledge: London, pp. 123-144.

The Gleaner. 2018. "Jisco Gets a Pass on Bauxite Levy, but Not Income Tax." *Business Jamaica Gleaner*, November 9.

Thomas, Marcelle. 2020. "PM Says Gov't Continuing with China-Funded Broadband Project." *Stabroek News*, November 8

UNCTAD (United Nations Conference on Trade and Development). 2022. "Global foreign direct investment flows over the last 30 years." UNCTAD: Geneva.

US House Foreign Affairs Committee. 2022. *China Regional Snapshot: The Caribbean*. Committee on Foreign Affairs: Washington, D.C.

Vlcek, William. 2010. "Byways and Highways of Direct Investment: China and the Offshore World." *Journal of Current Chinese Affairs* 39(4), pp. 111–42.

Vlcek, William. 2013. "From Road Town to Shanghai: Situating the Caribbean in Global Capital Flows to China." *The British Journal of Politics and International Relations* 16(3), pp. 534–53.

Wenner, Mark and Clarke, Dillon. "Chinese rise in the Caribbean: what does it mean for Caribbean stakeholders?" IDB *Technical Note* 107.

White, James R. 2002. *Subject: Information on Federal Contractors That Are Incorporated Offshore*. USGAO: Washington, D.C.

World Bank. 2022. *The World Bank. Data. Cayman Islands*. World Bank: Washington, D.C.

XL Group PLC. 2018. "XL Group PLC Announces Acquisition of Catlin Group Limited." *Cision PR Newswire*, January 9.

Zhang, Zoey. 2020. "China's Foreign Investment Access: Draft 2020 Encouraged Catalogue." *China Briefing*, August 4.

4.
CENTRAL AMERICAN OFDI TO CHINA

Rafael Arias-Achio and Rafael Arias-Ramírez

Introduction

While Chinese outward foreign direct investment (OFDI) to Central American countries has been increasingly studied, we know of no studies or empirical evidence on Central American OFDI to China. In the context of growing trade between China and the Central American region, we examine possible avenues and opportunities for Central American countries to invest in China. To answer this question, we develop a prospective analysis through the identification of market sectors, industries, and occupations where Central American economies could benefit from investing in China.

Red ALC-China has undergone an extensive search for case studies of OFDI from Latin American countries to China. While information on specific OFDI experience exists for many of the region's larger economies, Central American OFDI in China lacks reliable data and information: key informants (Vinicio Ruiz[1] and

1 Marco Vinicio Ruiz is an economist, specialist on issues related to economic development and international trade. Former Ambassador of Costa Rica in China during the presidency of Laura Chinchilla (2010-2014).

Espinoza[2]) confirm the existence of OFDI from the region to China, but there is insufficient knowledge and monitoring of these cases. However, this does not limit our capacity to analyze possible scenarios of Central American OFDI toward China.

With this in mind, we analyze the potential for OFDI in China by Central American countries. We do so through a prospective analysis that studies possible avenues for future investment between the two parties. We focus on two potential sectors for OFDI, the agroindustry, represented by coffee, and the digital economy and services sector. This is an exploratory analysis and represents initial ideas on how Central America could benefit from OFDI to China.

This study analyzes the investment opportunities in China from Central American economies by identifying potential market sectors and industries relevant to Central American countries. We contribute to an emerging literature on economic and trade relations between China and Central America and use scenario analysis, a form of prospective analysis to hypothesize the advantages and disadvantages of Central American OFDI in China. We apply scenario analysis to each of the two case studies mentioned above.

1. Brief Literature Review

Most of the research literature, if not all, regarding foreign direct investment (FDI) between Central American countries and China has focused on China's investments in Central American countries. The most relevant research regarding foreign direct investment is that of the *Red Académica de América Latina y el Caribe sobre China* (Red ALC-China). China's interest in Central American countries has been motivated by its geographic advantages, competitive advantages, and potential for the development of investments in energy sources, logistics to reduce transport costs, and

2 Eduardo Espinoza is an economist and director of Centro de Estudios para la Integración Económica of SIECA (Secretaría de Integración Centroamericana).

linkages to global value chains. As a result, China has invested significantly in the development of infrastructure in the Central American region (Arias and Vargas 2019; Zhu 2013).

Central American countries have established diplomatic relations with China in recent years, opening avenues for Chinese investments in the region, as well as increased Chinese participation in bilateral and multilateral relationships and organizations (Vadell 2022). While these Chinese and Central American relationships were initially driven by economic interests, these have opened avenues for greater political and policy-related participation of China in the region (Vadell 2022). To get to this point, Emmanuel (2022) argues that Latin American countries framed these relationships as motivated by economic opportunity in the context of strong geopolitical and economic ties between the United States and China.

It is through this discourse of economic opportunities that the presence of China in the region has not caused any significant conflict between the United States and China. Nevertheless, the United States has kept a close eye on the evolution of these economic and diplomatic relationships (Emmanuel 2022; Rod and Himmer 2021). In this regard, Rod and Himmer (2021) identify the use of economic and diplomatic tools, with both hard and soft power characteristics, on behalf of the United States to respond to China's incursion in Central America.

Central America has slowly formalized diplomatic relations with China. Currently, China has diplomatic relationships with Costa Rica, El Salvador, Honduras, Nicaragua, and Panama. The most recent additions to this short list are Nicaragua (2021) and Honduras (2023). Guatemala maintains diplomatic relations with Taiwan and has reaffirmed its relationship with official visits as recently as 2023 (AP 2023). However, Guatemala maintains economic relations with China, which is one of its main trade partners in coffee imports.

Figure 1. Central America: Exports to the US and China ($ US in thousands) (1994-2022)

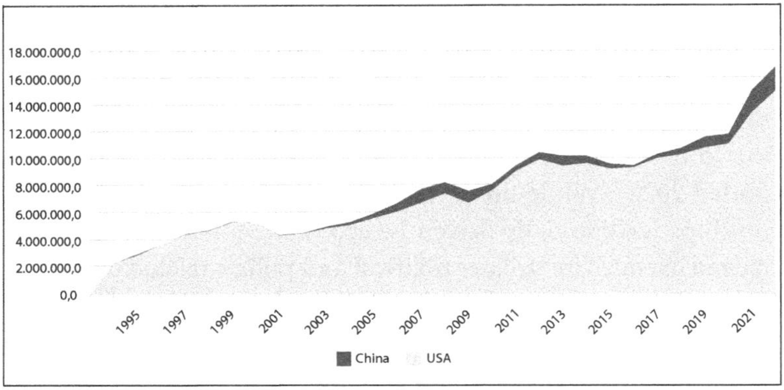

Source: own elaboration based on SIECA (2023).[3]

Figure 2. Central America: Exports by Country ($ US in thousands) (1994-2022)

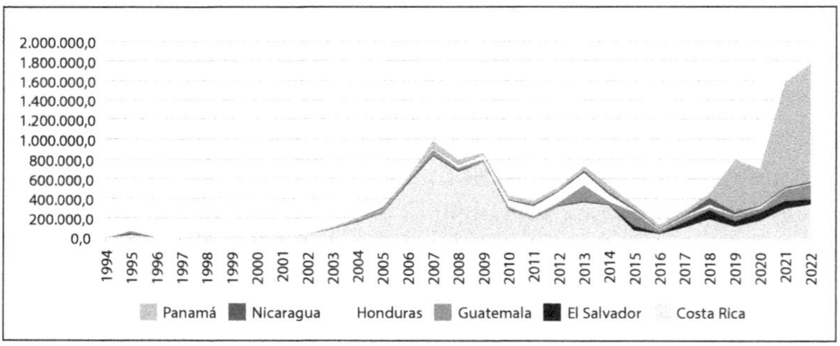

Source: own elaboration based on SIECA (2023).

The United States is still the main trade partner and market for the Central American region. However, exports to China have steadily grown, as shown in Figure 1, in Central America and will continue to grow as countries in the region negotiate trade agreements and participate in Chinese projects at an international level. Figure 2

3 SIECA´s trade information does not include exports of electronic components and devices, mostly by INTEL, for inconsistencies in data.

illustrates how growing diplomatic relationships have increased Central American exports to China. There has been an association between growing diplomatic relations, the signing of several trade agreements and the increasing commercial relations between the region and China in the last decade (Arce 2016).

We understand FDI and OFDI as a form of soft power in China's economic and political rise in the global economy. Foreign direct investment is understood as investments in a country that come from foreign actors and capital. Rather than achieving international objectives by force, China has sought to attract partners and change the preferences of countries by offering economic and investment opportunities. With this in mind, we conceptualize China's economic and political expansion in Central America as a form of soft power where China's economic power and ability to significantly invest in Central American countries leads them to consider China as a priority trade partner (Emmanuel 2022; Nye 2008; Vadell 2022).

As mentioned by Nye (2006), soft power is dependent on a country's culture, political values, and foreign policies. While the political values of China may seem foreign to Central American nations (Emmanuel 2022), their foreign policies of investment and trade are attractive. Lastly, cultural initiatives have slowly taken off with the purpose of promoting Chinese languages and culture (Zhu 2013). While China promotes itself in the region, we ask what opportunities exist for Central American countries to promote themselves and influence Central American-Chinese relations further to their benefit. Because of the minute size of Central American economies relative to China, a soft power-oriented strategy of foreign direct investment on behalf of Central American countries in China may offer significant gains to Central American economies.

This chapter is aimed to explore the possibilities and avenues for foreign direct investment in Central American economies in China. While much has been written about investments from China toward Central America, this chapter looks at the reverse and asks if FDI is plausible for Central American countries and what challenges exist in making any attempt at FDI in China beneficial for Central American economies.

2. Methodology

We apply a prospective research design by implementing scenario analysis to better understand possible avenues for FDI on behalf of Central American countries in China. Scenario analysis allows us to explore how different variables may interact in the future. Through this analysis, we can explore possible paths of development of Central American FDI and communicate or stimulate discussion around the prospect of Central American FDI in China, which allows us to better frame economic goals and decision-making in the region (Kosow and Gaßner 2008).

We use several databases to search for and review research literature on economic relations between Central America and China. We specifically search through JSTOR, Google Scholar, Springer Link, and Sage Publications. We also rely heavily on previous publications by the Red ALC-China, as well as statistics available through the USDA, WTO, and Doublethink. Through a review of the literature and economic and trade statistics, we identify two possible scenarios for Central American OFDI to China.

We base these scenarios on several assumptions. The first assumption is that Central American countries are interested in expanding their economic and trade presence abroad, i.e. rather than settling with their usual partners in trade, Central American countries seek to diversify partners and markets. This is noticeable in the shift from sustaining diplomatic relations with Taiwan to later breaking these so as to establish relations with China. The second assumption is that there is a common interest among Central American countries to maximize their gains through Chinese investment and trade. Consequently, one can think that Central American investment will consolidate trade and investment relationships with China while taking advantage of growing economic relations with the Asian giant.

3. Prospective Analysis

In this section, we explore the potential of Central American OFDI to China through two scenarios. The first scenario is related to a historic crop of the Central American region, coffee. We study China's growing coffee market and consumption as a possible investment opportunity for Central American countries, both by increasing exports of coffee to China, as well as investing in the countries market and the development of the coffee value chain in the country The second scenario relates to investment in the services market, specifically in specialized services related to commercial and technology services. This market has had significant growth in both China and Central America, making it an interesting option for FDI in both small and large businesses.

3.1. Scenario Analysis

Through scenario analysis, we look to better understand how plausible OFDI to China is for Central American countries. We identify two relevant scenarios for Central American OFDI to China, one related to the growing Chinese coffee market, and the other related to opportunities in digital markets. Through these scenarios, we analyze how the region's specialization in coffee production could be an entry point to investing in China as well as other agrobusiness activities. We can also analyze how the Central American region can take advantage of China's participation in the digital and service markets, considering some of the region's countries are experienced in these areas.

Scenario analysis is used to understand how the future may develop regarding specific interests and decisions (Duinker and Greig 2007). Porter (1985, quoted in Duinker and Greig 2007:209) defines scenario analysis as "... an internally consistent view of what the future might turn out to be –not a forecast, but one possible future outcome." Emphasis is made on this distinction between visualizing and forecasting a possible future outcome, scenario analysis only looks to visualize (Duinker and Greig 2007). It can be used to assess risks and ways of managing these and to brainstorm new ideas on a certain issue (Duinker and Greig 2007; Kelly *et al.* 2004). This paper seeks to achieve the latter, by wondering about the plausibility of Central American OFDI to China.

3.2. Central American OFDI Scenarios to China

While we have little to no data on Central American OFDI to China, we can identify two scenarios where investments may flourish if pursued. These scenarios are based on growing agro-industrial trade between the parts, as well as the emergence of the digital economy in both Central America and China. Regarding agro-industrial ventures, we focus on the coffee market in China and Central America's comparative advantages in the coffee market. For our second scenario, we focus on the growth and opportunities that the Chinese digital economy presents for Central America. With this in mind, we ask:

1. How can Central American agroindustry benefit from investing in the Chinese production and commercialization of agricultural products?
2. How can Central America benefit from investing in the development of the Chinese digital economy?

Through these questions, we hypothesize three different scenarios related to Central American investment in China. We analyze the forces of change at play in each scenario, their issues and trends, and the level of impact and uncertainty they represent to Central America.

3.2.1. Scenario 1: Agro-industry and the Coffee Market

Taking into consideration China's large market, there are many opportunities for exports from Central American agro-industries to China. One would expect that a logical next step in commercial relations is the investment on behalf of the parties. We analyze how Central America could benefit from investing in the Chinese agro-industry using coffee as an example. Coffee is an emblematic export for Central America, which explains the considerable rise of coffee exports toward China as shown in Figure 3.

Figure 3. Central America: Total Exports of Coffee and Similar Products to China ($US thousands) (1994-2022)

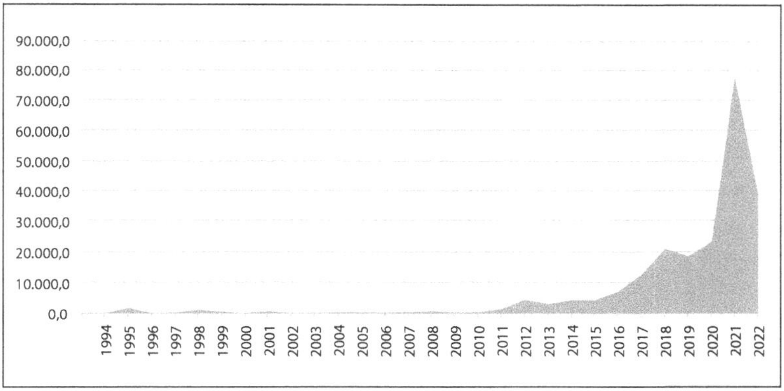

Source: own elaboration based on SIECA (2023).

Forces of Change. We identify three main forces of change that can motivate Central American investment in China's agro-industry. The first is that China has become an increasingly important actor in agro-industrial value chains, specifically in coffee value chains. Neilson and Zoe Wang (2019) observe that the Chinese coffee market is reshaping coffee's global value chains and has developed along with a growing coffee industry in the Yunnan province. Secondly, we argue that there is a growing diversity in Chinese preferences and demands around the quality of crops. In the coffee market, we notice a higher demand for specialized and high-quality coffee in recent years (Deloite China 2019). Lastly, we argue that the growing ties between Central America and China should motivate investments on behalf of both parties. We offer insights into how this may benefit Central American investment.

Issues and Trends. We can identify issues and trends for the Central American coffee agro-industry and the Chinese coffee market. While Central American nations are not the largest producers of coffee, they have built reputations for exporting specialized and high-quality coffee (Harvey *et al.* 2021). Along with this, Central American countries have vast experience with FDI in their coffee production and market. This OFDI has seen the entrance of large foreign-owned firms, such as Starbucks and Nestle as well as investments oriented towards research and innovation. Lastly, Central America has begun efforts to innovate coffee production in the face of climate change and sustainability issues. As for the Chinese coffee market, Deloitte China (2021) states that there is both an increasing demand for coffee and an increased attention to its quality among Chinese consumers. Along with this, consumers are concentrated in "1st and 2nd tier cities" (Deloitte China 2021:2) which present greater opportunities for FDI at different scales. Around 2018, Chinese consumers began to look for a

Figure 4. Central America: Exports by Country of Coffee and Similar Products to China ($US dollar) (1994-2022)

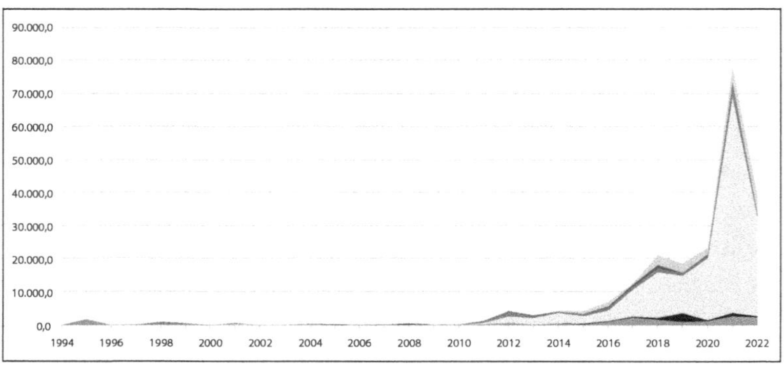

Source: own elaboration based on SIECA (2023).

greater variety and quality of coffee options, an advantage for FDI initiatives (Deloitte China 2021). Along with the consumption of coffee, its production has also grown significantly, although China still relies heavily on imports of coffee to supply demand. Currently, Guatemala is one of China's main coffee trade partners. Out of Central American countries, Guatemala concentrated most of the recent exports from the region to China as demonstrated in Figure 4.

Level of Impact and Uncertainty. We consider this scenario as one of high impact and high uncertainty. Investing in the Chinese coffee market would offer great benefits to Central American investments. Not only can Central America invest in the production of coffee, where knowledge and best practices are an asset to Central Americana countries, but also enter other stages of coffee value chains. Central America has specialized in its production of coffee and offers high-quality Arabica coffee. With growing concerns regarding land quality and climate change, emerging coffee production in China presents an interesting investment opportunity for Central America.

Along with production, Central America can invest in the emergence of quality-oriented chain brands as well as coffee shops. Central American investment can take advantage of niche coffee brands and shops, especially those that are focused on coffee quality as well as its environmental implications (Deloitte China 2021). This offers us the opportunity to link OFDI in coffee with investment in environmental and touristic services, another potential area of OFDI. Uncertainty can stem from several aspects of China's economy and the current global context. Initiatives such as the Belt and Road include actors and markets of different stages of a value chain. That is, they cover a wide range of activities that span from product production to after-sales. China's presence in global value chains stems from its manufacturing power, as well as its increased digital infrastructure and economy. However, the COVID-19 pandemic caused significant challenges to GVCs and gave way to the diversification of GVCs away from China. The pandemic and the Russian-Ukraine war have also trumped advances in the Belt and Road initiative (McBride *et al.* 2023). Xing (2022) argues that further opening the Chinese market to foreign investment could be a way to mitigate the effects of these events. Investing in the Chinese market implies greater investments in logistics, as well as new risks of a developing market with evolving preferences. Deloitte China (2021) has characterized the coffee market as one that is highly competitive and will soon be dominated by chain-store coffee shops. It also notes that consumer preferences are increasingly geared toward high-quality coffee. While the Central American experience with high-quality coffee is an asset, more concerns arise with consolidating Central American investments in China.

Final Scenario Logic. The underlying logic of this scenario is that, given the vast experience of Central American countries in agroindustry and exports, the next plausible step is to invest in other agro-industrial markets. We use coffee as an example of how this may happen. We observe a growing market for coffee production and commerce within China. We consider that Central America has a series of competitive advantages that could influence the success of its investments in a coffee market with evolving preferences. However, we note that consolidating these investments in such a competitive market may be difficult.

3.2.2. Scenario 2: Investing in the Chinese Digital Economy

Central America represents an interesting region to trade with and also to invest in. Its geopolitical location offers the region an attractive advantage in transportation, logistics, and trade. China has greatly invested in trade and logistics initiatives in recent years, this is an advantage for Central America as their exports of services are mainly concentrated in transportation and travel, these are followed by business services, intellectual property, financial services, and IT services (Figure 5). Furthermore, the Central American region has experienced an increase in the use of digital economies, or aspects related to the digital economy. An example of this is the prevalence of the use of fintech in the region, eCommerce, and eServices. Moreover, users of the digital economy have grown substantially in Central American countries with greater barriers to access to technology. Lastly, there is an important experience in the region with receiving FDI in the services and technological sectors. Large companies such as Intel have invested in Central America, these experiences should translate to Central American investments elsewhere.

Figure 5. Central America: Exports of Services ($ US thousands)(2017-2021)

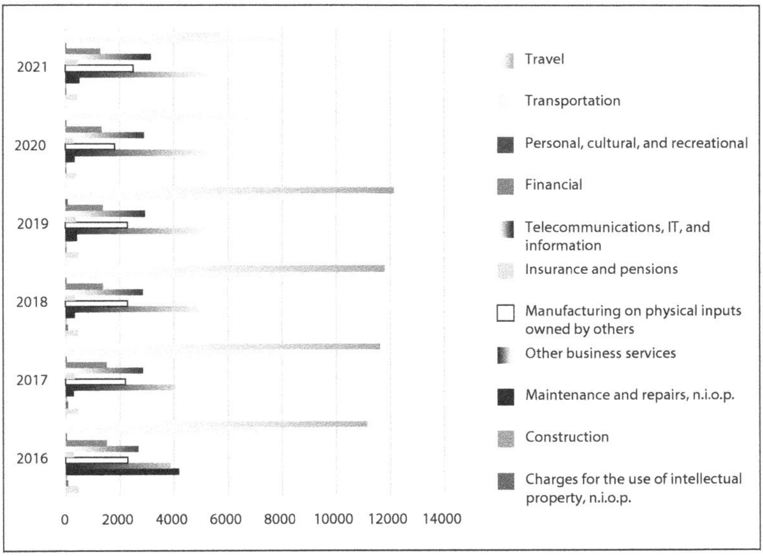

Source: own elaboration based on SIECA (2023).

Central America has experienced an increase in users of the digital economy and information technologies. Nevertheless, there are still important gaps in digital skills in the region. We analyze how investing in the Chinese digital economy could galvanize Central American businesses, as well as improve digital skills across the region.

Forces of Change. The first force of change we identify is technological innovation in commerce. The introduction of the internet, social networks, and now artificial intelligence will continue to transform commerce and commercial opportunities (Zhang and Chen 2019). Secondly, specific technologies have emerged for things such as eCommerce and eServices; this technological transformation needs to be coupled with an increase in digital skills. Lastly, commerce has now centered on user experience and related services as production and consumption become more automated (Kruger *et al.* 2016).

Issues and Trends. China is currently growing its presence in the digital economy (McKinsey, 2018). The growth of the digital economy in China, see Figure 6, has presented several challenges related to its size and the logistics that are required for it to work. Consequently, China has heavily invested in information infrastructure and has sought to join strategic partnerships regarding the digital economy (Sun 2022). One of these partnerships is the Digital Economy Partnership Agreement (DEPA) whose members are New Zealand, Singapore, and Chile. China requested to join the agreement in 2022 (Sun 2022).

Figure 6. China: Market Size of the Digital Economy ($ RMB trillion) (2005-2021)

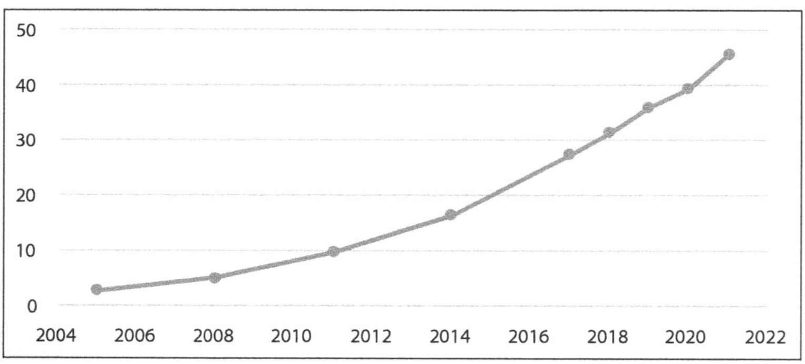

Source: own elaboration based on CAICT (2022) and STATISTA (2023).

Along with these global initiatives on behalf of China, a push toward technological and scientific innovation also forms part of

China's hegemonic aspirations. State policies and attraction of investment in China are focusing on becoming an innovation leader on a global scale. Much of this push for innovation has to do with the need of the Chinese economy and society, but also with presenting China as a center for technological innovation and not just manufacturing (MOFCOM 2021). Beyond just the size of China's digital economy, there is a more profound transformation in China's overall economy. As noted by Gereffi *et al.* (2022), China has transitioned from focusing on consumer goods to becoming a technological leader in information technologies. With this transition, China gained a presence in new global value chains and has further diversified its economy. While investment is mainly concentrated in the manufacturing industry, a majority of countries that invest in the Chinese markets do so in technology, finance, and business services. Of investments from the United States, 35 % of the realized FDI value is in the services sector. In the case of the European Union, services represent 24.8 % of the realized FDI value (MOFCOM 2021).

Figure 7. Central America: Digital Economy User Growth (2019)

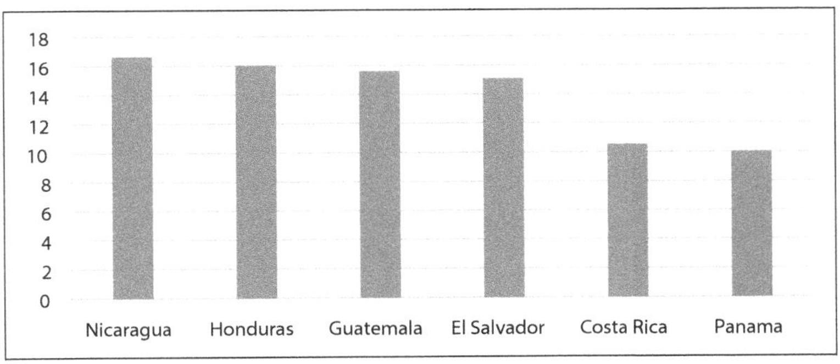

Source: own elaboration based on Del Carmen *et al.* (2020) and BID with data from STATISTA.

As for Central America, it is also experiencing growth in its digital economy as well as an increase in its users, see Figure 7. Fintechs dominate Central America's digital economy, with certain countries having important income from eCommerce, and online transportation services (Del Carmen *et al.* 2020). Central American countries have made important strides in their digitalization processes (Forbes Centroamerica 2021).

However, much is needed in terms of digital infrastructure and digital skills to close gaps across Central American countries (Del Carmen *et al.* 2020). Policies should be geared towards translating an increase in digital skills and infrastructure with an increase in service exports and OFDI. As shown in Figure 8, there are large gaps between countries in exporting information technology related services.

Figure 8. Central America: Total Telecom Exports of Services ($US million) (2016-2021)

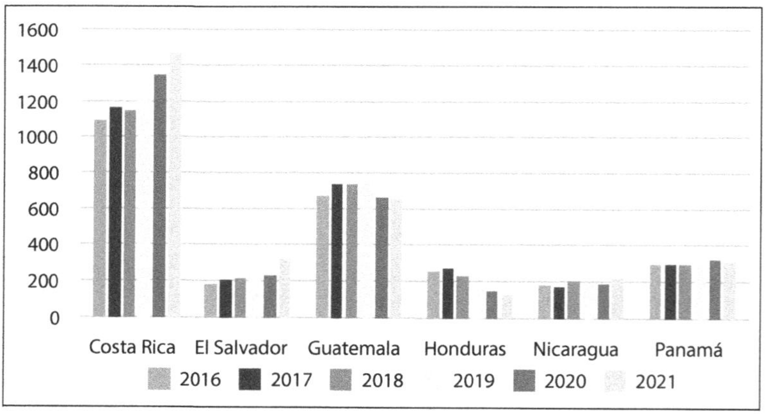

Source: own elaboration based on SIECA (2023).

Level of Impact and Uncertainty. We consider this scenario to be of high impact and medium uncertainty. The impact of investing in the Chinese digital economy can contribute to an increase in users of the digital economy, and in the competitive capacity of businesses that have transitioned, to provide eCommerce and eServices options. The Chinese digital economy allows Central American businesses to test their luck in foreign markets without needing to be there physically (Del Carmen *et al.* 2020). Investing in such a large digital market like China's could also be an opportunity for the digitalization of traditional markets (Cruz 2019; Del Carmen *et al.* 2020). As mentioned beforehand, businesses related to coffee, as well as other high-potential activities, could be successful in the Chinese digital economy. There are, however, important challenges for Central American countries to keep up with the pace of growth and demand in the Chinese digital economy. The first is the need for greater development of digital skills, as well as digital infrastructure. Along with these two needs, Central America needs to develop regional strategies regarding the digital economy, as well as policies for regulating that market (Cruz 2019; del Carmen *et al.* 2020). Nevertheless, a cautious entry into the Chinese digital economy can offset many of the risks associated with the digital economy.

Final Scenario Logic. There has been significant growth in the digital economy in China. This presents two unique opportunities for Central American countries: the first is to invest in the digital economy and its service, as well as to transfer technology and knowledge through investments. Not only could Central America benefit commercially, but also in the development of human capital and digital skills in the region. As noted in the previous scenarios, China has increased its role in global value chains, specifically those related to the digital economy. This increased participation is accompanied by large-scale commerce and trade initiatives such as the Belt and Road Initiatives. Lastly, there has been a sustained expansion of China through establishing new diplomatic or commercial relations while pursuing its "One-China" policy and geo-political presence. It is through this last force of change that Central America can take advantage and pursue further economic opportunities through investment in Chinese value chains.

4. Conclusions and Policy Proposals

After an exhaustive search for case studies of Central American OFDI in China, the lack of data and reliable information motivated an exploration of scenarios for Central American OFDI. Scenarios analysis is a valuable exercise for policy proposals and policy design and in this chapter we develop two scenarios and consider the contextual factors that can condition each scenarios development. The following section discusses these factors and the future of Central American OFDI in China.

Soft power and the restructuring of global value chains. Voci and Luo (2018:2) explain that soft power can be seen through a utilitarian view where states pursue their objectives "not by defeating enemies, but rather by seeking alliances". In measures of soft power, China ranks in the top 30 nations to use soft power throughout the existence of the SoftPower30 index[4]. Within this index, China frequently ranked in the top 10 of soft power through culture and engagement. This indicates a clear intention of China to expand alliances and diffuse Chinese culture. With what end? China's growth is motivated by economic competitiveness at a global scale, as well as symbolic and cultural prestige (Voci and Luo 2018). From a Central American perspective, economic opportunities through alliances with China makes sense. However, the shift in diplomatic relations between Central American countries and China may present challenges for Central American countries in the long term. The extent of future geopolitical tensions between USA and China are unknown and require careful maneuvering by Central American nations. While outward foreign direct investment from Central America to China may not deepen tensions between China and the United States, it does complicate the convergence of Central American interests with both the United States and China. Because of this, the use of Soft Power is key for Central American countries as tensions between both

4 See: https://softpower30.com/what-is-soft-power/.

superpowers develop. According to Eduardo Espinoza (personal interview), chief economist of SIECA, the region has promising opportunities in its present and future economic relations with China. There is specific potential in terms of the localization advantages that the region, including Panama, can offer to FDI from China and vice versa. This is particularly evident in activities related to agribusiness and associated chains of value (tropical fruits, coffee, sugar, pork, and bovine meat, cardamon and other species), medical devices, clean energies and outsourcing and nearshoring of several economic activities such as electric automobile, logistic of oversea transport, digital services. Other important advantages in a reciprocal connection between OFDI to China and FDI from China in the region have to do with the economies of scale, specialization, and the reduction of transactions costs (transportation costs). The Central American regions offers great opportunities to invest in logistics, specialized services with the potential to expand those investments throughout the Pacific Basin. This will require a collective political will and action by Central American governments and the government of China in order to find the avenues for designing and consolidating a joint strategy based on a governance framework that can create the conditions for a better business climate and clear rules for public and private investments in both directions (Ruiz, personal interview).

Regional integration as a challenge to overcome in Central America. Throughout this chapter we have discussed Central America as a consolidated group, made up of Costa Rica, El Salvador Guatemala, Honduras, Nicaragua and Panama. However, regional integration has been a historic challenge for the region. Caldentey (2014) notes that in recent decades Central American integration has achieved greater foreign interest in the Central American market, there has been growth in trade and cooperation within the region, and a greater will to pursue regional objectives. This is also proven by the growing importance of trade between China and the region (Arce 2016)

However, Caldentey (2014) also notes that the region requires a clear agenda and plan of action at the regional scale. This is necessary if it wants to benefit from trade and investment opportunities, regional interest convergence and greater coordination in the region's actions in other international arenas. The region is still facing barriers due to a history of internal conflicts, political violence, institutional instability, and political tensions between its members. However, there are important regional initiatives that relate to the scenarios presented in this chapter. Regional strategies are in place to deal with climate changes and sustainable energy, as well as digital access and infrastructure (SG-SICA 2016; CEPAL 2020). Regarding climate changes and energy, Central America has proposed changes in how agro-industries function and produce. The region is specifically concerned with the uses of biomass and biofuels in agro-industrial production. Regarding the digital economy, Central America is recognized as a digital region in which the smartphone has driven its digitalization. Central America is focused on this and has a regional strategy in place since 2016 (SG-SICA 2016), nevertheless, the strategy needs to be updated so the region can improve on regional regulations that can guide the development of Central America's digital infrastructure, digital skills, and investments (CENPROMYPE 2022).

According to Marco Vinicio Ruiz (personal interview), economist and former ambassador of Costa Rica in China, there are already OFDI flows between Central America and China, but these are no that transparent, especially in commerce and food industry. These relations, however, are happening on a very small scale, which is an obstacle for the consolidation of some potential activities. Central American enterprises and investments in China not only have to deal with problems of scale, but also with competitiveness in a market where big corporations play with their own advantages and rules.

Ruiz also argues that the region has failed to design and implement a joint strategy to promote OFDI in China and better understand the dynamics of China's economic interests and relations in Central America. This requires studying the Chinese economy to explore opportunities and market segments that can be reachable for the region. A collective and consensual action is necessary to create an institutional framework that allows a negotiation with China as a region, just like some regions in Africa have done. For instance, Central America must define a strategic and prospective plan (5 years plan that can identify activities with high potential to participate in market segments or articulate with global value chains in China) that includes the signing of a joint project with China to promote investments in strategic activities with potential to be part of global value chains. This project must be separated from free trade agreements that the different countries already have signed with China. It is necessary to put the efforts in signing a program of investments on strategic sectors, which must be a step forward in the political and economic relations between Central America and China (Ruiz, personal interview).

The unknown avenues of technological development and innovation. Lastly, the policy implications of technological development are unpredictable. As we enter an era of artificial intelligence and innovation in information communication technology (ICT), digital skills will make a sharp difference in the region's economic growth and development. As noted by Kavanagh (2019), the advancement of new tech implies new challenge and threats to governance. Given the magnitude of technological changes, especially those related to Artificial Intelligence (AI), preparedness through policies and regulations can have significant impacts on the outcomes of these technological changes (Kavangh 2019). China is set to be a major player in the future of technological innovation and the digital economy. As China shifts from manufacturing to technological innovation, Central America could greatly benefit from its investment and participation in the development of China's digital economy and technological sector.

References

Arce Alvarado, Randall. 2016. "Mercado Común Centroamericano y República Popular China: retos del vínculo comercial de cara a la integración del MCCA". In, Dussel Peters, Enrique (coord.). *La nueva relación comercial de América Latina y el Caribe con China. ¿Integración o desintegración regional?* Red ALC-China, UDUAL and UNAM/Cechimex: Mexico, pp. 97-140.

Arias, Rafael and Vargas, Luis. 2019. "Chinese OFDI in Costa Rica". In, Dussel Peters, Enrique (coord.). *China's Foreign Direct Investment in Latin American and the Caribbean. Conditions and Challenges.* Red ALC-China, UDUAL and UNAM/Cechimex: Mexico, pp. 253-270.

CAICT (China Academy of Information and Communication Technology). 2022. *Report on the Development of China´s Digital Economy 2022.* CAICT: Beijing.

Caldentey del Pozo, Pedro. 2014. *Los desafíos estratégicos de la integración centroamericana.* CEPAL: Mexico.

CEPAL (Economic Commission for Latin America and the Caribbean). 2016. *Innovation and internationalization of Latin American services.* CEPAL: Santiago de Chile.

CEPAL. 2020. *Estrategia Energética Sustentable 2030 de los países del SICA.* CEPAL: Santiago de Chile.

Del Carmen, Giselle, Díaz, Karen, and Ruiz-Arranz, Marta. 2020. *A un clic de la transición: Economía digital en Centroamérica y la República Dominicana.* IADB: Washington, D.C.

McKinsey. 2018. "China's fast climb up the value chain". *McKinsey Quarterly*, May 9.

Cruz, Guillermo. 2019. *Economía digital y desarrollo productivo en Centroamérica.* ALAI: Montevideo.

Deloitte China. 2021. *White Paper on China's Freshly Brewed Coffee Industry.* Deloitte China: Beijing.

Duinker, Peter. N. and Greig, Lorne. A. 2007. "Scenario analysis in environmental impact assessment: Improving explorations of the future". Environmental Impact Assessment Review 27(3), pp. 206-219.

Dussel Peters, Enrique (coord.). 2019. *China's Foreign Direct Investment in Latin America and the Caribbean. Conditions and Challenges.* Red ALC-China, UDUAL and UNAM/Cechimex: Mexico.

Forbes Centroamérica. 2021. "La economía digital avanza en Centroamérica". *Forbes Centroamérica*, April 22.

Forbes Mexico. 2015. "Starbucks conquista poco a poco a Centroamérica". *Forbes México*, September 21.

Gereffi, Gary, Bamber, Penny and Fernandez-Stark, Karina. 2022. *China's New Development Strategies: Upgrading from Above and from Below in Global Value Chains.* Palgrave Macmillan: Singapore.

AP News. 2023. "Guatemala leader in Taiwan expresses "rock-solid friendship". AP, April 25.

Harvey, Celia A., Pritts, Aalyssa A., Zwetsloot, Marie J., Jansen, Kees, Pulleman, Mirjam M., Armbrecht, Inge, and Valencia, Vivian. 2021. "Transformation of coffee-growing landscapes across Latin America. A review". *Agronomy for Sustainable Development*, 41(5), Article 62.

Kelly, Ruth, Sirr, Lorcan and Ratcliffe, John. 2004. "Futures thinking to achieve sustainable development at local level in Ireland". *Foresight* 6(2), pp. 80-90.

Kosow, Hannah, Gaßner, Robert. 2008. *Methods of Future and Scenario Analysis: Overview, Assessment, and Selection Criteria.* DIE/GDI: Bonn.

Kruger, Rendani, Gelderblom, Helene and Beukes, Wynand. 2016. *The value of comparative usability and UX evaluation for e-commerce organisations.* CONF-IRM 2016 Proceedings: South Africa.

McBride, James, Berman, Noah and Chatzky, Andrew. 2023. "China's Massive Belt and Road Initiative". *Backgrounder* (Council on Foreign Relations), February 2.

MOFCOM (Ministry of Commerce of the People's Republic of China). 2021. *Foreign Investment Guide of the People's Republic of China.* MOFCOM: Beijing.

Rod, Zdeněk and Himmer, Michal. 2021. "The great powers in Central America: US response to Chinese activities in the region". *Latin American Policy* 12(2), pp. 236-249.

SG-SICA (Secretaría General-Sistema de Integración Centroamericana). 2016. *Estrategia Regional Digital para el desarrollo de la Sociedad de la información y el conocimiento en el SICA*. SG-SICA: El Salvador.

SIECA (Secretaría de Integración Económica Centroamericana). 2023. *Sistema de Estadísticas de Comercio de Centroamérica.* Retrieved on July 10 at: http://www.sec.sieca.int/.

Sun, Shaoyan. 2022. "China's Digital Economy: Development, Impacts, and Policies". *China Institute-University of Alberta*, November 30.

STATISTA. 2023. "Market size of the digital economy in China in selected years from 2005 to 2021". Retrieved on August 1, at: https://www.statista.com/statistics/1250080/china-digital-economy-size/.

USAID (US Agency for International Development). 2020. *Fact Sheet. Resilient Coffee in Central America.* USAID: El Salvador.

Vadell, Javier. 2022. "China's bilateral and minilateral relationship with Latin America and the Caribbean: the case of China–CELAC Forum". *Area Development and Policy* 7(2), pp. 187-203.

Xing, Yuqing. 2022. "China and global value chain restructuring". *China Economic Journal* 15(3), pp. 310-329.

Zhang, Longmei and Chen, Sally. 2019. "China's Digital Economy: Opportunities and Risks". *IMF Working Papers* 19/16, pp. 1-27.

5. CHILEAN OFDI TO CHINA

Dorotea López, Andrés Bórquez and Juan E. Serrano-Moreno[1]

Introduction

The emergence of China in the economic system is one of the most significant economic accomplishments of the twenty-first century, one which guarantees to radically modify the current economy and labour market. With the Asian nation being the leading destination for Chilean goods, trade relations between Chile and China have been steadily growing. However, this has not been the case for investments.

A burgeoning literature has focused on understanding capital flows from China to Chile. Indeed, when most researchers study foreign direct investment (FDI) and Chile, they often measure capital flows that go into the nation, that is, FDI inflows. Nonetheless, Chile's outflows or, outward foreign direct investment (OFDI) – money that Chile's investors invest outside the country– frequently flies under the radar (Latinometrics 2023). However, Chile invests more of its GDP overseas than China and the European Union (Latinometrics 2023).

1 The authors thank the editor for his detailed comments on an earlier version of the manuscript and gratefully acknowledge financial support to this project by ANID Millennium Science Initiative Program NSC2022 053.

There is not much literature that examines the reverse flow; that is Chile's OFDI in China. Understanding this enables us to explore the logics that leads to investment and the dynamics Chilean actors must experience in their interactions with China. In this sense, this exercise can be a relevant input for a parameter of comparison with the investment behaviour of other regions, such as developed countries that invest in China.

In Chile's case, studies conducted by the Chilean Ministry of Foreign Affairs are the only publicly available data. There are limited additional studies that analyse the issue. Therefore, this study gathers official data from Chilean company case studies based on firms' public financial statements, annual reports, and interviews with key players.

Two specific Chilean firms, Elecmetal and Codelco, are further investigated. This choice is justified as the industrial sector, specifically the mining industry, quantitatively dominates Chilean OFDI to China. Furthermore, comparing both companies enrich this study, as their scope and mission differ. Elecmetal, a world-leading private firm in mining equipment, sought to offshore some of its production to China in the early 2010s. Conversely, Codelco, a state-owned company, invested in China to provide trade services to the mother corporation, aiming first at the Chinese market and, more recently, at the overall Asian market. Likewise, their intentions differ. Whilst Elecmetal aims to access third markets, Codelco aspires to supply the Chinese market.

This study was conducted through interviews with critical informants from the companies under investigation, particularly those linked to international operations. More precisely, the interviewees are those in charge of the companies' investment decisions in China.

Following the introduction, the paper reviews existing literature on Chile-China relations, which, as indicated, is highly scarce. Thirdly, the general trends of the outward foreign direct investments to China until 2021 are examined. This assessment is first done to then analyse two solid case studies selected. Lastly, the results are discussed, along with some recommendations, so as to draw a conclusion considering the matters mentioned above.

1. Literature review

1.1. Prior Research on Chile-China Relations

Despite the increased importance of outward foreign direct investments (OFDI) to enhance economic development, literature regarding Chile's OFDI to China is highly scarce. Most authors study the topic from the opposite viewpoint (i.e., China's OFDI to Chile) or exclusively relate to trade relations, which in many aspects differs from investments (Dussel Peters 2022; Bórquez and Bravo 2021; Chen and Perez-Ludeña 2014). Although promising, this early empirical research is limited in scope and needs an update (Gachúz 2012; Heine 2016; Serrano-Moreno *et al.* 2021a). This review integrates existing literature on Chile-China relations, serving as a basis for understanding the reasons for the scarce literature on investments from Chile to China.

The milestones linking Chile and China are well-known, as Chile has a pioneering status in creating relations with China. In 1970, Chile was the first South American nation to forge diplomatic ties with the Asian economy (Guilisasti 2006; Pérez Le-Fort 2006; Wilhelmy 2001). Further, Chile was the first Latin American nation to agree on a joint venture with China in 1982 to support China's entry into the World Trade Organization (WTO) in 2001 and to recognise China as a market economy in 2004 (Heine 2016; Recabarren and Tso-Lee 2020). Consequently, Chile and China signed a free trade agreement (FTA) in 2005 during the Asia-Pacific Economic Cooperation (APEC) Leaders' Summit in Busan, becoming effective in October 2006 (Heine 2006). This FTA was China's first ever signed with an individual nation, granting Chile privileged duty-free access to the Chinese market. Following this FTA, China became Chile's principal trading partner.

1.1.1. Chinese OFDI to Chile

Hence, Chile has been at the forefront of Latin America's increasing relations with China. Following the China-Chile FTA, bilateral trade increased fivefold during the first ten years (i.e. 2006-2016) (Heine 2016). Nevertheless, Chinese direct investments in Chile were minimal until 2016 compared to elsewhere in Latin America, where Chinese OFDI took off in 2010 (Serrano-Moreno 2021:82). Nonetheless, this Chile-China paradox changed in 2016 as Chile and China established a strategic partnership in order to enhance foreign investments (Bórquez 2019), and Chile joined the Belt and Road Initiative in 2018 (Serrano-Moreno 2021, 2023; Serrano-Moreno *et al.* 2021b). This year was a turning point for Chilean OFDI in China (Serrano-Moreno 2021:87).

Between 2016 and 2021, Chile was the most dynamic Chinese OFDI recipient in Latin America, with 19 % of regional OFDI (Dussel Peters 2022:7). Serrano-Moreno (2021) confirms that Chinese OFDI grew in 2018 when Chile received US$ 6,777 million in investments from China. Since then, Chinese investments in Chile have amounted to more than US$ 2,000 million and US$ 3,000 million in 2019 and 2020, respectively (Serrano-Moreno 2021:87). Most notably, the OFDI amount per transaction from China to

Figure 1. China's OFDI Received by Chile (2016-2021)

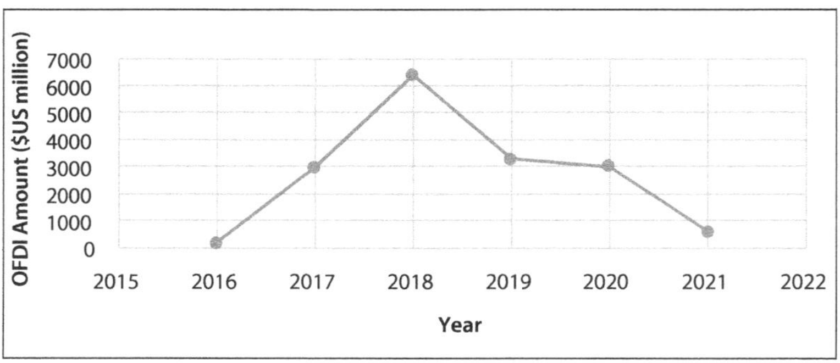

Source: own elaboration based on Dussel Peters (2022).

Chile amounted to US $458 million between 2015 and 2021 (Dussel Peters 2022:8). Figure 1 depicts China's OFDI received by Chile from 2016 to 2021. It is important to note that OFDI from China to Chile considerably decreased in 2021, most likely owing to the economic and financial crisis following the pandemic.

1.2. Bilateral Trade

China is Chile's main trading partner since 2010 (p.655, Heine 2010), receiving a 38.3 % share of Chilean exports and delivering 29.5 % of imports in 2021 (SUBREI 2022). Chinese-Chilean relations entered a new phase in 2019 after a protocol upgraded the FTA to promote trade liberalisation, deepen economic cooperation, and ultimately strengthen the strategic partnership (Serrano-Moreno *et al.* 2021/a). The Chinese Commerce Ministry (2019) claimed that this was the first FTA upgrading agreement between China and a Latin American nation. Following this agreement, the Chile-China Free Trade Area became China's most open free-trade zone, as trade in goods increased fivefold compared to previous levels (MOFCOM 2019). Hence, the Chile-China FTA is the cornerstone of the bilateral relationship, and its successful implementation has consolidated China as Chile's first trading partner (SUBREI 2015). In 2021, China concentrated roughly 39 % of Chile's total export value, of which 76.6 % were goods from the mining sector (Chile Customs 2021). From the mining export basket, 62.3 % of total exports were copper ores and concentrates, and 29.1 % were copper (Chile Customs 2021). Similarly, China provided approximately 28.3 % of Chile's imports in 2021 (Chile Customs 2021). As the following section shows, Chilean copper exports to China has highly influenced the Chilean OFDI to the Asian nation, which is primarily concentrated in the mining sector.

1.3 Policies to Enhance OFDI to China

So far, the Chilean government has not pursued explicit policies to encourage Chilean companies to invest abroad. Nonetheless, two public agencies, ProChile and InvestChile, are worth considering. The former enhances Chilean exports, whilst the latter attracts investments into Chile. Formally, these institutions are not responsible for promoting Chilean investments abroad. However, ProChile has offices in China that may assist Trade Representation Offices (TRO) which offer services to their mother companies in Chile. Indeed, our research confirms that there are no actual public policies to support Chilean investments in China. The interviews confirm that, although ProChile could potentially help Chilean companies that open TROs, the aforementioned public agency has no impact.

It is generally known that since the mid-1970s, Chile started opening to outside competition by promoting trade and financial liberalisation, deregulation, and privatisation (UNCTAD 2007). In 1974, ProChile, the Chilean Ministry of Foreign Affairs institution, was founded to foster the export of Chilean goods and services abroad. This corporation provides Chilean firms that have export potential with the needed knowledge and information to facilitate the internationalisation process. For this aim, ProChile has five offices in China (Beijing, Chengdu, Guangzhou, Shanghai, and Hong Kong) and one in Taiwan (Taipei) (ProChile 2022).

Similarly, InvestChile is a government agency that implements initiatives to promote and coordinate actions with the aim of attracting foreign direct investment into Chile. This institution offers specialised services to align the interests of foreign investors to business opportunities in Chile. Providing information on the Chilean economic, social, and legal environment and informing on the procedures and regulations with which investors must comply, InvestChile brings FDI into the nation. Our research suggests that this institution could provide expertise and experience in designing new policies to enhance Chilean OFDI abroad, as discussed in the last section.

2. Chile's OFDI to China until 2021

2.1 Global Trends of Chilean OFDI

Between 1990 and 2019, approximately 1,250 Chilean firms executed more than 3,300 projects abroad through trade agreements in goods and services and capital movements (SUBREI 2021). Total Chilean outward foreign direct investments (OFDI) abroad within this period reached US$ 128,832 million distributed among countries in five distinct regions, as displayed in Figure 2 (SUBREI 2021). Annual investment outflows from Chile to other economies between 1990 and 2021 are shown in Figure 3. Whilst data from 1990 is only available from the SUBREI, data from the UNCTAD is collected for the period 2016-2021. However, both data sources depict similar trends.

Figure 2. Chilean OFDI: Annual Flows by World Regions (percentage) (1990–2019)

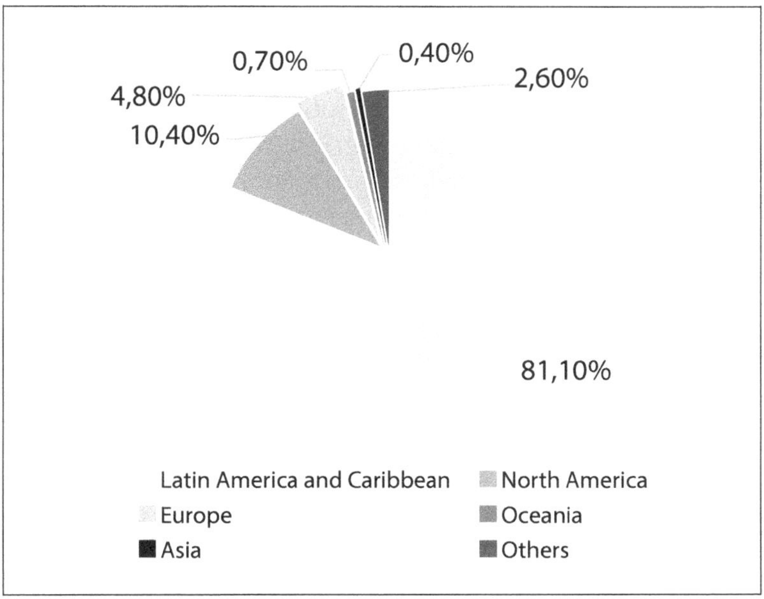

Source: own elaboration based on SUBREI (2020).

Figure 3. Chilean Total OFDI ($ US million) (1990-2019)

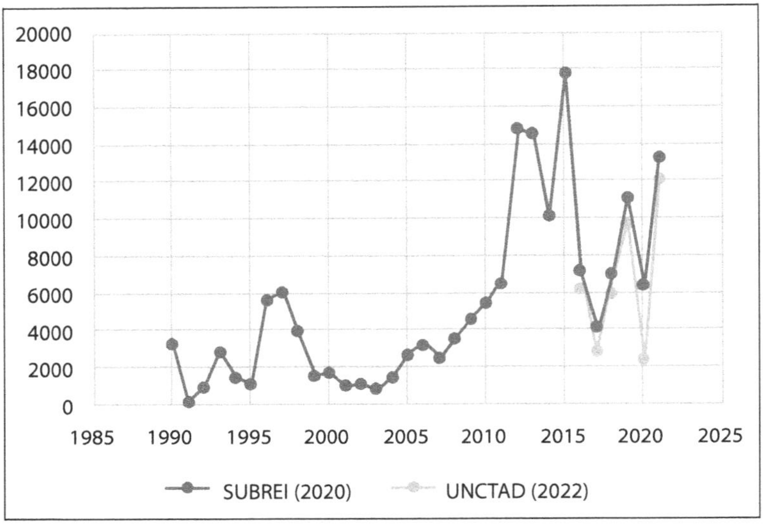

Source: own elaboration based on SUBREI (2020) and UNCTAD (2022)[2].

Latin American economies are the leading destinations for Chilean outward direct investments (81.1 % of the total OFDI), with relatively steady growth and concentrated primarily in Brazil, Peru, Colombia, and Argentina (SUBREI 2021). These four countries account for a total volume of US $ 94,099 million or, similarly, 73.10 % of total investments (SUBREI 2021). Table 1 illustrates these countries' share of Chilean OFDI worldwide, showing that the top ten nations account for 92.2 % of investments.

2 The data regarding total Chilean OFDI abroad from 1990 until 2021 (marked in blue) is obtained from SUBREI (2020). From 2016 until 2021, the data is retrieved from the UNCTAD (2022). It is observed that the data in the common years (i.e., 2016-2021) from both sources follow a similar trend. Chilean authorities from the SUBREI attribute the slight difference to how one understands the concepts of materialized investment and capital inflows.

Table 1. Chilean Total OFDI by Countries (1990-2019) ($US million)

Rank	Top Destinations	Total Amount Invested, $ US million	Percentage of Total Amount Investment Abroad
1	Brazil	37,385	29,00 %
2	Peru	19,970	15,50 %
3	Colombia	18,511	14,40 %
4	Argentina	18,233	14,20 %
5	United States	13,225	10,30 %
6	Uruguay	4,835	3,80 %
7	Mexico	1,930	1,50 %
8	Canada	1,825	1,40 %
9	Germany	1,507	1,20 %
10	Spain	1,196	0,90 %
11	Croatia	1,006	0,80 %
12	Ecuador	987	0,80 %
13	Belgium	938	0,70 %
14	France	909	0,70 %
15	Panama	906	0,70 %
16	Australia	873	0,70 %
17	Egypt	581	0,50 %
18	Venezuela	545	0,40 %
19	**China**	**408**	**0,30 %**
20	England	367	0,30 %
	Others	2695	1,90 %
	Total	**128,832**	**100,00 %**

Source: own elaboration based on SUBREI (2021).

2.2 Chilean OFDI in China

China is the 19th destination worldwide for Chilean FDI and the second destination among Asia-Pacific economies after Australia (SUBREI 2020b). From 1990 to December 2018, direct investments from nearly 60 Chilean companies to China amounted to

US $408 million, representing 0.3% of the total amount invested abroad (SUBREI 2020a). Figure 2 shows that Asia captures 0.4% of total Chilean OFDI, corresponding to three-fourths of this to China. Figure 4 depicts the Chilean OFDI evolution in China from 1990 to 2018.

Figure 4. Evolution of Chilean OFDI to China ($US million) (1990- 2018)

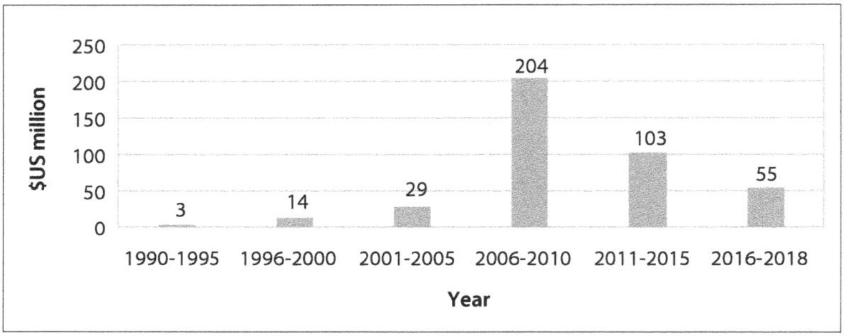

Source: own elaboration based on SUBREI (2020).

Three main sectors constitute the total US $408 million invested in China until 2018 (Figure 5). The Chinese industrial sector received US$326 million from Chile between 1990 and 2018, representing 79.9% of the total direct investments to China (SUBREI 2020a).

Figure 5. Chilean OFDI in China by Sectors (1990- 2018)

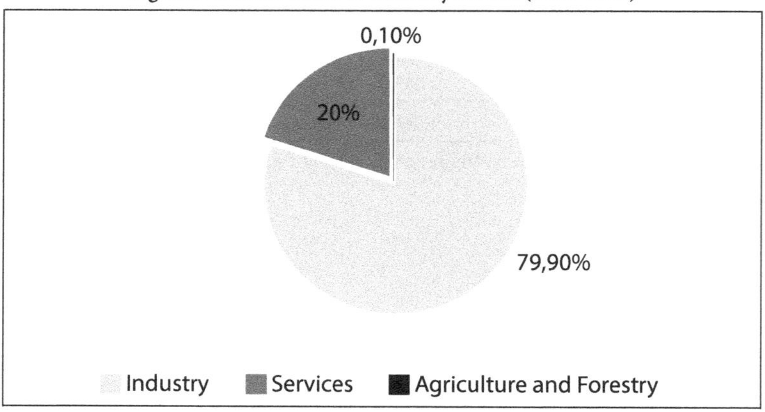

Source: own elaboration based on SUBREI (2020).

Secondly, Chilean direct investments in the services sector, mainly associated with maritime transport and minerals trade, amount to US $82 million, constituting 20% of the total invested. Third is the agricultural sector, with an amount close to US $1 million and a share of less than 0.1%. The concentration of OFDI in the industrial sector is a direct consequence of the dominance of copper in Chilean exports to China. Indeed, Chilean mining companies (i.e., Codelco, Elecmetal, and Sigdo Koppers) opened their Trade Representation Offices (TROs) to facilitate their minerals and mining equipment exports to China.

To enter the Chinese market, Chilean firms mainly established TROs in Shanghai, Beijing, Hong Kong, and Chengdu. Further, companies also create subsidiaries in China to offshore production (SUBREI 2020/a). Lastly, joint ventures with Chinese partners or other foreign businesspeople are steadily growing (SUBREI 2021:5). Table 2 outlines Chilean companies from distinct sectors that have performed direct investments in China, highlighting their sector, investment destination, and business entity type. Two specific Chilean companies, Elecmetal and Codelco, are worth investigating in further detail.

Table 2. Relevant Chilean Companies Investing in China

Investing Company Name	Sector	Investment Destination	Business entity type	Project Date
Banco de Chile	Financial services	Hong Kong	Subsidiary	2004
		Shanghai	Subsidiary	2005
		Beijing	TRO	2006
		Shanghai	Subsidiary	2011
Bci	Financial services	Hong Kong	TRO	2006
Azurian	Software & IT services	Shanghai	TRO	2008
Distribución y Servicio (D&S)	Food & Beverages	Shanghai	TRO	2009

Chilemat	Consumer products	Not Specified	Not specified	2009
Compañía Chilena De Navegación Interoceánica (CCNI)	Transportation & Warehousing	Hong Kong	TRO	2009
Agencias Universales (Agunsa)	Transportation & Warehousing	Hong Kong	Subsidiary	2010
Celulosa Arauco y Constitución	Wood products	Shanghai	Subsidiary	2010
Codelco	Metals	Shanghai	Subsidiary	2011
Compañía Electro Metalúrgica (Elecmetal)	Metals	Changshu	Joint Venture + Plant	2011
		Changzhou	Subsidiary + Plant	2012
	Metals	Changshu	Joint Venture	2018
Vina Errazuriz	Food & Beverages	Shanghai	TRO	2012
Agrosuper	Food & Beverages	Shanghai	Subsidiary + TRO	2012
		Hong Kong	Subsidiary + TRO	2012
		Chengdu	TRO	
		Qingdao	TRO	
Viña Montes	Food & Beverages	Shanghai	TRO	2013
Compañía de Aceros del Pacifico (CAP)	Metals	Hong Kong	Subsidiary	2013
Compañía de Aceros del Pacifico (CAP)	Metals	Hong Kong	Subsidiary	2013
Banco Security	Financial services	Hong Kong	TRO	2013

Grupo Gordillo	Industrial equipment	Beijing	TRO	2019
Agrosuper	Food & Beverages	Chengdu	TRO	2020
OXIQUIM	Chemical Industry	N/A	Plant	
		Beijing	TRC	
Falabella	Textile Manufacturing	Hong Kong	Subsidiary	
		Shenzhen	Subsidiary	
		Shanghai	Subsidiary + TRO	
		Hong Kong	Investment	
Sigdo Koppers	Metallurgical Industry	Jiangyin	Investments in Associates	
		Zibo	Investments in Associates	
		Suzhou	Subsidiary	
		Wuxi	Subsidiary	
		Chengdu	TRO	
SQM	Mining (Fertilisers)	Shanghai	Subsidiary	
		Qingdao	Joint Venture	
		Beijing	Subsidiary + TRO	
		Chengdu	Joint Venture	
		N/A	Plant (Lithium)	
Mosaico	Manufacturing	Ningbo	Operations Center	
Caimi	Textile Manufacturing	Hangzhou	N/A	
Sodimac	Metallurgical Industry	Shanghai	N/A	

Source: own elaboration based on each company's website and Red ALC-China.

2.3 Case studies of Chilean Companies in China

2.3.1 Elecmetal

2.3.1.1. History and Reasons for Setting up in China

ME Elecmetal is a world-leading producer and marketer of high-end grinding media, steel parts and other goods and services for the mining market, owning TROs in all world regions (ME Elecmetal 2017:22). According to Elecmetal's consolidated financial statements, as of December 31st 2022, the consolidated net sales revenue amounted to ThCLP $1,149,631,195 (ThCLP $882,367,637 in 2021)[3]. From this, ThCLP $63,978,715 (ThCLP $56,487,902 in 2021) were generated in China, or similarly, 5.6% of sales revenues[4] (ME Elecmetal 2022/a:46). Figure 6 shows the sales revenues in percentages, distinguishing the four main countries.

Figure 6. Elecmetal's Net Sales Revenues by Four Top Countries (as of December 30, 2022)

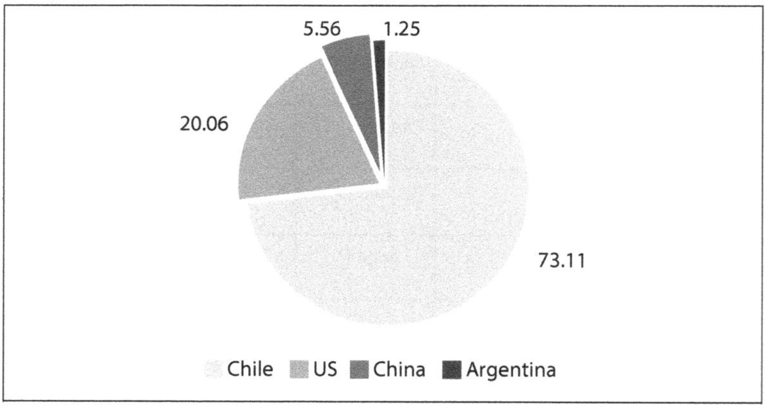

Source: own elaboration based on ME Elecmetal Annual Report (2022/b:144).

3 ThCLP$ = Thousands of Chilean pesos.

4 It is important to note that ThCLP $840,555,021 (ThCh $675,429,880 in 2021) was generated in Chile, ThCLP $230,666,102 (ThCh $136,979,598 in 2021) in the United States, and ThCLP $14,431,357 (ThCh $13,470,257 in 2021) in Argentina.

Of the total consolidated revenues generated in Chile as of December 31st 2022, 52 % corresponds to the metallurgical segment, 27 % to the glass packaging segment, 20 % to the wine segment and 1 % to the media segment. The percentages by segment as of the same date in 2021 were 43 % 29 % 27 % and 1 %, respectively. Notably, 100 % of sales revenue generated in China and the United States as of December 31st of 2022 and 2021 corresponded to the metallurgical business segment. Further, of the total consolidated revenues generated in Argentina as of December 31st, 2022 and 2021, 100 % corresponds to the wine segment (ME Elecmetal 2022/b:73).

Headquartered in Santiago, ME Elecmetal's factories are in Chile, the United States, and China (p.26, ME Elecmetal 2017). The firm under consideration has extensive strategic alliances, licenses, and joint ventures with multinational corporations worldwide. Strategic alliances with Chinese firms include representation and product development agreements with Jiangxi Naipu Mining Machinery and New Materials Co. Ltd, two corporations that supply rubber and steel parts for mill coating (ME Elecmetal 2017:22).

In 2011, Elecmetal arrived in China. The firm and a private steel company in Changshu (China), LongTeng Special Steel Co., Ltd, established a 50/50 joint venture in the Asian nation (ME Elecmetal 2021:10). Under the name of "ME Long Teng Grinding Media (Changshu) Co. Ltd." (in short, "ME Long Teng"), the joint venture company constructed a manufacturing plant to produce grinding balls and bars in Changshu (Jiangsu province), two products that ME Elecmetal markets directly worldwide (ME Elecmetal 2021:24). ME Long Teng annually produces 500,000 tons of grinding balls in Changshu, using ME Elecmetal specifications and technology (ME Elecmetal 2021:10). These grinding balls are then used to pulverise materials (i.e., ceramics, paints, ores, or chemicals) into thin powders. Through manufacturing agreements with LongTeng Special Steel Co. Ltd., Elecmetal successfully started commercialising two new grinding balls worldwide: "ME Super SAG" and "ME Ultragrind" (ME Elecmetal 2017:24). These Elecmetal products are certified under several International

Organization Standardization (ISO) standards. More precisely, the grinding media manufacturing plant is certified in the following ISO standards (ME Elecmetal, n.d.):

- ISO 9001: 2008 Certified Quality Management Standards.
- OSHAS 18001: 2007 Certified Environmental Management Standards.
- ISO 14001: 2004 Certified Occupational Health and Safety Standards.

As of December 31, 2022, ME Long Teng Grinding Media Ltd. (Changsu) registered ThCLP $96,694,665 in assets and ThCLP $21,698,274 in liabilities (ME Elecmetal 2022/b:166). Comparing these numbers to the revenues registered on the same date of the previous year is interesting. Assets amounted to ThCLP $100,007,154 and liabilities to ThCLP $27,109,125 as of December 31, 2021. Further, the joint venture in Changshu made a revenue of ThCLP $76,662,743 in 2022, depicting an increase compared to ThCLP $68,509,163 made by December 31, 2021.[5]

According to the interviews, regarding employment, all of its labour force is local, except the Chilean Finance and Quality managers. The general manager acknowledges that nowadays it is easier to control Chinese operations from Chile.

Interviewees state that the firm decided to invest in China with the purpose of gaining competitiveness in accessing international markets other than the Chinese. In addition to lower production costs, the infrastructure (in this case, waterways and transport) was highly relevant. Elecmetal initially sought to export from its Chinese plant to Russia and other mining countries in the Asia Pacific region. Indeed, the firm did not aim to supply the domestic market as its products were considered too expensive and too technologically advanced for the Chinese mining sector at the time.

---

5 There are no exact estimates on Elecmetal's total OFDI amount in China. The only available data that could provide an estimate are the assets and liabilities of the 50/50 joint venture, ME Long Teng Grinding Media Ltd.

Nonetheless, the conflict in Crimea in 2014 and the subsequent sanctions against Russia hampered this objective.

In 2012, Elecmetal established a fully-owned subsidiary named ME Elecmetal China Co., Ltd in Changzhou, Jiangsu province, China. More precisely, the location is in Changzhou Export Processing Zone. This zone is on the southern bank of the Yangtze River and is well connected to Shanghai's port, thus facilitating the import and export process. With a net worth of US$ 36,310 thousand, this subsidiary is a completely foreign-owned enterprise focused on manufacturing and selling steel parts (Elecmetal 2021:71). In 2014, this subsidiary built a specialised steel foundry plant in Changzhou with a total annual production capacity of 30,000 tons of spare parts for grinding equipment (Elecmetal 2021:19). However, their most valued products manufactured in the Changzhou plant are their high-end armour for large-scale grinding mills, a piece of essential equipment for the global mining industry. This plant obtained in 2016 an ISO-9000 and ISO-14000 certifications, indicating both the high-quality and the high clean manufacturing standards (ME Elecmetal 2017:25) of the products. Lastly, via the subsidiary "Elecmetal Investments Ltd." in China, ME Elecmetal makes indirect and permanent investments in China and Hong Kong (ME Elecmetal 2022:33).

2.3.1.2. Learning processes

The interviewees claim that, since Elecmetal's establishment in China in 2011, the firm learned that it is essential to abide by the rules given, as there are conditions such as limitations of the property of land or special tax assessments. Initially, they were hesitant to settle in China without a domestic partner as they were unfamiliar with the business culture. However, the Changzhou National Hi-tech District (CND), a state-owned Hi-tech Zone in China that successfully attracts foreign investment into the Jiangsu province, insisted the company set up alone. Initially, the CND was critical in enabling Elecmetal to continue with their investment even if they did not have a local partner, as the CND supported them by assisting in the interaction process with the customs agency and tax office. In financial matters, the CND helped the Chilean company work with two specific local banks, the China Construction Bank and the Hong Kong and Shanghai Banking Corporation (HSBC). The CND still supports Elecmetal today, easing their apprehensions.

The CND is in Changzhou prefecture-level city in southern Jiangsu province, in the heart of the Yangtze River Delta Shanghai Economic Ring. It is the most sophisticated and high-end industrial area in Changzhou. The CND encourages domestic and foreign investors to establish scientific research institutions and high-tech companies with an export focus (Ferrari 2008). Another feature positively valued by companies about CND is the presence of highly skilled labour, which is possible thanks to the multiple educational and training institutions in this Hi-tech Zone (Dezan Shira & Associates n.d.). In line with this, this high-tech district has more than 11,000 industrial enterprises, including approximately 1,800 foreign-invested firms from 68 countries and regions. Also, the CND is the only high-tech district that integrates different types of transport infrastructure (i.e., roads, airports, ports, subways, and high-speed railways) (AMCHAM n.d.). This infrastructure contributes to its strategic position, reducing travel times to nearby major cities such as Shanghai and Nanjing. Consequently, Elecmetal learned that the waterways and support from the CND were essential during the pandemic.

Further, the firm is aware that trust is a vital element, more than in other markets, and it takes a long time to develop. In the interviewees' words: "Doing business in China requires trust, and this takes time, especially with the local partners." The interviewees shared a telling example: "On the opening day of the Changzhou plant, the CND installed, as a surprise and as a gift, a complete garden at the plant's entrance." This anecdote reveals the importance of cultivating interpersonal relationships for building trust. Hence, Elecmetal's interviewees know that it is necessary to demonstrate a long-term interest in Chinese partners.

CND's support contrasts with Elecmetal's relationships with the Chilean authorities in China. The interviewees explain that the firm has "good relations with the embassy" (sic.), and they are regularly invited to social gatherings but never need their support. The interviewees stated that Elecmetal's success in penetrating the Chinese market and integrating into the nation was attributed to Chinese local authorities and not to Chilean governmental institutions in China.

2.3.1.3. Challenges and expectations

Furthermore, the company has also experienced difficulties since its establishment in China. Competition regarding automation and robotisation in their production process is their primary concern. The interviewees claim Elecmetal's biggest challenge is automating its production process before competitors. Further, geopolitics also poses a challenge, although to a lesser extent. The China-Taiwan tension worries them, but protectionism and potential tariffs are critical challenges (ME Elecmetal 2022/b).

In this regard, Elecmetal's annual report (2022/b:32) stated:

> "Resulting from US-China bilateral announcements, from July 2018, the US government applied tariff measures primarily against Chinese imports to a list of products. This list included the crusher replacement parts that subsidiary ME Global imports from China using its designs and technical specifications to satisfy the needs of its customers in the United States. Subsequently, the US established a new list of Chinese products subject to these measures, including a 10 % tariff on imports of steel grinding media. Elecmetal's subsidiary imports this product from China, where they are manufactured according to their own designs and technical specifications by the joint venture, ME Long Teng Grinding Media (Changshu) Co., Ltd. The latter tariff was increased from 10% to 25% in 2019, which very significantly affected the company's ability to compete in this market" (Elecmetal 2022/b:32).

Nonetheless, the interviewees highlight that Elecmetal has managed to evade US sanctions against the grinding balls produced in China because the firm also has plants in Zambia. In this sense, Elecmetal can avoid the tariffs against China and continue exporting to the US thanks to their plants in other nations.

Next, high labour costs in China are risky and could create a significant difference compared to competing firms. The competition produces similar goods at lower prices, as their plants are in Indonesia, India, and the Philippines, where the labour costs are cheaper than in China. Consequently, though, the competing firms offer lower-quality goods. For this reason, the interviewees explain that Elecmetal aims to produce high-end equipment in China for the Asia-Pacific markets. They highlighted that China offers comparative advantages in terms of high-qualified human resources and infrastructure, which contributes to the firm's production of higher-quality goods compared to the competition. However, the company expects the demand for their products to grow in the Chinese market in the following years, as the Chinese mining sector is becoming more sophisticated and requires more advanced equipment than it did when Elecmetal arrived in China in 2011.

2.3.2 Codelco

2.3.2.1. History and Reasons for the Establishment in China

Codelco is an independent company wholly owned by the Chilean government, created in 1971 (Codelco 2015). As Chile's largest mining firm, Codelco's core business is to extract and process mineral resources. The company converts such resources into refined copper and by-products to market them internationally. From its foundation and until 2015, the firm produced 20% of Chilean exports, being Asia the most important market (Codelco 2015).

Codelco began considering Asia as a susceptible market for its shipments in the 1990s. Initially, the firm decided to open an office in Singapore in 1992, as it involved growth that in Asia was in demand. Subsequently, as China became more important than any other country in the region, Codelco relocated the office to Shanghai in 2002. Unlike other companies at that time that opted for Beijing to enhance relations with the political elites, Codelco opted for Shanghai to establish stronger ties with businesspeople. Codelco's key decision-makers perceived that Shanghai offered a better context to develop business opportunities.

In 2005, the firm "China Minmetals Corporation" signed an agreement with Codelco to secure its long-term copper supply (Guilisasti 2006; Heine 2006). Headquartered in Beijing, Minmetals is a metals and mineral trading firm created in 1950. It is worth considering that Minmetals is a state-owned company under the direct control of China's state-owned Assets Supervision and Administration Commission (Fitch Ratings 2021). Hence, the Chinese government made Minmetals responsible for producing and trading metals and minerals (Codelco 2005). This strategic alliance implied that Minmetals would agree to buy copper for fifteen years to secure its supply, and Codelco would obtain funds to finance its investment plans (Codelco 2005). It is important to note that this Codelco-Minmetals agreement occurred prior to the Chile-China FTA, and this operation created conditions for accelerating the FTA negotiation (Codelco 2005).

In this context, Codelco's exports to China started to increase dramatically since 2005 and the company realised it needed a more significant presence in China. Consequently, on November 2, 2011, Codelco created a fully-owned sales subsidiary in Shanghai named Codelco Shanghai Company Limited (Codelco, n.d. -a.). The subscribed and paid-up capital as of 2021 amounted to US$ 2,000,000 (Codelco 2021). Notably, Codelco Shanghai Co. Ltd. is a sales and commercial subsidiary and does not produce mining products (Codelco 2021). This limited liability firm in Shanghai has two primary business purposes directly related to importing and exporting copper, molybdenum, and other metals. First, it acts as a procurement agency providing services to purchase mining goods (Codelco 2021). Second, the subsidiary provides sales agency services to sell copper, molybdenum and other by-products to China, Hong Kong, Malaysia, Korea, Taiwan, Indonesia, Thailand, Myanmar, and Vietnam (Codelco 2016). Indeed, Codelco Shanghai Co. Ltd. is Codelco's only copper and molybdenum Sales Representative in Asia (Codelco n.d./b).

Regarding the firm's finances, in 2021, Codelco's total sales revenue amounted to US $20,023 million (Codelco 2021). Asia, including China, was a key market for copper sales. Codelco distributed to Asia 46.1 % of their refined copper sales in 2021, implying receiving US$9,230 million revenues from the sales subsidiary in China (Codelco 2021). Nonetheless, Codelco aims to perform geographic diversification for refined copper sales (Codelco 2021). In 2021, Codelco increased sales in Southeast Asia but reduced exposure to China and traders (Codelco 2021). Amid production challenges and subsequent copper output reduction, Codelco will halve its copper sales to China in 2023 (Luk 2022).

Regarding employment, as for Elecmetal, the entirety of Codelco's current labour force in China is local. According to the interviewees, Codelco Shanghai Co. Ltd. comprises 23 local employees, as the three Chilean managers left China during the COVID-19 pandemic. Like Elecmetal, Codelco's interviewees acknowledge that it could be easier to control operations "via Zoom" (sic.) without a direct physical presence on the field nowadays. Therefore, the main objective of Codelco's presence in Shanghai is "to cultivate relations with local customers and authorities in order to trade in optimal conditions" (sic.).

2.3.2.2. Learning Processes

Due to its supply history, Codelco's progressively built-up internal knowledge of the Chinese market helped expand its presence. Hence, the firm autonomously set up and developed its networks in China without the help of Chilean state agencies whose understanding of China is "very limited" (sic.), according to the interviewees. This possibility results from accumulated experience in the field and deepening interpersonal and long-term relations. For instance, Chinese employees moved from Shanghai to Santiago, enhancing the capacities of the internal firm. Also, the interviewees explain that Codelco imported to Chile heavy equipment produced by their Chinese clients, despite its quality, to cultivate relationships.

Therefore, for Codelco, establishing trust relationships with Chinese clients is critical, as these are key for solving misunderstandings or tense situations. Codelco learned that in China, disagreements are resolved by encouraging negotiations and alluding to long-term relations. Further, the interviewees state that learning Chinese law is relevant, but, contrary to other countries, conflicts with local clients should be solved through informal and interpersonal interactions avoiding legal disputes at all costs.

Similarly, the interviewees point out the importance of participating in international and local fairs, seminars, and conferences in Asia, such as the Shanghai Forum, in which businesses are generated, negotiated, and undertaken. Next, the firm learned that unlike the fairs in Western countries —for instance, the London Metal Exchange Week—, here they are focused on presentations and exhibitions; in Asia, they are vital for negotiating concrete projects, closing business deals, and cultivating long-term relationships.

However, the interviewees are critical towards Codelco's long-term strategy or, to be more precise, its lack of. The firm did not take full advantage of its privileged access to the Chinese market as it limited itself to selling copper as a raw material with no added value. Hence, aside from copper, Chilean products are considered good and cheap. However, Codelco's investment in research and development is marginal. This situation is challenging to reverse compared to other actors, such as New Zealand, which has better positioned its agro-industrial high-end products, thus obtaining higher benefits.

2.3.2.3. Challenges and Expectations

Since China is Codelco's most significant and prominent market, the company is committed to maintaining its trading company in China. It is important to note that the Shanghai office is not strictly vital for firm operations, as mentioned. Instead, the office primarily aims to maintain long-term relationships with local actors so there will not be a change in the current export flows to China. Indeed, the mission is to preserve its current clients, not to necessarily find new ones. Further, China may increasingly become a supplier of inputs and machinery to Chilean mining.

Nonetheless, while we write these lines, Codelco is also looking to grow in Southeast Asia and India, so the firm is opening a trading company in Singapore. The reason for expanding in Southeast Asia is that China is at a stage where its demand for minerals is stabilising due to its industrial development. At this point, the interviewees state that the market demand will come from the inland areas that have yet to be developed. Further, they point out that Chile, as far as possible, should not take sides in geopolitical tensions between China and the United States. However, any involvement should consider Chile's interests and improve its negotiating position.

3. Conclusions and Policy Proposals

3.1. Conclusions

Over the last two decades, China has become an attractive destination for foreign investment, especially for large firms, including Latin American companies. Our findings confirm that the Chilean economy's specialization in the mining sector determines the nature and the OFDI flows to China. The mining sector received 79.9% of the total direct investments to China between 1990 and 2018 (SUBREI 2020/a). Also, our findings show that the Asian country built a dynamic and attractive environment so that companies can offshore their industries, access the Chinese market and, in the best cases, achieve both alternatives. This chapter explores the Chilean case; although it is far from being a significant case in terms of the volume of investment from the region to China, it allows us to understand the logic that drives this trend and to contrast the experience of a Chilean state-owned company (Codelco) and a private company (Elecmetal) investing in China.

After the signing of the FTA between the two countries in 2005, China quickly became in 2010 the primary destination market for Chilean shipments. Chile mainly exports raw materials, including minerals, forestry resources and foodstuffs. However, investment has been less active than trade, with around thirty cases over the last 20 years. According to data from the Secretary for International Economic Relations (SUBREI), from 1990 until 2019, Chile's direct investment in China had reached US$408 million dollars whilst total OFDI abroad amounted to US$128,832 million. This is 0.3% of the total amount invested abroad. Similarly, the UNCTAD (2022) records that Chilean OFDI abroad from 2016 to 2021 amount to US $42,341 million.

The question is: what has driven these investments in the case of Chile? Several factors explain the presence of Chilean capital in China. One of the main ones is Chilean companies' search for new markets. This is the case of Codelco, which sought to expand in Asia, and China has been an attractive option due to its large population and growing middle class. Another critical factor is the Chinese government's policy of promoting foreign investment. China has implemented numerous policies that make it easier for foreign companies to invest in China, especially those looking to manufacture and export. This includes reducing tariff barriers and implementing tax incentives for companies that invest in industrial development. In particular, the Chinese government has created special economic zones to favour productive linkages and optimise export logistics. Thirdly, Chilean companies emphasise that high levels of infrastructure and connectivity have been vital to investing in China. The Asian nation manages to establish platforms to operationalise trade competitively.

The first Chilean investments in China focused on financial services, transportation and manufacturing sectors of household products and construction materials exported to Chile. In this category, cases like Elecmetal invested in China by opening factories to export products to the world market in general and the Asia Pacific region in particular. In the 2010s, Chilean companies started investing in developing services related to international trade, such as the opening of TROs (Codelco, Agrosuper and Viña Concha y Toro).

However, investing in China also entails difficulties for Chilean companies. One of the main concerns is the lack of knowledge and understanding of the Chinese market. China has a particular investment system where each province has its agencies to attract investment. This makes managing the domestic regulatory processes more complex, particularly in deciding where to invest. In Codelco's case, this point was mitigated because they had opened an office in Singapore in 1992 that allowed them to travel to China often and learn about specific country aspects regularly. In fact, with the information gathered during these trips, they could select the city of Shanghai for their first office in China, unlike most foreign companies that initially bet on Beijing, a city with more political than business characteristics than Shanghai. In Elecmetal's case, these initial decisions were resolved through the intermediation of CND in Jiangsu province, which played an essential role in selecting the province and dealing with local authorities and banks.

Cultural differences and language barriers are also elements that hinder communication and negotiation with Chinese partners or clients. On this point, a consensus among the cases analysed is that knowledge of the culture can be vital in dealing with the day-to-day difficulties of investing in China. In this sense, the Codelco and Elecmetal offices create business relationships, build networks with their counterparts, understand them, and identify sensitive points when generating daily interactions. Both companies emphasise that in China, disagreements are resolved by encouraging negotiations and alluding to long-term relationships.

Learning Chinese law is relevant in this configuration, but the long-term resolution is worked out under relational parameters.

This chapter also focused on the long-term challenges for Chilean investment in China. In both cases, China will continue to be an important place to do business, but a maintenance strategy prevails. Growth and new business creation will shift to South and Southeast Asia. There is a consensus that the new geopolitical scenario affects the integration strategy of China-based supply chains.

Regarding this point, it was possible to confirm a perception of more significant uncertainty about the future. The United States and China are the two largest economies in the world and have a strong presence in the Chilean market. Tensions between these powers may reduce international trade and investment, while new trading blocs may emerge, leading to less integrated trade. The international scenario increases risk exposure for the Chilean economy and capital abroad. Consequently, both companies took action to diversify their businesses in the long term. Codelco recently decided to open a new office in Singapore that will serve as a platform for doing business in Southeast Asia. Similarly, Elecmetal opted to reorient production in Africa to avoid tariff hikes caused by the trade war between China and the United States.

This study found that the role of promotion agencies and other Chilean state initiatives has not significantly impacted investment or the development of new projects in China. Both companies studied have the resources for managing their relations with China.

3.2 Policy Proposals

On April 11, 2023, Chilean news published that foreign direct investment from other nations to Chile kicked off in 2023 (Forbes 2023). Chile's Central Bank reported that the flow of inward FDI received as of February 2023 reached US$4,677 million, representing an increase of 46% compared to the same period in 2022 (Forbes 2023). According to an analysis conducted by

InvestChile, this number is 10% higher than the average of the last five years (US$ 4,260 million). More precisely, the inflow in February amounted to US$ 2,999 million, an amount that is above the average of the last 12 months, which reached US$ 1,826 million (Forbes 2023).

Given the challenging economic environment this year, the Chilean government is working hard to attract more foreign investment to the nation. Chile's economy minister, Nicolás Grau, states that "to increase investment, the government has implemented several measures, including the deployment of investment attachés in five points globally, which join the existing attaché office in Tokyo, in order to promote Chile as an investment destination in strategic countries; and also very intense agendas that we are promoting in specific sectors, such as green hydrogen and soon in lithium" (Forbes 2022).

Nonetheless, little is done by Chilean authorities to enhance the opposite; that is, there are no policies that would enhance OFDI from Chile to other nations. Considering the small size of the Chilean market, OFDI from Chile is a strategic need for many Chilean companies. Today, domestic market saturation and competitive pressure are critical push factors for Chilean OFDI (UNCTAD 2007). As globalisation grows, Chilean firms cannot solely count on home markets as a source of secure profit. Competition from foreign companies steadily rises through imports, inward FDI, and non-equity participation modes (UNCTAD 2007). Indeed, Chile is a more active investor worldwide than most developed economies, including the EU, Japan, and the US, relative to its GDP (Latinometrics 2023). Given the relevance of the points mentioned above, the Chilean authorities should have an ambitious policy supporting OFDI.

With several Asian countries, and in particular with China, there is a relationship of economic complementarity. In this logic, investments in these markets enable having access to the production of products that are not possible to develop in local industries. At the same time, these markets have a natural demand for domestic products. Therefore, the opening of associated services will allow the dynamization of exports and the detection of new opportunities for Chilean capital. Consequently, the investment of Chilean capitals in Asia can mean learning processes in key industrial and logistical issues to improve performance and make companies more resilient both locally and internationally.

The World Economic Forum (2022) published a report on OFDI policy for sustainable development, proposing several measures that home-country governments could employ to support OFDI. General guidelines from the report that could be applied to Chile include the following areas:

Firstly, institutional arrangements could be performed to regulate and facilitate OFDI to specific target markets. Given China's increasing attractiveness to Chilean firms, new institutions should be designated to enhance Chile's absorptive capacity. Secondly, since geopolitics can challenge operations in China, the Chilean authorities should offer political risk insurance and early support services. Thirdly, financial support is critical for promoting OFDI. Otherwise, Chile could target small and medium-sized enterprises to help them overcome their financial limitations in OFDI and subsequent competitive disadvantages.

More precisely, based on Elecmetal's and Codelco's challenges in their expansion to China, capacity building, market intelligence, and incentives are policies that should be implemented to enhance Chilean OFDI to China. Moreover, the Chilean embassy in China and Chilean commercial attaches are critical for supporting firm internationalisation.

Regarding firm capacity building, Chilean authorities should communicate the necessary information to strengthen Chilean firms' capacity to expand into the Chinese market. Chilean companies must improve their understanding of OFDI's advantages, risks, and challenges. Increasing knowledge of multicultural challenges and international business management issues that could be encountered while operating in China is critical to enhancing OFDI. Next, the Chilean government should provide relevant information and market intelligence on investment opportunities in China, including consultancy services to aid Chilean-based companies to grow and succeed through OFDI in China. An institution coordinating initiatives and providing direct assistance to national firms would improve their market intelligence, helping them mitigate risk and overcome obstacles in venturing into China.

Thirdly, fiscal and financial incentives via the provision of loans can similarly encourage Chilean domestic companies to invest in China. Otherwise, the Chilean Central Bank should offer backup to investors in their investments for financial support. The Chilean embassy in China should have a double responsibility. First, it should guide Chilean firms in their landing process in China by informing companies about Chinese legislation and regulations is critical. Second, the embassy should ensure sustainability in the Chinese market, providing constant support and supervision. Providing techniques for companies to build trust with local partners seems relevant for them to sustain long-term. Lastly, Chilean experts in Chinese commercial matters should promote Chilean OFDI to China by supporting the commercial actions of Chilean firms operating in China.

References

AMCHAM (American Chamber of Commerce in Shanghai). n.d. "Changzhou National High-tech District (CND)". Retrieved April 4, 2023, at https://www.amcham-shanghai.org/en/industrial-park/changzhou-national-hi-tech-district-cnd

Bórquez, Andrés. 2019. "Exploring the non-traditional foreign investment in Sino–Latin American relations: The Chilean case". *Competition and Regulation in Network Industries* 21(1), pp. 18–33.

Bórquez, Andrés and Bravo, Carlos. 2021, "Who are China's strategic economic partners in South America?". *Asian Education and Development Studies*, Vol. 10 No. 3, pp. 445-456.

Chile Customs. 2021. "Entre enero y abril exportaciones chilenas a China crecieron 44,6 % y sumaron US$ 11.472,8 millones".

Retrieved April 24, 2023, at https://www.aduana.cl/entre-enero-y-abril-exportaciones-chilenas-a-china-crecieron-44-6-y/aduana/2021-05-11/144056.html

Codelco (Corporación Nacional Del Cobre Chile). 2005. "Presidente Ejecutivo explica acuerdo Codelco-Minmetals". Retrieved on April 24, 2023, at https://www.codelco.com/noticias/2005/presidente-ejecutivo-explica-acuerdo-codelco-minmetals#:~:text=A %20Codelco %20le %20interesa %20posicionarse,proveedor %20de %20metales %20y %20minerales.

Codelco. 2015. *Annual Report 2015*. Codelco: Santiago de Chile.

Codelco. 2016. "Offices, subsidiaries and sales representatives". Retrieved on April 11 2023, at https://www.codelco.com/memoria2016/en/pdf/mem2016codelco-subsidiaries.pdf

Codelco. 2021. *Memoria Anual 2021*. Codelco: Santiago de Chile.

Codelco. (n.d.-a). "Filiales". Retrieved on April 24, 2023, at https://www.codelco.com/transparencia/filiales

Codelco. (n.d.-b). "Ventas". Retrieved on April 24, 2023, at https://www.codelco.com/nosotros/ventas/ventas

Dezan Shira & Associates. n.d. "Changzhou National High–Tech District – Updates". *Dezan Shira & Associates* - Your Partner for Growth in Asia. Retrieved on April 24, 2023, at https://www.dezshira.com/updates/2013/07/changzhou-national-high-tech-district.html

Dussel Peters, Enrique. 2022. *Monitor of Chinese* OFDI *in Latin America and the Caribbean 2022*. Red ALC-China: Mexico

Ferrari, Marco. 2008. "Changzhou National Hi-Tech District Attracts Overseas Investors". *China Briefing News*, July 31.

Fitch Ratings. 2021. "Rating Report China Minmetals Corporation." *FitchRatings*, August 16.

Forbes. 2023. "Inversión extranjera en Chile durante febrero logra un alza de 46 % con respecto al mismo mes de 2022." *Forbes Chile*, April 12.

Gachúz, Juan Carlos. 2012. "Chile's economic and political relationship with China." *Journal of Current Chinese Affairs*, *41*(1), pp. 133-154.

Errazuriz Guilisasti, Octavio. 2011. "Las relaciones de Chile y China: del simbolismo a la acción." *Estudios Internacionales 39*(154), pp. 169–178.

Heine, Jorge. 2006. "China, Chile and free trade agreements." *Estudios Internacionales 38*(152), pp. 143–147.

Heine, Jorge. 2016." The Chile-China Paradox: Burgeoning Trade, Little Investment. *Asian Perspective*, *40*(4), pp. 653–673.

Latinometrics. 2023. "Chile Invests More of its GDP Abroad Than the EU & China". *Latinometrics*, April 17.

Luk, Julian. 2022. "Codelco to slash copper sales to China by 50 % amid production challenges, sources say". *Fastmarkets*, November 23

ME Elecmetal. n.d. "ME Ultragrind for regrinding." Retrieved on April 24, 2023, at https://www.me-elecmetal.com/wp-content/uploads/2021/09/ME-Ultra-Grind-1.pdf.

ME Elecmetal. 2017. ME *Elecmetal Annual Report 2017*. ME Elecmetal: Chile.

ME Elecmetal. 2020. *Compañía Electro Metalúrgica S.A. Annual Report 2021*. ME Elecmetal: Chile.

ME Elecmetal. 2021. "Compañía Electro Metalúrgica S.A y Afiliadas." Retrieved on April 24, 2023, at https://www.me-elecmetal.com/wp-content/uploads/2022/05/EEFF-Elecmetal-03.2022.pdf.

ME Elecmetal. 2022/a. *Estados Financieros Consolidados Intermedios al 30 de junio de 2022 y por los períodos de seis y tres meses terminados el 30 de junio de 2022*. ME Elecmetal: Chile.

ME Elecmetal. 2022/b. *Memorias anuales de* ME *Elecmetal*. ME Elecmetal: Chile.

MOFCOM (Ministry of Commerce People's Republic of China). 2019. "The Protocol Upgrading China-Chile Free Trade Agreement Comes into Force Today". MOFCOM, March 1.

Pérez Le-Fort, Martin. 2006. "Relaciones sino-chilenas bajo nuevas circunstancias." *Instituto de Estudios Internacionales de la Universidad de Chile*, *38*(152), pp. 123-136.

Recabarren Silva, Javier Eduardo and Lee, Yun-Tso. 2020. "La diplomacia parlamentaria chilena en la profundización de las relaciones entre Chile y China. 2000-2016." *Universidad Militar Nueva Granada*. https://doi.org/10.18359/ries.4251

Serrano Moreno, Juan Enrique, Pérez Ceballos, Alejandra and De Abreu Negrón, Maria Gabriela. 2021/a. "Beyond copper: China and Chile relations." *Asian Education and Development Studies* 10 (3), pp. 1-16.

Serrano-Moreno, Juan Enrique, Telias, Diego and Urdinez, Francisco. 2021/b. "Deconstructing the Belt and Road Initiative in Latin America". *Asian Education and Development Studies*. Vol. 10 (3), pp. 337-347.

Serrano-Moreno, Juan Enrique. 2021, "La retórica de la conectividad de la Iniciativa de la Franja y la Ruta en América Latina". In, Sahd, Jorge (ed.). *China y América Latina: Claves para el futuro*. CEIUC and Konrad Adenauer Stiftung: Santiago, pp. 151-173.

Serrano-Moreno, Juan Enrique. 2023. "Latin America and the Caribbean: How the Belt and Road Initiative diminished the United States influence". In, Regilme, S.S. (ed.). *The United States and China in the Era of Global Transformations: Geographies of Rivalry*. Bristol University Press: Bristol (forthcoming).

SUBREI (Subsecretaría de Relaciones Económicas Internacionales). 2015. *Análisis de las relaciones comerciales entre Chile y China en el marco del tratado de libre comercio*. SUBREI: Chile.

SUBREI. 2020/a. *Presencia de Inversiones Directas de Capitales Chilenos en China 1990 – diciembre 2018*. SUBREI: Chile.

SUBREI. 2020/b. *Presencia de Inversiones Directas de Capitales Chilenos en las Economías Miembros del Foro de Cooperación Económica Asia-Pacifico (APEC) 1990-diciembre 2018*. SUBREI: Chile.

SUBREI. 2021. *Presencia de Inversiones Directas de Capitales Chilenos en el Mundo 1990-diciembre 2020*. SUBREI: Chile.

SUBREI. 2022. "Comercio exterior de Chile crece 41% en 2021 impulsado por envíos no cobre y servicios." SUBREI, January 1.

Taotao, Chen and Pérez Ludeña, Miguel. 2014. "Chinese foreign direct investment in Latin America and the Caribbean." *Production Development Series* 195 (ECLAC), pp. 1-30.

UNCTAD (United Nations Conference on Trade and Development). 2007. *Global Players From Emerging Markets. Strengthening Enterprise Competitiveness through Outward Investment.* UNCTAD: Geneva.

Wilhelmy, Manfred. 2001. "China y América Latina." *Instituto de Estudios Internacionales de la Universidad de Chile*, pp. 3-11.

World Economic Forum. 2022. *Outward Foreign Direct Investment Policy Toolkit for Sustainable Development. Insight Report.* UN-ESCAP and WEF: Geneva.

6.
MEXICO'S OFDI TO CHINA

Enrique Dussel Peters

Introduction

The socioeconomic relationship between Mexico and the People's Republic of China —China in what follows— has increased exponentially during the 21st century in any imaginable field, including trade, China's overseas foreign direct investments (OFDI), infrastructure projects and in the generation of employment, and with respective micro, meso, macro, and regional impacts. From a socioeconomic perspective it has been one of the most outstanding performances for Mexico in the 21st century generating new learning processes and challenges at all mentioned levels.

There is a widespread literature regarding the impact of foreign direct investment on growth and development, while differentiating between developed and developing countries (Blomström and Persson 1983; Dunning 1999; Jiang 2003; Lall and Narula 2006; Lim 2001; UNCTAD 2021; Xing 2006). In addition, there is an increasing literature regarding China's outward foreign direct investment (OFDI) in Latin America and the Caribbean (LAC) (Dussel Peters 2019, 2023/b; ECLAC 2021; MOFCOM, NBS and SAFE 2021). However, the research of Latin American and the Caribbean's (LAC) as well as Mexico's OFDI to China has been practically non-existent, with important exceptions (Basave and

Gutiérrez Haces 2011, 2013; Dussel Peters 2012; EMGP 2021; Goldstein and Toulan 2007; Grosse and Mesquita 2007; IDB 2012).

Based on this brief assessment the goal of the document is to analyze Mexico's OFDI to China during 2000-2022 including micro, meso, and macro aspects. The first section briefly examines the overall Mexico-China socioeconomic aspects relevant for Mexico's OFDI to Mexico: the formal diplomatic, institutional, and economic framework, the trade exchange and infrastructure projects, among others, are important for understanding the performance of Mexico's OFDI to China, which will be discussed in the second part. This second section includes general OFDI trends from Mexico, specifically to China, and two case studies (Bimbo and Interceramic) to elucidate the reasons, conditions, and challenges of Mexico's OFDI in China. The final part of the document highlights the main results of the analysis and stresses some policy and research recommendations.

The document will integrate specific references to methodological, statistical, and conceptual debates regarding OFDI in general and for Mexico specifically, although it will not explicitly attempt to generate a methodological and conceptual framework for OFDI, which would go far beyond the scope of the analysis.

1. Overall Socioeconomic Mexico-China Relationship

The Mexico-China socioeconomic relationship has been examined in detail in the last decade (Dussel Peters 2022/a), and in particular through business chambers and academic institutions such as the Center for Chinese-Mexican Studies (Cechimex) at the School of Economics of the National Autonomous University of Mexico (UNAM), among others. In what follows we will only focus on four relevant issues to embed the next chapter on Mexico's OFDI to China: the existing institutional framework between Mexico and China, the increasing relevance of China's presence in Mexico's international trade, China's OFDI to Mexico, and the new triangular relationship between Mexico, China and the United States in the context of NAFTA (North American Free Trade Agreement implemented in 1994)/USMCA (United States, Mexico and Canada Agreement, since 2020). This will allow for an understanding of the second chapter of this analysis.

In 2022, and after 50 years of diplomatic relations since 1972, Mexico and China account for a profound and complex institutional framework of cooperation in all socioeconomic fields. Dozens of socioeconomic institutions —including in the legislative, executive, business organizations, as well as universities and academic entities— have generated sporadically and in a few cases periodic exchanges.1 Today Mexico and China account for four main bilateral institutions with periodic and mostly annual exchanges: the Binational Commission (created in 2004), the High Level Group (GAN) (since 2013), the High Level Group on Economics and Business (GANE) (since 2013), and the High Level Group on Investments (GANI) (since 2014). These bilateral cooperation institutions function in addition to regional institutions such as the CELAC (the Community of Latin American and Caribbean States)-China Forum (since 2014), the China-LAC Business Summit since 2007, and several academic and think-tank periodic meetings since the 2010s, among other regional institutions. While the bilateral institutions have focused in their work in different years on potential sectors of interest (including topics such as investment statistics and their differences according to different methodological approaches, tourism, and autoparts-automobiles, among many others), in general there has not been a periodic monitoring and evaluation on these and other FDI-related topics, even less so from a pro-active and concrete perspective regarding new fields of cooperation and investments regarding tourism, e-commerce, new technologies in electric vehicles, telecommunications, and the global value chain of lithium, among many others.

1 The assessment of dozens of public, private, and academic institutions after 50 years of diplomatic relations (Dussel Peters 2022/a) allows for an understanding of the increasingly mature, complex, and heterogeneous institutional relationship between Mexico and China.

Nevertheless, since 2013 both countries defined their relation as an "integral strategic association" and signed in 2008 a reciprocal investment agreement (APPRI) that enables for an institutional bilateral framework on the promotion of FDI flows and dispute settlements; the aforementioned integral strategic association has after 10 years not allowed for a monitoring and evaluation process so far.

A second topic to understand the in-depth socioeconomic relationship between China and Mexico refers to the substantial and dynamic performance in international trade in the 21st century. China has become Mexico's second largest trading partner since 2003, only behind the US. While China's share in Mexico's trade increased from less than 1 % in 2000 to 10.96 % in 2022, the US' fell from 80.73 % to 62.37 % for the same period; this performance has also continued since the overall confrontation between the US and China since 2018 (figure 1). At least three characteristics in the Mexico-China trade are relevant: 1. Mexico's trade with China has increased drastically during 2000-2022 particularly through imports, and even under the 2020-2022 COVID-19 period. While it is true that Chinas has become Mexico's third export destination (and accounting for its highest share of 1.89 % of Mexican exports in 2022), imports from China increased from less than 1 % in 1996 to 19.63 % in 2022, resulting in a massive trade deficit and a 11:1 import/export coefficient in 2022, 2. The LAC-China trade reflects that in the 21st century trade by technological level presents huge and increasing gaps: until 2020 Chinese imports from LAC of products of medium and high technological level accounted for less than 7 %, while Chinese exports to LAC by medium and high technological level did so with more than 50 % in 2020 (Dussel Peters 2022/b). Mexico is an exception in LAC: in 2020 49 % of its exports to China included medium and high technology level products, while its imports accounted for 72 %, i.e. Mexico exported copper and other low value-added products to China, but it also exported autoparts, automobiles, electronics, and telecommunications, 3. An additional element of the Mexico-China trade is relevant for understanding its increasing dynamics and complexity: while it is true that Mexico presents a dramatic trade balance deficit with China, by far the largest with any country in the last decade, it is also crucial to understand that around 91 % of Mexican imports from China are intermediate and capital goods, and only 9 % consumption goods; i.e. most of Chinese goods are transformed in Mexico for consumption either in the domestic market or to be exported. Thus, Mexico-China trade has not only increased quantitatively, but it has also allowed for an important qualitative change during the 21st century: by substituting imports from the US and the European Union, it has integrated these imports for its domestic manufacturing sector for both domestic consumption and exports.

Figure 1. Mexico: Foreign Trade with the US and China (as a percentage of respective total) (1993-2022)

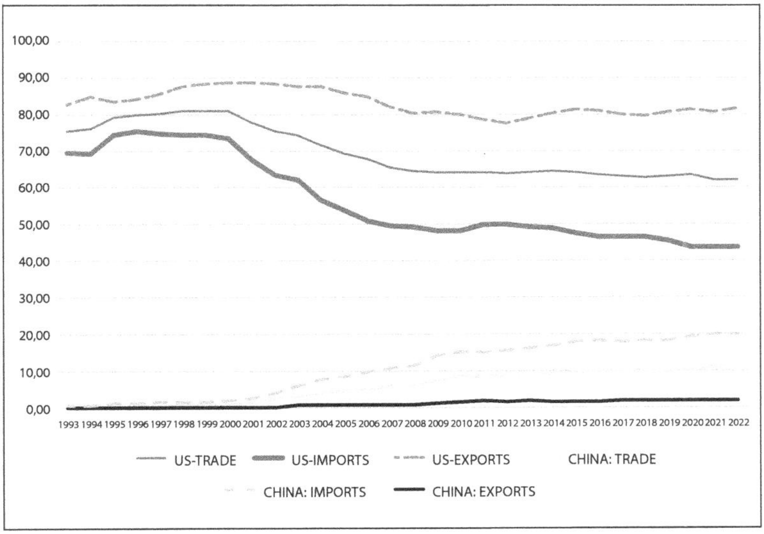

Source: elaborated on Banxico (Cechimex 2023).

The third relevant topic to understand the next section is China's OFDI to Mexico. Based on an increasing literature in LAC on China's OFDI that includes methodological and statistical issues, as well as analysis by country, regions, and firm-level examinations[2], at least three items are relevant on this topic.[3] First, it is important not to exaggerate China's OFDI in LAC. While it is true that it has been extremely dynamic in the 21st century, until 2022 600 OFDI-transactions for $ 184 billion accounted for 6.05 % of LA's total FDI during 2000-2022 (and 8.81 % for 2020-2022), i.e. other countries and regions such as the US and the European Union are still far more significant for LAC in this field. Second, Chinese OFDI in LAC has diversified substantially in the 21st century by country, sector, property of the Chinese firm, as well as by generated employment. Two examples: by country during 2000-2004 Chinese OFDI concentrated in Brazil (accounting for 40.94 % in Chinese OFDI in LAC), and continued to be the largest recipient (with 20.96 %) during 2020-2022, but countries such as Argentina, and Chile, and particularly Mexico, increased significantly; Chinese OFDI to Mexico increased from $ 500 million for 2000-2004 to $ 12.4 billion during 2015-2019 and $ 5.7 billion in 2020-2022, becoming the second largest OFDI recipient from China in LAC during 2020-2022. By sector Chinese OFDI has also diversified importantly going far beyond raw materials; they accounted in LAC for 81.39 % of total Chinese OFDI in 2000-2004 and fell to 41.28 % in 2020-2022. Third, in Mexico's case, Chinese OFDI has not only been very dynamic in the more recent periods (as highlighted above) but has also had significant employment generation above LAC's average (representing

2 Red ALC-China has been leading this discussion for more than a decade through its annual *Monitor of Chinese* OFDI *in Latin America and the Caribbean* (https://www.redalc-china.org/monitor/index.php?option=com_content&view=article&id=437) and dozens of publications, conferences, and annual statistics; Cechimex has also contributed importantly through conferences, working papers and discussions on methodological topics, case studies, and overall debates on Chinese OFDI in LAC (http://www.economia.unam.mx/cechimex/index.php/es/publicaciones-menu). The statistical discussion on Chinese OFDI in LAC is substantial, considering that Mexico´s public sources account for an accumulated Chinese OFDI of $ 3 billion until 2021, while the *Monitor* registers $ 16.9 billion (Dussel Peters 2023/b). However, and even including these substantial differences, Chinese OFDI accounts for less than 2.7 % of Mexico´s accumulated FDI until 2021.

3 For a detailed analysis see: Dussel Peters (2023/a/b).

24.07 % of Chinese employment generation through OFDI during 2000-2021) and lower OFDI per transaction levels than the rest of LAC. These performances are strongly associated with Chinese OFDI in Mexico characterized by sector (mainly in manufacturing), and the increasing importance of Chinese private firms, in both cases in contrast to the rest of LAC (Dussel Peters 2023/b).

Fourth, the new triangular relationship between the US, China and Mexico is a general issue that has already affected the Mexico-China relationship in all the aforementioned topics (trade and OFDI, among many others), as well as in the context of NAFTA / USMCA. Considering the overall confrontation between the US and China since 2018 (Anguiano Roch 2021) and debates on friend-shoring and ally-shoring, countries such as Mexico could greatly benefit from these tensions in terms of trade and OFDI from the US and China (Oropeza García 2021). There is an ongoing debate regarding Mexico's effective capacity in realizing this potential, particularly *vis a vis* other Asian countries such as Vietnam.

2. Mexico's OFDI to China (2000-2022)

This chapter will begin with an overall assessment on Mexico's global and Chinese OFDI, followed by detailed case studies for Bimbo and Interceramic in China, and some additional analysis on Mexico's OFDI to China resulting from interviews.

2.1.1. Overall Performance of Mexico's OFDI to China (2000-2022)

Contrary to overall and specific instruments to promote FDI in Mexico (Dussel Peters 2000; SE 2023), Mexico has so far not elaborated on mechanisms to facilitate overseas foreign direct investments (OFDI). The lack of public instruments on Mexico's

OFDI is related to limitations on the understanding of the qualitative and quantitative flows of Mexican OFDI, as well as to the overall sentiment that a country such as Mexico should not export capital, but rather attract it (see the overview in Introduction).

2.1.1. Overall Mexican OFDI

Based on UNCTAD's (2023) analysis and statistics, Table 1 reflects important shifts of global OFDI during 2000-2021 and its increasing relevance for LAC. Historically the European Union (EU) was the main global source of OFDI, accounting for up to 58.55% of international OFDI in 2005, followed by the United States, with levels above 20% in the late 1990s. These structures have changed substantially since than: Asia became the main source of OFDI since 2012 —accounting for 50.28% during 2018-2021— and Japan, the United States and China have become the top OFDI emitters for the most recent 2018-2021 period. LAC has played a small but increasing role in flows of international OFDI: from levels below 1% until 1991 to 2.01% of total OFDI in 2018-2021 (table 1). For the two largest economies of LAC, Mexico has substantially surpassed Brazil in terms of OFDI and, in average, accounted annually for $6,920 million during 2000-2021 (figure 2). Several issues are relevant in this regard. First, OFDI from Brazil and Mexico declined importantly comparing the periods 2000-2017, and 2018-2021; Asia, China and Japan are important global exceptions for this general performance (table 1). Second, Mexico and Brazil only accounted for 28.27% and 17.83% of LAC's OFDI during 2000-2021, i.e. other countries have also played an important role regarding LAC's OFDI.4 Third, Mexico's OFDI was particularly strong after the 2009 crisis and for the period 2009-2015 (with $13.4 billion annually in average), and has fallen considerably since then. Finally, Table 1 also calculates the OFDI/FDI coefficient: for the most recent period (2018-2021),

4 For a full analysis, see: Dussel Peters (2023/a).

the European Union, the US, and particularly Japan have become net exporters of FDI, while Asia and China are still net importers of FDI. In the case of LAC, the coefficient has been relatively stable for 2000-2021 with the defined subperiods at around 20 %, i.e. LAC is still a massive net importer of FDI. This is also the case for Mexico and Brazil, although with significant differences: for 2018-2021, for example, the OFDI / FDI coefficient was of 16.40 % and 6.30 %, respectively (table 1).[5]

Table 1. FDI and OFDI for Selected Countries and Regions (2000-2021)

	2000-2017	2018-2021
	FDI (in $million)	
Asia	6,372,220	2,345,656
China	1,703,297	609,829
Japan	137,870	59,073
European Union	6,424,955	1,115,075
LAC	2,172,253	531,352
Brazil	789,947	203,874
Mexico	496,996	128,056
United States	4,010,799	946,546
World total	24,039,607	5,474,351
	OFDI (in $million)	
Asia	5,829,436	2,289,399
China	1,149,847	578,843
Japan	1,544,014	620,058
European Union	8,126,777	1,125,723
LAC	447,121	91,388
Brazil	83,175	12,844
Mexico	131,252	20,997
United States	4,561,604	509,210
World total	23,134,875	4,553,260

5 Considering the importance of Mexico's OFDI during 2009-2015 (for $ 93.7 billion), the coefficient accounted for 45.33 %.

FDI (share over total FDI)		
Asia	26.51	42.85
China	7.09	11.14
Japan	0.57	1.08
European Union	26.73	20.37
LAC	9.04	9.71
Brazil	3.29	3.72
Mexico	2.07	2.34
United States	16.68	17.29
World total	100.00	100.00
OFDI (share over total OFDI)		
Asia	25.20	50.28
China	4.97	12.71
Japan	6.67	13.62
European Union	35.13	24.72
LAC	1.93	2.01
Brazil	0.36	0.28
Mexico	0.57	0.46
United States	19.72	11.18
World total	100.00	100.00
OFDI / FDI (percentage)		
Asia	91.48	97.60
China	67.51	94.92
Japan	1,119.90	1,049.65
European Union	126.49	100.95
LAC	20.58	17.20
Brazil	10.53	6.30
Mexico	26.41	16.40
United States	113.73	53.80
World total	96.24	83.17

Source: own elaboration based on UNCTAD (2023).

Figure. 2 LAC: Annual Average of FDI and OFDI (in $million) (2000-2021).

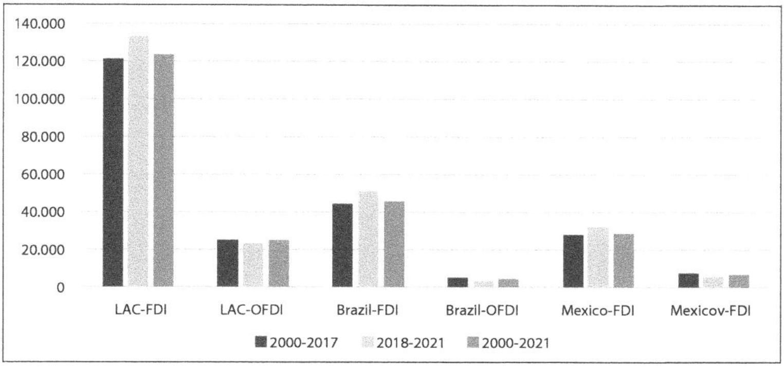

Source: own elaboration based on UNCTAD (2023).

Four additional issues are important for understanding Mexico's OFDI in general and to China.

First. Surprisingly, and given the macroeconomic relevance of Mexico's OFDI, as discussed above, there is very little analysis on Mexico's OFDI, particularly if compared to existing analysis on its FDI. The work in the last decades of Jorge Basave Kunhardt, done with other colleagues, has been seminal for understanding Mexico's OFDI and multinational corporations (MCN) to several countries. He highlights that Mexican OFDI could be understood for different reasons in "waves": one in the 1970s and a second since the last decade of the 20th century and up to 2008 because of changes in international production (Basave Kunhardt 2022:192). LAC and Central America became the center for Mexican OFDI as a result of their previous trade relations and advantages in property (Basave Kunhardt 2016/a:37-40). His analysis on specific industrial groups and in countries (Basave Kunhardt 2022; Basave Kunhardt and Gutiérrez Haces 2013) reflects that in the US, for example, mergers and acquisitions (M&A) played a fundamental role for Mexican OFDI (Basave Kunhardt 2022:199-203). OFDI in the most recent wave resulted from industrial groups that were already dominant in Mexico for several decades and with historical trade and export experiences previous to OFDI, also as a "defensive strategy against the opening of Mexico's economy" (Basave Kunhardt 2016/b:13), i.e. to expand their markets and in some cases the further acquisition of specific assets through M&A. In addition, it reflects that Mexico, until today, does not count with any statistics on Mexico's OFDI[6]; in general, research on the topic depends on the recipient country.

Second. A recent analysis on Mexico's and LAC's OFDI, based on transaction level statistics,[7] highlights that intra-LAC (or intra-regional) OFDI has achieved substantially higher levels than intraregional trade: for the last 2018-2021 period, for example, intraregional trade accounted for 14.6 %, while intraregional OFDI did so with 65.5 %; these gaps do also exist for most of LAC's subregions (Dussel Peters 2023/b). According to this analysis Mexico has become the most dynamic source of LAC's OFDI (with 30.77 % of LAC's OFDI) during 2018-2021, followed by Chile (18.18 %), Bermuda (12.16 %) and Brazil (10.33 %). From a recipient's perspective, LAC's OFDI to LAC during 2018-2021 accounted for 65.51 % to LAC (or intraregional OFDI) and particularly to Peru, Brazil and Colombia; Mexico received 11.3 % of LAC's OFDI during this recent period.

Third. Considering the limitations on official data sources on Mexico's OFDI in general, both statistics and analysis on Mexico's OFDI to China is even scarcer, with some exceptions. IDB's (2012) approach was the first to systematically attempt to understand LAC's conditions and challenges, particularly at the level of firms with a sample of 85 major MNC in LAC. While acknowledging that these firms "remains the exception rather than the rule" (IDB 2012:5), LAC's OFDI to China was on the rise; economics of scale

6 The research of Basave Kunhardt and Gutiérrez Haces since the 2010s includes statistics for the top 20 Mexican non-financial MNC but would require a far more detailed registration of these and hundreds of other Mexican firms engaging in these transactions. There are no public statistics that offer this information in LAC and in Mexico (IDB 2012:15); the Brazil-China Business Council is a notable exception (Frischtak and Soares 2012)

7 This analysis is based on 5,204 OFDI transactions reported by FDI Markets. While LAC´s OFDI in 2021 and according to macroeconomic data of LAC´s central banks accounted for $ 57.4 billion, it was of $ 9.6 billion according to FDI Markets (Dussel Peters 2023/a).

played an important role for understanding the dynamics of these *multi* or *translatinas* and their OFDI was highly concentrated in the US. Based on this sample, 55% of LAC's OFDI to China concentrated in manufacturing, 28% in services and 17% in the primary sector; since the early 2000s new firms entering the Chinese market increased rapidly (IDB 2012:16-24). IDB's distinction between firms' representatives (sales, marketing, and other support activities) versus those producing or offering services in China is important; the latter firms were the minority at that point in time, particularly in services (IT, software, transportation, restaurants, and finance) (IDB 2012:22), with a heterogeneous mix of greenfield and M&A transactions. Specifically, regarding Mexico's OFDI to China, two analyses stand out. On the one hand the efforts by Basave Kunhardt and Gutiérrez-Haces (2013) attempting to overcome statistical limitations (see above): until 2009, 16 Mexican MNC invested in China, although with no detailed presentation of amounts, employment, and other characteristics. The same authors highlight that "market seeking" has become the "main determining factor behind OFDI in China" (Basave Kunhardt and Gutiérrez-Haces 2013:248) based on their experiences in the Mexican domestic market, such as in the case of Bimbo and Nemak. The second contribution to this topic (Dussel Peters 2012) accounts for Mexico's OFDI to China of less than 0.01% over total Chinese FDI during 1996-2010 and examines in detail the cases of Bimbo, Nemak, Softek and Maseca, among others. In most of the cases, Mexican firms investing in China result from quasi-monopolies in Mexico and are looking for for China's domestic market with their global branding (such as Bimbo, Grupo Modelo, and Cemex), and in a few cases they invest in China as export platform activities and efficiency (Nemak, Softtek and Worcester, among others). Practically all Mexican transactions that initiated through M&A in China required substantial product adaptations for the Chinese consumer and clients and were oriented towards the upper-end middle and higher-class segments with differentiated and high-quality products (Dussel Peters 2012:16-17).

Finally, we do present Mexico's OFDI to China based on two different sources, in addition to UNCTAD's (2023) aggregated results discussed above (table 1 and figure 2). The first, based on China's Ministry of Commerce (NBS, several years), considering important methodological limitations[8], reflects that China received $ 152 million from Mexico during 2003-2021, particularly during 2003-2017 ($ 130 million). Brazil ($ 679 million), Panama ($ 483), Belize ($ 412 million) and Mexico were the largest source of Chinese FDI during 2003-2021 (annex 1). Based on transaction-level statistics registered by FDI Markets (2022)[9] for 2003-2021, Mexico's 23 OFDI transactions to China accumulated $ 1.1 billion and more than 5,000 jobs (i.e. substantially higher then Chinese official sources examined earlier); in terms of the OFDI amount Mexico was only second to Brazil (with $ 3.5 billion). Interestingly, Mexico's employment per transaction was one of the highest for the LAC countries —of 218 jobs per transaction—, as well as one of the highest employment / OFDI amount, of 4.73 jobs per $ million, reflecting labor intensive OFDI-activities in China compared to the rest of LAC (annex 2). Finally, and based on the same source and its limitations, Annex 3 presents the 23 investment transactions in China by Mexico during 2003-2021. Three findings are relevant based on this dataset: a. Manufacturing and services —not including food & beverages— are by far the most relevant activities of Mexico's OFDI to China, accounting for 64.96 % of total Mexico's OFDI for the period, b. Several

8 The methodological shortcomings of China's NBS and MOFCOM on FDI and OFDI have been examined in detail (Dussel Peters 2023/b), particularly registering statistics according to its first country of destination in OFDI and last country before entering China for FDI, rather than the effective destination and source of OFDI and FDI, i.e. for 2003-2021 LAC accounted for 10.27 % of China's FDI, but Cayman and Virgin Islands accounted for 95.85 % of LAC's FDI to China.

9 In general, the database includes greenfield transactions, although there are also ome M&A. In the future, researchers should revise each of the 187 registered investment transactions of LAC in China during 2003-2021, and enrich it through additional databases and sources, such as Red ALC-China does with Chinese OFDI transactions in LAC (Dussel Peters 2023/b). The transactions by Bimbo and ICC, which will be examined in depth in the next section, are not registered in this database; initial research confirms two transactions by United Logistics Services by the same amount to Shanghai and Shenzhen in 2013.

internationally competitive Mexican firms have been able to integrate to China's domestic market in automotive components, software, and IT Services such as Katcon, Nemak, Yalo, and Softek, and c. Only three Mexican firms (Gruma, United Logistics Services, and Nemak) accounted for Mexican OFDI to China for $ 592 million or 55.77 %, i.e. in the Mexican case OFDI to China is still highly concentrated in a small number of Mexican MNC.

2.2. Case Studies

In addition to prior research (Dussel Peters 2012) and the cycle of Conferences of Cechimex in which Chinese and Mexican firms have participated since 2005[10], as well as an exhaustive literature and news review, the following analysis is based on interviews held in China during November 2022-March 2023 with Bimbo and Interceramic, and with almost a dozen Mexican and Chinese experts. In most of the cases firms are not interested and are also very cautious in presenting detailed statistics of their activities in China, particularly on their clients and suppliers; unless otherwise stated, the information is a result of the interviews.

2.2.1. Grupo Industrial Bimbo S.A. de C.V. (Bimbo)

Grupo Industrial Bimbo (or Bin Bao宾堡 in China) is the largest bakery company in the world in 2023. Founded in 1945 in Mexico City, Bimbo began its internationalization strategy in the mid-1980s with exports to the United States, and initial OFDI to Guatemala (1990) and massive investments since 1996 (Dussel Peters 2012). In 2022 Bimbo accounted $ 19.8 billion net sales, more than 9,000 different products fabricated in 34 countries, 3.3 million points of sale, 214 production plants, more than 100 brands worldwide, and almost 140,000 employees; its distribution

10 See: http://economia.unam.mx/cechimex/1index.php/es/actividades-academicas.

network includes 55,000 international routes (Bimbo 2022; Sáenz Arelle 2020). Bimbo has allowed for a profound diversification of its sales: North America (Canada and the United States) represented 50.9 % of net sales in the first quarter of 2023, followed by Mexico (30 %), Latin America (9.6 %) and Europe, Asia and Africa (9.5 %).[11] Another relevant issue is its increasing commitment with the environment, considering that in 2022, 85 % of its global facilities used renewable energy sources (Bimbo 2022:11-12). While Bimbo is the global bakery leader, it also specializes in snacks, artisan breads and premium bread products, tortillas, multi-grain, and organic breads, including bread made with vegetables. While North America, Europe and even Mexico and Latin America reflect levels of relative saturation and mature markets, Asia and China offer the highest growth potential: Europe's per capita consumption of bread and baked products was of 57 kilograms per capita, compared with 7.2 kgs in China (Seeking Alpha 2023).

Bimbo initiated its activities in China in 2006, also as the result of the generational change in Bimbo and the personal experience of Daniel Servitje,[12] Grupo Bimbo CEO's since 1997. With the first acquisition of the Spanish baker Panrico Beijing Food Processing Center in 2006 for $ 11 million, Bimbo began a slow and difficult learning process in China. With this acquisition Bimbo bought a firm with more than 10 years of experience operating in China and acquired 800 workers, a plant outside of Beijing and a distribution network around Beijing and Tianjin, with sales of $ 11.5 million in 2005. Panrico already accounted for a 55 % and 35 % market share in bread and sweet bread (Dussel Peters 2012). It took Bimbo at least five years to get to know the Chinese custom-

11 According to Daniel Servitje, Bimbo's international operations already represented over 2/3 of its operations in 2015 (RIR 2015).

12 According to Daniel Servitje in 2012: "From my perspective, if you want to be in any business today, you have to be close to what's happening in China ... The Chinese market is very positive. It is very dynamic, and it is a market that demands a lot of flexibility. It also changes rapidly. We need to adapt our views more to the reality of the Chinese market." (Bimbo 2012); in the same interview Daniel Servitje recounts that he travelled to China for the first time in 1982 as a college student.

er and to integrate Panrico to Bimbo's structure. Originally Bimbo attempted to concentrate on bread, croissants, sweets, and chocolates —not tortillas— and introduced products from Mexico and other countries such as "*gansitos*" from Mexico. Bimbo, however, found out very quickly that the Chinese consumer is completely different than in other countries and had to integrate its plant and production to China's tastes and customs; today 100 % of Bimbo's products in China are unique for the country.

After this initial process Bimbo acquired in 2009 the local brand Baiwanzhuangyuan and in 2010 Jin Hong Wei (for $ 63 million), East Balt Bakeries (2017), and in 2018, Mankattan (for $ 200 million), by far the largest investment of Bimbo in China. The period 2006-2010 was a particularly slow process full of learning experiences, which also resulted in cautious and conservative scenarios in terms of its sales in China.[13] Another crucial learning process was the acquisition, since 2009, of Chinese bakery firms with their brands and distribution networks, including their previous local and regional knowledge, contrary to Panrico; i.e. Bimbo learned to "adapt our business model and of distribution to local practices, not leaving aside our characteristic model of direct distribution" (David Colín in Sáenz Arelle 2020:79). The acquisition of these Chinese local and regional brands allowed the company to enhance local production and substantially expand its products; in the first years Bimbo's products —through Panrico— were highly concentrated in a group of baked goods for the local market produced in one plant in the outskirts of Beijing and with some presence in Beijing and Tianjin. After the long learning process through the acquisition of Jin Hong Wei, and Million Land during 2009-2010,[14] in the late 2010s Bimbo was able to begin with a

13 Up to 2010, Bimbo's sales in China accounted for $ 35 million dollars or around 2 % of its global sales (Bimbo 2012).

14 In the 2009 Annual Report Bimbo (2009:6) acknowledges that "our operations in China are focused to better learn tastes and preferences of consumers and to allow for the maximal growth through the extension our operations organically and through acquisitions". In the same report (Bimbo 2009:12) Bimbo confirms that consumers related Bimbo's products as wheat-related (*mian shi*), and contrary to the much more traditional *mantou* (unfilled steamed bun) and *baozi* (filled bun, with meat or vegetarian)

much more aggressive strategy and, thanks to investments through East Balt Baker (2017) and Mankattan (2018), it became the second largest baked goods player in China. East Balt Baker[15] and Mankattan's acquisition for $ 200 million dollar were particularly relevant in terms of new products —such as sliced bread, cakes, buns and Yudane (a Japanese-style sandwich bread), with strong links to fast-food channels—, integrating 1,900 workers and four new plants in Beijing, Shanghai, Sichuan, and Guangdong (Bimbo 2018). As a result, in 2021, Bimbo has presence in China in Beijing, Shanghai, Sichuan, Guangdong, Shenyang, Tianjin, Wuhan and Hangzhou (David Colin in Sáenz Arelle 2020:80).

Finally, a group of specific reflections arise according to the interviews.

1. Panrico was probably a necessary step for Bimbo to begin activities in China, considering that it held product trials in Mexico and in China (Dussel Peters 2012). The acquired plant, products, and distribution networks were allowed Bimbo to begin a long learning process in which China and its consumers proved to be substantially different —in terms of tastes, customs, regulations, etc.— than in any other country where Bimbo had invested before 2006; local and regional differences within China proved to be as relevant in this process. In addition, Panrico came from a similar (Spanish) culture than Bimbo; at this point Bimbo was probably not ready for acquiring Chinese firms, as it did several years later. Each acquisition by Bimbo since 2006

15 Bimbo acquired for $ 650 millions dollars East Balt Bakery which operated 21 plants in 11 countries; in China it specialized in buns, English muffins, hard and soft rolls, bagels, artisanal bread, and particularly in the food service industry (in 2017 East Balt China received by McDonald the Year Award for superior performance in quality, food safety, innovation and people practice in China (SFWB 2017). It accounted for bakery facilities in Beijing, Shanghai, Shenyang, Wuhan, Zhengzhou, Hangzhou and Tianjin.

required enormous human and technical capabilities to integrate new products and plants.[16]

2. With the acquisition of Jin Hong Wei, East Balt Bakery and Mankattan, Bimbo is today an experienced and mature player in China's bakery market, but also with important investments in new markets and regions in China. After almost 20 years of experiences in China with hundreds of different products —and failures in some cases— and plants in very different provinces, cities, and cultures within China, Bimbo is ready to expand substantially based on these experiences. Economics of scale, experiences with suppliers and clients, historical incursions in new local and regional markets, and the integration of new plants, among other issues, are all relevant topics for Bimbo's future expansion in China's dynamic and competitive bakery market.
3. Since 2006, Bimbo has learned to supply most of its inputs locally requiring the highest quality standards for overall services and ingredients; it also relies on global partners for ingredients that are used in most of its plants, i.e. it substantially benefits from economics of scale like few other competitors in China.
4. In the more recent experiences Bimbo has also learned that China's bakery market is not only extremely dynamic and with high expectations in terms of growth in the next decades, but also that the Chinese consumer is extremely demanding in terms of quality; boutique bakeries, for example, offer new high-quality products reflecting these new demands and segments of bakery products and services in China. Parallel R & D investments by Bimbo together with local suppliers are, in Bimbo's experience, critical for

16 The presentations by Elizondo Huerta (2010) and Zermeño (2017) reflect these enormous challenges i.e., the acquisition of Panrico in 2016, for example, allowed for the incursion of Bimbo in China in prepared bakery products such as sandwiches and hamburgers, as well as Chinese traditional products, generating important human, technical and financial requirements for this learning and integration processes; the challenges were much more significant with the larger and later acquisitions.

developing new products and continuing integrating to these dynamic markets.

5. Regarding Bimbo's clients today, local clients are the basis for Bimbo and account for the highest share in sales: supermarkets and little neighborhood shops that share Bimbo's historical experience in developing distribution networks through bicycles, and electric vehicles increasingly; these clients are in addition to other global clients such as Walmart, Costco, and McDonalds. Adapting in the last years to massive e-commerce and cashless transactions has also been an important learning process for Bimbo in China (Zermeño 2017) and for the rest of Bimbo Group globally.
6. Finally, in 2022 the portfolio of bakery products that Bimbo offers in China is mainly oriented towards the respective local markets, in some cases nationally. These products are only developed and sold in China.

2.2.2. Internacional de Cerámica (Interceramic)

Interceramic was founded in Chihuahua in 1979 and is the largest glazed floor tile manufacturer in North America. In 2022 it distributed and traded products in Mexico, United States, Central America and, since 2010, in China. In Mexico it accounts for 327 franchise showrooms and 83 points of sale through Home Depot; in the US, 12 showrooms (Interceramic Tile & Stone Gallery) and 50 independent distributors are the main sale channels, while 3 company-owned stores in Guatemala add to the international structure of Interceramic (Interceramic 2023). It accounts for 10 production plants; in addition to its production sites in Chihuahua, it also has a production facility in Texas that represents 5.5 % of Interceramic's production (Interceramic 2023:17).

In general, Interceramic specializes in the production and distribution of ceramic floor tile and wall tile in the superior-quality products, customer service, and price segment; since 1989 its R & D Center in Chihuahua guarantees state of the art production and products. Interceramic offers a large selection of ceramic, porcelain, glass and natural stone products for floor and walls, bathroom fixtures, backerboards and shower pan liners, tile cleaning and maintenance materials, decorative floor, and wall borders, as well as wet saws, cutters, and hand tools. With annual sales of around $700 million in 2022 —and an impressive growth rate of net sales of 30% during 2020-2022— Interceramic produced in 2022 48 million square meters of tile in its 10 production plants; Mexico accounts for more than 76% of Interceramic's sales, the US 22.3%, and the rest, including Central America and China, 1.5% (Interceramic 2023:29). During 2020-2022 Interceramic's employees have been relatively stable at around 5,650 workers.

ICC (Interceramic China) announced in 2010 its first franchise showroom in Foshan, province of Guangzhou, China. ICC's activities in China have been linked to Guangdong Kito Ceramics Co., LTD since its agreement in 2010 to create the joint venture "Guangdong Xinfenging Ceramics, Co. LTD" (Interceramic accounts for 50% and Kito 50%); this joint venture has the goal to distribute products fabricated by Interceramic and Kito, as well as by third companies. The basis of this company is the granting of licenses for the distribution to local firms interested in trading ICC's and Kito's products and services. For Interceramic the joint venture did not only open the playing field for sales in a market with a great potential such as China, with the support of Kito, but also for supplying locally and in China to export to Mexico and the US based on Kito's expertise. ICC has today 23 employees in China (Interceramic 2023:25-27).

A group of qualitative and quantitative aspects are of particular interest to understand ICC's experience in China.

First. Interceramic's efforts in China —before the formal creation of ICC in 2010— began in 2004-2005 as a source of global outsourcing; Chinese suppliers were cheap, particularly for polished tile in large formats that was not produced in Mexico.[17]

17 ICC's first exports from China to the United States (in 2002) included large polished 60 cms x 60 cms tiles; in 2022 they are being produced and exported from India.

As a result Interceramic began importing these products to Mexico and they became the most profitable products for the company (in some cases the import price was of 50 Mexican pesos and they were sold to the consumer for $ 100 Mexican pesos). However, drastically growing imports required Interceramic's presence in China. In 2022 ICC generated a gross volume —sales in China and imports from China to Mexico— of $ 100 million dollar, i.e. in addition to ICC, Interceramic also operates a sales representative office for its imports to Mexico.

Second. Interceramic witnessed since then a profound change in China's tile production and distribution; this process began in the first decade of the 20th century —in the early 2000s very few firms accounted for the standards to export to the US and Mexico— and allowed a group of Chinese firms to importantly innovate in production and distribution formats. In addition, Interceramic had an important portfolio of products and services in Mexico and the United States that did not exist in China.[18] These factors were crucial for understanding the creation of ICC in 2010. In addition, since 2015, and more importantly since 2019, it has included distribution of Italian production under the ICC brand with exclusivity in China.

Third. In 2022, ICC in China has become an agent of change with important global experiences in design and new concepts for selling tile and related products.[19] [20] The joint venture with Kito in 2010 allowed ICC to present its products and services initially in Foshan, in 2022, there were 130+ specialty stores in different

18 The sales of Mexican production in China, however, has decreased in the last decade, mainly because of increasing transportation costs and its lack of attractiveness to China. In China porcelain products are very desirable, while in Mexico it is ceramics; porcelain tile is usually made from a finer clay, fired at higher temperatures than ceramic ones, and absorb less water.

19 For three years in a row the original and innovative designs of ICC have received the "Top Ten Glazed Porcelain Brands" in China. At its website in China ICC offers 7 types of products: wood style tile, full polished tile, stone style tile, 3D ART tile, cement style, and the special imported collection from North America and Europe (https://www.tiles86.com/brands/all-tiles/foshan-icc-ceramics.html).

20 As a result, Chinese ceramic firms are starting to invest in countries like Mexico (Diario Plaza Juárez 2023).

cities and provinces in China (80 % of them in China's coastal regions)[21]; as in Mexico and the US, it continues specializing in high-end products.[22]

Fourth. Surprisingly, in the more recent period and until 2022, 88 % of sales of ICC in China are manufactured in China: 50 %-60 % in Kito's plants and another 30 % provided by other 8 Chinese suppliers; the rest (around 12 %) are supplied from Italy under ICC's brand.[23] This performance is related to the former highlighted topic of the extreme dynamism and learning process in China within the tile industry: particularly in terms of design, that is to say, importing machinery from Italy and top-quality inputs (including digital printing which have been rapidly closing the gap with Italian competition). As a result, ICC has been increasingly learning in and from China in the last years. In construction and the tile industry, Chinese showrooms, and "malls", for example in Shanghai and Hangzhou, have become the global points of reference.

Fifth. Independently of the former analysis based on Interceramic's annual reports, ICC in China accounted in 2022 for around 100 employees (around 80 in offices and 20 in warehouses); 130 showrooms with an average of 20-30 persons including another 3,200 employees. Initially ICC invested $ 5 million and throughout the period more than $ 54 million until 2022.

---

21 ICC's showrooms in China are fundamental: "The first is the selection of products, which must be trendy, high-end, and highly recognizable products. For example, the Italian ABK slate ... The second is space collocation ... The third is the sense of experience of the store, which is the design orientation that ICC has always adhered to" (Min.News 2023).

22 "As a high-end Antique brick brand, ICC's advantage is not only a wealth of products, but also it also has international leading resources, technology, design, and production teams to support the establishment and continuation of the brand´s product system, so that ICC no matter what the market trend is. With changes, brands can always be at the forefront of fashion trends and guide market consumption" (Humberto Valle in Min.News 2023).

23 The production in China from Kito and the other eight Chinese suppliers would have an important potential to be exported to Mexico, but antidumping duties of $ 6.78 dollar per square meter, in addition to transportation costs, make them unprofitable.

In these 15 years of experience of ICC in China it has been able to substantially change its functions and processes. While it has maintained its joint venture with Kito and substantially expanded relations with other suppliers in China, cost increments in China also required ICC to search for new suppliers in Asia (Malaysia and particularly Vietnam). The ICC Design Club, inaugurated in March 2023, has deepened ICC's commitment in China and in Foshan (now the "Ceramics City" in China).

2.2.3. Other Cases and Discussions

Based on almost half a dozen of interviews in China, other discussions are relevant for understanding Mexico's OFDI to China.

First. Mexico represents a country with important OFDI transactions in China in the 21st century, including firms such as Aeroméxico, Bimbo, Cemex, Grupo Kuo, Grupo Omnilife, ICC, Italika, Katcon, Liverpool, Maseca, Metalsa, Nemak, Softek, Televisa, and Worcester, among others. So far, these large Mexican firms have not been examined in detail. It is important to distinguish firms that do trading or procurement with representation in China —Italika and Liverpool— while another group such as Bimbo, ICC, Maseca, Metalsa, Nemak, Softek, and Worcester have effectively invested in larger service facilities and plants.

Second. These large Mexican firms with economic activities in China and OFDI have in most of the cases a company structure that allows them to prepare for their activities in China. Medium and smaller Mexican firms, however, do have substantial entry-barriers for initiating economic activities in China; mainly liquidity constraints —at least 2 years without profits, capital expenditures to visit several Chinese firms to understand the respective markets, clients, and suppliers, as well as increasingly expensive labor power, and the costs of overall regulations— are all bottlenecks for smaller Mexican firms that want to operate in China.

Inventories, the costs of e-commerce,[24] and high transportation costs add to the challenges of smaller firms. Most Mexican firms, particularly the smaller ones, are ill-prepared to do business in China since they do not do sufficient, if any, due diligence on potential Chinese counterparts (clients, suppliers, etc.) and are not aware of the legal record of Chinese firms regarding trade and obligation failure which are available in online platforms in Chinese.

Third. Hong Kong offers important tax incentives —corporate and value-added taxes— compared to mainland China. Hong Kong's attractiveness is particularly relevant for a firm's representations and procurement, less so for (Mexican) firms that wish to do OFDI in China. In the latter cases, for example in the food and autoparts-automobile global value chains, investing in China is critical. The effective registration of foreign firms in China has improved significantly, historically from 4-5 months to a week in cities such as Beijing.

Fourth. Mexico's public sector has so far not played an important role in supporting Mexican firms to invest in China or to export from Mexico to China. Further innovation and production differentiation could become crucial in the short term for Mexico's OFDI in China.

Fifth. From a qualitative perspective, and to be examined in the future in detail, the first two decades of the 21st century were relatively "easy" in terms of rapid growth in Chinese demand for foreign and high-quality goods. Today, however, competition with Chinese and foreign firms has increased drastically in all imaginable global value chains, also through e-commerce; sanitary and phytosanitary regulations, for example, have very much increased in the last decade, also generating new barriers for (Mexican) foreign firms in China.

Sixth. Italika —the leader in Mexico's motorcycles with a market share of more than 60%—, as part of Grupo Salinas and one

24 Large firms that offer online and mobile marketplace opportunities in retail and wholesale trade in China require deposits of up to $ 150,000 dollars, sufficient inventories, a well-functioning, updated, and serviced website, follow-up services, etc. that in most of the cases cannot be satisfied by medium and small Mexican firms.

of the largest industrial and services groups in Mexico, provides a good example of the increasing role of Mexican traders and representations in China. Created in 2004, Italika began importing motorcycles from South Korea and shifted its imports from China in 2007-2008. Since its beginning, Italika implements CDK (Completely Knocked-Down) processes, i.e. it imports all parts and components from China and assembles them in several plants in Mexico. Its main suppliers —Lancin 40 %, Rato 35 %, and Zhongshen 25 %— have become critical for developing new models specifically for Mexico, including adaptations according to the population and geography. Given the increasing relationship with its suppliers and sales, Italika has been able to develop more than 90 different motorcycle models and sub models, slowly also in the lithium battery niche. In 2022 Italika exported from China to Mexico more than 6,500 containers and has also been able to diversify components from India, Thailand, and Vietnam. In general, Italika's OFDI in China have been minimal and account for 35 employees in 2022.

3. Conclusions and Recommendations

Global OFDI flows have become a significant socioeconomic factor in the last decades —parallel to FDI flows—, although not sufficiently acknowledged in literature and by policy makers. This is particularly the case for developing countries, South-South capital flows, and even more so for LAC-China OFDI trends in the 21st century.

As discussed in detail in the first chapter, Mexico and China today account for a mature socioeconomic relationship after more than 50 years of diplomatic ties. With a group of bilateral and regional institutions, growing trade, Chinese OFDI to Mexico, and infrastructure projects, both countries present conditions for learning processes and improving existing socioeconomic relations in the next decades. The lack of monitoring and evaluation of these institutions and main socioeconomic events in the last decades, however, also do reflect some of the main challenges for both countries. The 10th anniversary of the "strategic integral association" in 2023 and increasing pressures resulting from the confrontation between the US and China since 2018 reflect the need to substantially improve existing bilateral institutions and deepen options in specific fields of the bilateral relationship, as discussed in chapter 1. While socioeconomic cooperation has improved importantly in health and under COVID-19, for example, other topics such as trade, bilateral OFDI flows, tourism, among many others, have not been examined pro-actively by the existing bilateral institutions.

As discussed in detail in chapter 1, trade, Chinese OFDI in Mexico, and infrastructure projects have become the most dynamitc issues in the bilateral economic relationship; Mexico's OFDI to China, so far, have not been included explicitly in the bilateral agenda.

Chapter 2 begins examining general trends in global OFDI and particularly for LAC and its main countries. One of the first outstanding results are the enormous differences of OFDI flows globally, but also for LAC, Brazil, and Mexico according to UNCTAD, other international sources, and the respective national sources in LAC countries. Based on UNCTAD the global traditional OFDI sources —the European Union and the US— have declined in their global share, and particularly Asia, Japan and China have increased drastically their OFDI flows in the last decade: Asia became the main source of OFDI in 2012 and, during the last decade China, Japan and the US have become the principal exporters of capital in this specific form. LAC and its main countries are important FDI importers —with OFDI / FDI coefficients significantly below 100%—; nevertheless, LAC's OFDI accounted for $539 billion during 2000-2021 and has become an important macroeconomic factor for the region, considering important differences by country (table 1). In the case of Mexico, "waves" of OFDI processes have been established since the 1990s reflecting internationalization processes of Mexico's large MNCs, including companies such as Bimbo and Interceramic. With few exceptions the performance has not been examined in detail for Mexican MNCs in general, and specifically for OFDI flows to China; there are no official statistics neither on Mexico's total OFDI nor to China.

Chapter 2 establishes at least 23 OFDI transactions from Mexico to China until 2021 accounting for $ 1.1. billion dollars; only three Mexican MNCs (Gruma, United Logistics Services, and Nemak) concentrated 55.77 % of Mexico's OFDI to China until 2021. Based on a literature review and mainly interviews, this chapter elucidates how Mexican MNCs began in the early 20th century performing OFDI transactions in China; in most of the cases as a result of their transnationalization process and with little support from Mexican authorities. They started this process through trade and further acquisitions mainly in the US, Central America, and the rest of LAC, and later in Asia and China. Most of these MNCs began their activities through trading and procurement, and in later "waves", specifically through the acquisitions of existing plants. Thus, these large Mexican MNCs already accounted for important international experiences before entering China, although in most of the cases, with little antecedents in Asia and China.

The case studies of Bimbo and Interceramic (and ICC in China) are substantial from a group of perspectives.

First, these both very large Mexican MNCs required a very long learning process starting with procurement and trading activities (Interceramic) and relatively small acquisitions (Bimbo) in the early 2000s to begin "understanding" the Chinese market in their respective market niches. Based on these initial learning processes, both large MNCs were able to deepen their activities in China through further acquisitions (Bimbo) and joint ventures (Interceramic through the creation of ICC), or a "second wave" of OFDI activities in China. Both "waves" required more than a decade and a long patience by their respective headquarters, particularly in the case of Bimbo, also considering initial low profitability and increasing OFDI. After these rather long processes both firms are well suited to compete in China, based on their historical experiences with suppliers, clients, local and national regulations, as well as in developing innovations and dealing with changes under COVID-19 in China and globally, and with changing transportation costs, among many other topics.

Second. In both cases, Bimbo and Interceramic attempted to introduce Mexican and international products to China. However, they quickly found out that Chinese consumers —in terms of culture, taste, and other regional and national consumption patterns depending on the market niches of both firms— were different to those that had experienced in other international markets. In both cases Bimbo and Interceramic had to develop and innovate in several years new suppliers, products and distribution networks based on several years of experiences in China. In 2022 both firms practically in its totality depend on in-China innovations and fabrication —100 % in the case of Bimbo and 88 % in the case of ICC— to supply the Chinese market; this is an outstanding performance after more than a decade of learning processes.

Third. In both cases Mexican MNCs have been able to develop new brands —based on the former learning processes— that practically make them indistinguishable from Chinese brands: Bin Bao 宾堡 and ICC are for the Chinese consumer Chinese firms and brands, not Mexican MNCs or *translatinas*.[25] Considering Chinese idiosyncrasies, consumption patterns, and also the increasing confrontation between China and the US, Bimbo's and ICC's proposals are very valuable.

Fourth. As it happens with investment flows, firms interact and learn in doing their OFDI transactions, but also learn from their recipient country. Both Bimbo in China and ICC have become important sources for transmitting crucial learning processes for their headquarters in general —for example in terms of e-commerce and cashless transactions—, but also in terms of design and showrooms (ICC), as well as through the development of new products and processes (Bimbo), i.e. Mexican MNCs OFDI processes in China allowed for innovating processes in their overall international groups. Their experiences in China, in addition, also

25 This has also been my personal experience in the last years i.e., colleagues and friends in China were not aware that Bin Bao宾堡 was a Mexican firm but considered it a Chinese one.

supported transactions in other Asian countries (India, Japan, Malaysia, and Vietnam) with the purpose of further supporting their transnationalization processes.

At least three recommendations result from the analysis.

First, to further deepen and extend LAC's and Mexico's OFDI processes from a macro, meso, micro and territorial perspective. For LAC and Mexico they have become increasingly relevant at all mentioned levels; also related to the fact that these processes are in general, and with some exceptions, of particular relevance for large MNCs, and much less so for small and medium firms. As discussed in chapter 2, Mexico's OFDI during 2009-2015 accounted for $93.7 billion or 45.33% of Mexico's FDI. Policy makers in China and in LAC and Mexico should improve official and bilateral statistics and begin to reflect on these important capital flows; researchers also have to improve the understanding of OFDI, their causes and bilateral economic effects.

Second. As discussed recently (Dussel Peters 2023/a), OFDI transactions in LAC have played a yet unrecognized important role in intraregional integration in LAC, at least as important as intraregional trade. From this perspective, and not demeriting the importance of trade, OFDI transactions by LAC countries and from Mexico to China play and could further increase their role in socioeconomic integration with China and specifically regarding the integral strategic association since 2013. LAC and Chinese officials, as well as researchers, should improve and systematize these processes to discuss in detail the potential of bilateral integration and deepening.

Third, and finally. It is not clear if the public sector in LAC should enhance these OFDI transactions in general and to China, also considering important bottlenecks and structural limitation in accessing capital. Nevertheless, LAC's and Mexican MNCs will further expand and deepen their transnationalization processes, such as the cases discussed in chapter 2. Regional institutions such as BID and ECLAC, but also national agencies, together with academic, researchers, firms, and business organizations, should explicitly promote events discussing these important recent trends and their micro, meso, macro and territorial impacts in LAC and in Mexico. As discussed throughout the paper, OFDI flows are quantitatively and qualitatively not only relevant *per se*, but also in terms of capital flows and development in general.

REFERENCES

Anguiano Roch, Eugenio. 2021. "Confrontación entre Estados Unidos y la República Popular China". *Cuadernos de Trabajo del Cechimex* 1, pp. 1-16.

Basave Kunhardt, Jorge. 2016/a. *Multinacionales mexicanas, surgimiento y evolución.* Editorial Siglo XXI: México.

Basave Kunhardt, Jorge. 2016/b. "IED de las empresas multinacionales mexicanas y estrategias de "catch up" tecnológico". *Economía Informa* 399, pp. 3-15.

Basave Kunhardt, Jorge. 2022. "Inversión extranjera directa de grandes empresas mexicanas en Estados Unidos". *Problemas del Desarrollo* 53(209), pp. 189-219.

Basave Kunhardt, Jorge and Gutiérrez Haces, María Teresa. 2011. "Mexico´s Global Players". In, Sauvant, Karl (edit.). *MNS´s from Emerging Markets: New Players in the World* FDI *Market.* Vale Columbia Center, New York, pp. 2159-2209.

Basave Kunhardt, Jorge and Gutiérrez Haces, María Teresa. 2013. "Mexican OFDI in China -Ownership Advantages to Gain New Markets: Two Case Studies". *China* USA *Business Review* 21(3), pp. 241-253.

Bimbo. 2009. *Informe Anual 2009.* Mexico City: Bimbo.

Bimbo. 2012. "Baking in Beijing rises for Mexico´s *Bimbo*". Bimbo, July 10.

Bimbo. 2018. "Grupo Bimbo to Acquire Mankattan in China". Bimbo, February 12.

Bimbo. 2022. *Informe Anual Integrado 2022.* Mexico City: Bimbo.

Blomström, Magnus and Persson, Hakan. 1983. "Foreign investment and spillover efficiency in an underdeveloped economy:

evidence from Mexican manufacturing industry". *World Development* 11, pp. 493-550.

CCSI (Columbia Center on Sustainable Investment). 2017. *The Uneven Trends of Mexican MNEs: Between sluggishness and strength in the international markets.* IIE and CCSI: New Yorck.

Diario Plaza Juárez. 2023. "Time Ceramics se instalará en Emiliano Zapata, con una inversión de dos mil 700 mdp". *Diario Plaza Juárez,* May 11th.

Dunning, John H. 1998. "Globalization and the new geography of foreign direct investment". *Oxford Development Studies* 26(1), pp. 47-69.

Dussel Peters, Enrique. 2000. *Polarizing Mexico. The Impact of Liberalization Strategy.* Lynne & Rienner: Boulder/London.

Dussel Peters, Enrique. 2012. "Mexican Firms Investing in China 2000-2011". Discussion Paper 255 (IDB), pp. 1-18.

Dussel Peters, Enrique (edit.). 2014. *La inversión extranjera directa china en México: 10 casos de estudio.* Red ALC-China, UDUAL and UNAM/Cechimex: México.

Dussel Peters, Enrique (edit.). 2019. *China´s Foreign Direct Investment in Latin America and the Caribbean. Conditions and Challenges.* Red ALC-China, UDUAL and UNAM/Cechimex: México.

Dussel Peters, Enrique (coord.). 2022/a. *50 años de relaciones diplomáticas entre México y China. Pasado, presente y futuro.* UNAM/Cechimex, Senado de la República y UDUAL: México.

Dussel Peters, Enrique. 2022/b. "Capitalismo con características chinas. Conceptos y desarrollo en la tercera década del siglo XXI". *El Trimestre Económico* LXXXIX (2), nr. 354, pp. 467-489.

Dussel Peters, Enrique. 2023/a. "El proceso de integración de América Latina más allá del comercio: el caso de la OFDI intrarregional". En, Blanco Estévez, Adrián (editor). *Global LATAM 2022. Series Inversión Extranjera.* Secretaría General Iberoamericana e ICEX: Madrid, pp. 57-77.

Dussel Peters, Enrique. 2023/b. *Monitor of China´s OFDI in Latin America and the Caribbean 2023.* Red ALC-China: México.

ECLAC (Economic Commission for Latin America and the Caribbean). 2021. *Latin America and Caribbean* FDI *2021*. ECLAC: Santiago de Chile.

Elizondo Huerta, Pablo. 2010. "Incursión de Grupo Bimbo en China". *Ciclo de Conferencias del Cechimex*, March 24th.

EMGP (Emerging Markets Global Players). 2021. EMGP Data. EMGP: New Yorck. Available at: https://emgp.org/data/.

Frischtak, Claudio and Soares, André. 2012. *Empresas Brasileiras na China: Presenca e Experiencias*. BCBC: Brazil.

Goldstein, Andrea and Toulan, Omar. 2007. "Multilatinas Go to China: Two Case Studies". In, Grosse, Robert and Mesquita, Luiz F. 2007. *Can Latin American Firms Compete?* Oxford University Press: Cambridge, pp. 269-292.

Grosse, Robert and Mesquita, Luiz F. 2007. *Can Latin American Firms Compete?* Oxford University Press: Cambridge.

IDB (Inter-American Development Bank). 2012. *Pathways to China: The Story of Latin American Firms in the Chinese Market*. IDB: Washington, D.C.

Interceramic. 2023. *Reporte anual 2022*. Interceramic: México.

Jiang, Xiaojuan. 2003. "Geographical Distribution of Foreign Investment in China: Industrial Clusters and Their Significance". *China & World Economy* 1, pp. 16-24.

Lall, Sanjaya and Narula, Rajneesh. 2006. "FDI and its Role in Economic in Economic Development: Do we need a new agenda?". In Narula, Rajneesh and Lall, Sanjaya (edit.). *Understanding* FDI *Assisted Economic Development*. Routledge: London/New York, pp. 1-18.

Lim, Ewe-Ghee. 2001. 1999. "Determinants of, and the Relation Between, Foreign Direct Investment and Growth: A Summary of the Recent Literature". *IMF Working Paper* 2001/175, pp. 1-28.

Min.News. 2023. "11 years in China: this ceramic brand, from abiding by original design to an international brand that is respected by the world". *Min.News*, May 28th (at: https://min.news/en/home/fa773f38390d7acdeffa27098aefe47d.html).

MOFCOM (Ministry of Commerce), NBS (National Bureau of Statistics and SAFE (State Administration of Foreign Exchange).

2021. *2020 Statistical Bulletin of China´s Outward Foreign Direct Investment.* MOFCOM, NBS and SAFE: Beijing.

NBS (National Bureau of Statistics). Several years. *China Statistical Yearbook.* NBS: Beijing.

Oropeza García, Arturo. 2021. *China-Estados Unidos ¿la guerra sigilosa?* IIJ/UNAM: México.

RIR (Revista InfoRetail). 2015. "Las claves de la internacionalización de Bimbo". *RIR*, May 28th.

Sáenz Arelle, Susana. 2020. "La cruzada de Grupo Bimbo en el gigante asiático". *Comercio Exterior* 24 (octubre-diciembre), pp. 78-80.

SE (Secretaría de Economía). 2023. Invest in Mexico. Your best option for the long term. SE: Mexico.

SFWB (Snack Food & Wholesale Bakery). 2017. "East Balt Bakeries China earns McDonald´s Supplier of the Year Award". *SFWB*, February 27.

Seeking Alpha. 2023. "Grupo Bimbo: World´s Leading Baking Player Worth A Look". *Seeking Alpha*, May 9.

UNCTAD (United Nations Conference on Trade and Development). 2021. *World Investment Report 2021. Investing in Sustainable Recovery.* Geneva: UNCTAD.

UNCTAD. 2023. *UNCTADSTAT* (at: https://unctadstat.unctad.org/wds/TableViewer/tableView.aspx?ReportId=96740).

Xing, Yuqing. 2006. "Why is China so attractive for FDI? The role of exchange rates". *China Economic Review* 17, pp. 198-209.

Zermeño, Bernardo. 2017. "La experiencia de Bimbo en China durante una década". Cycle of Conferences of Cechimex, April 19th.

Annex 1. China: FDI Flows by Region and Country (2003-2021)

	2003-2017	2018-2021	2003-2021	2003-2017	2018-2021	2003-2021	2003-2017	2018-2021	2003-2021
	(in $million)			(annual average in $million)			(percentage)		
Total	1,448,584	590,953	2,039,537	96,572	147,738	107,344	100.00	100.00	100.00
Asia	1,060,919	501,572	1,562,490	70,728	125,393	82,236	73.24	84.88	76.61
Hong Kong	803,349	423,766	1,227,115	53,557	105,941	64,585	55.46	71.71	60.17
Japan	71,680	14,806	86,487	4,779	3,702	4,552	4.95	2.51	4.24
Macao	9,392	7,407	16,799	626	1,852	884	0.65	1.25	0.82
Republic of Korea	57,072	17,864	74,936	3,805	4,466	3,944	3.94	3.02	3.67
Singapore	68,355	30,813	99,169	4,557	7,703	5,219	4.72	5.21	4.86
Taiwan	27,951	4,914	32,865	1,863	1,228	1,730	1.93	0.83	1.61
Africa	17,222	2,876	20,098	1,148	719	1,058	1.19	0.49	0.99
Europe	92,608	33,853	126,462	6,174	8,463	6,656	6.39	5.73	6.20
Germany	21,701	8,367	30,068	1,447	2,092	1,583	1.50	1.42	1.47
France	10,963	3,027	13,990	731	757	736	0.76	0.51	0.69
Luxemburg	4,977	1,629	6,606	332	407	348	0.34	0.28	0.32
Netherlands	13,855	6,728	20,584	924	1,682	1,083	0.96	1.14	1.01
United Kingdom	8,995	3,339	12,334	600	835	649	0.62	0.56	0.60
Latin America	176,965	32,483	209,448	11,798	8,121	11,024	12.22	5.50	10.27
Argentina	124	3	127	8	1	7	0.01	0.00	0.01
Barbados	4,527	205	4,732	302	51	249	0.31	0.03	0.23
Belize	358	54	412	24	14	22	0.02	0.01	0.02
Brazil	599	80	679	40	20	36	0.04	0.01	0.03

Cayman Islands	33,661	11,860	45,522	2,244	2,965	2,396	2.32	2.01	2.23
Chile	118	18	136	8	4	7	0.01	0.00	0.01
Colombia	2	0	2	0	0	0	0.00	0.00	0.00
Cuba	60	0	60	4	0	3	0.00	0.00	0.00
Ecuador	5	0	5	0	0	0	0.00	0.00	0.00
Guatemala	3	1	4	0	0	0	0.00	0.00	0.00
Guyana	0	1	1	0	0	0	0.00	0.00	0.00
Mexico	130	21	152	9	5	8	0.01	0.00	0.01
Panama	445	38	483	30	9	25	0.03	0.01	0.02
Peru	19	3	22	1	1	1	0.00	0.00	0.00
Saint Vincent & Grenadines	14	0	14	1	0	1	0.00	0.00	0.00
St. Kitts-Nevis	87	7	94	6	2	5	0.01	0.00	0.00
urks & Caicos Islands	17	2	19	1	1	1	0.00	0.00	0.00
Uruguay	51	6	57	4	2	3	0.00	0.00	0.00
Virgin Islands, British	135,087	20,156	155,243	9,006	5,039	8,171	9.33	3.41	7.61
Australia	5,750	1,359	7,108	383	340	374	0.40	0.23	0.35
Canada	7,064	936	8,000	471	234	421	0.49	0.16	0.39
United States	42,471	10,148	52,618	2,831	2,537	2,769	2.93	1.72	2.58

Source: own elaboration based on NBS (several years).

Annex 2. LAC: OFDI to China (2003-2021)

	Number of Transactions (1)	Amount ($million) (2)	Employment (3)	Number of Transactions (1)	Amount (2)	Employment (3)	(2) / (1)	(3) / (1)	(3) / (2)
				(percentage over respective total)			(percentage)		
Argentina	8	173	600	4.28	2.18	2.10	21.65	75.00	3.46
Bermuda	22	591	3,250	11.76	7.44	11.37	26.86	147.73	5.50
Brazil	70	3,520	10,680	37.43	44.34	37.37	50.29	152.57	3.03
Cayman Island	24	831	5,442	12.83	10.46	19.04	34.61	226.75	6.55
Chile	22	681	1,531	11.76	8.58	5.36	30.95	69.59	2.25
Mexico	23	1,061	5,021	12.30	13.37	17.57	46.15	218.30	4.73
Venezuela	4	523	608	2.14	6.59	2.13	130.70	152.00	1.16
Rest	14	559	1,448	7.49	7.04	5.07	39.90	103.43	2.59
Total	187	7,939	28,580	100.00	100.00	100.00	42.45	152.83	3.60

Source: own ellaboration based on Dussel Peters (2023/a).

Annex 3. Mexican Firms Investing in China (2003-2021)

	Investing company	Sector	Activity	Employment	OFDI amount
2004	Gruma	Food & Beverages	Manufacturing	505	100
2004	Cristal Glass	Ceramics & glass	Manufacturing	400	30
2005	Grupo Molinero Garcia	Food & Beverages	Manufacturing	292	55
2005	Hylsamex	Metals	Manufacturing	174	64
2006	Gruma	Food & Beverages	Manufacturing	505	100
2007	El Fogoncito	Food & Beverages	Retail	1,033	51
2008	Softtek	Software & IT services	Research & Development	150	21
2009	Asiamex	Food & Beverages	Sales, Marketing & Support	8	14
2009	Softtek	Software & IT services	Customer Contact Centre	204	9
2009	Asiamex	Food & Beverages	Sales, Marketing & Support	23	14
2011	Nemak	Automotive components	Manufacturing	300	43
2012	Nemak	Automotive components	Manufacturing	282	46
2012	Naranya	Business services	Business Services	71	19
2013	United Logistics Services	Transportation & Warehousing	Logistics, Distribution & Transportation	127	151
2013	United Logistics Services	Transportation & Warehousing	Logistics, Distribution & Transportation	127	151
2014	Bancomext (Banco Nacional de Comercio Exterior)	Financial services	Business Services	72	59
2015	Linio	Consumer products	Sales, Marketing & Support	15	2

2015	Naranya	Business services	Business Services	71	19
2018	Katcon Global	Automotive components	Manufacturing	282	46
2018	Katcon Global	Automotive components	Manufacturing	150	21
2018	Yalo (Ayalo SAPI de CV)	Software & IT services	Sales, Marketing & Support	30	3
2019	Global Frut	Food & Beverages	Manufacturing	170	39
2021	Nowports	Software & IT services	Sales, Marketing & Support	30	3
TOTAL				5,021	1,061

Source: own ellaboration based on Dussel Peters (2023/a).

7.
PERU'S OFDI TO CHINA

Alan Fairlie

Introduction

The multiple dimensions of the Peru-China relationship is an issue that has been investigated before, from the historical presence of the Chinese population in Peru in the 19th century, to the most recent commercial relationship, especially after the Free Trade Agreement (FTA) entered into by the two countries.

For the study of the Free Trade Agreement and how this affects the trade relationship, information from MINCETUR (2021, 2022, 2023) and WTO (2019, 2021) has been systematized. Also some research on the effects of the FTA. Here, Fairlie (2019) presents the influence of this treaty on Peru's trade flows and concludes that, instead of helping to diversify the trade basket, primary exports have increased.

Similarly, in Moreno (2020) another problem of the FTA can be visualized, that is, that the textile industry is being hit by trade with China and the entry of its cheaper products. Meanwhile, there are contrary opinions such as those expressed in León Espinosa (2021), who analyzes the ties between the two countries and how they are stronger, Quesada (2021) publishes statements on this agreement, as well as Novelli and Chávez (2022), who found the benefits of the FTA in companies, like their greater growth and increased stability in the market.

Therefore, several studies analyze the gains from bilateral trade and Chinese investments in Peru. However, there has been limited research on Peruvian investment in China; and the contribution of this work is to document some cases with useful experiences so as to observe how they managed to position themselves in this Asian market.

The FTA between Peru and China strengthened the relationship between these countries and fostered the growth of trade and investment. As a consequence, there was a considerable growth in the trade relationship, thus contributing to the promotion of foreign investments and reinforcing national liberalization policies. In the Peruvian case, *Proinversion* and measures to increase investment in infrastructure were created, facilitating Chinese investments in mining, fishing and other sectors. In addition, different infrastructure projects were promoted by large companies, such as the Port of Chancay, the Chaglla Hydroelectric Power Plant, and Luz del Sur.

However, the case is different for Peruvian overseas foreign direct investments (OFDI) in China. Despite Chinese policies to increase foreign investment, some possible reasons have been found as to why there are not a large number of these investments: cultural differences, lack of entrepreneurial human capital, lack of knowledge of the Chinese market, etc. Even so, it has been possible to find a number, albeit small, of Peruvian companies with investments in China. These success stories are valuable as a guide for other companies that want to enter the Chinese market and contribute to the rarely studied topic of Peruvian investments in China.

Therefore, this paper is divided into two parts. In the first, we will look at the commercial characteristics, the investment between China and Peru and Chinese infrastructure projects in Peru. In the second part, we will analyze (with the available information) the cases of companies that have managed to reach the

Chinese market, such as Intercorp and Camposol S.A., and some of the challenges they have faced.

First, in the trade block between countries, we use the trade data provided by MINCETUR (2022), Trade Map (2023), the Office of Economic Studies and Trade Intelligence CIEN - ADEX (2023), and Song Yang (2023/a), which allow us to observe how the main trade variables behave over time.

Then, we refer to previous work such as that of Aquino Rodriguez (2019), who conducts a sectoral analysis of investments between Peru and China. Similarly, Song Yang (2023/b) studies the trade relationship between China and Peru and how these countries are economically correlated. Data on investments are taken from UNCTAD (2023), where there is data from the 1990s to 2021, for all countries linked to China. Alférez Murias (2020) analyzes Chinese investment in infrastructure in Peru based on the theories of international relations and Peruvian foreign policy, and argues that the PRC's actions in infrastructure investment in Peru have positioned the country at the regional level as an emerging power thanks to its status as a strategic partner and the reception of modern projects in the hemisphere. Similarly, the text of La Torre (2021) makes a study of the increase of Chinese FDI in the infrastructure sector in Peru between 2016 and 2019. CoperAcción (2023), systematizes the opinions of experts on the subject from an environmental perspective.

The analysis is also complemented by other sources such as Asociación Peruana de Agentes Marítimos (2017), which analyzes the port effects of the construction of the Port of Chancay; Osterloh (2019), providing an account of the main Chinese investments in infrastructure from 2016 to 2019; and the Bloomberg article, by Brambilla and Lepido (2023), which report on the most current Chinese investment in infrastructure.

On the other hand, Peruvian investments in China are quite limited.

Tang (2018) mentions that the FTA with China is not enough to succeed in Chinese business, rather it is necessary to go further, in the sense that entrepreneurs have knowledge of how the Chinese market works, from its commercial protocols to its social codes. Similarly, Vasquez (2021) brings up the importance of understanding the language of the people with whom the business relationship in China is going to be established, which may be in English, in order to obtain satisfactory and safe results in the negotiations. On the other hand, Millones Alvarado (2021) highlighted some of the actions that can be taken by the Peruvian State to help with a more fluid trade between China and Peru. Thus, he indicates that greater planning in highway infrastructure, technology transfer and more experienced human capital in management are needed to increase investment in China.

For the case studies, the first uses the information collected from Interbank (2023), which publishes the history of the company from its beginnings to the present. In addition, this is complemented by the interview with Ríos (2023), which provides details about the company's experience in China. The executive director of the Shanghai office comments on the difficulties and opportunities of being in such a dynamic market.

In the case of Camposol, the research of Ayala-Hernández (2019) and Ramírez *et al.* (2021) was studied. The first is an exhaustive analysis of the reality of the company and the industry in which it is located in order to subsequently be able to propose strategies with the goal of seeking the orderly growth of Camposol, which allows knowing the value chains of the company and how they are used abroad. Similarly, the second delves deeper into this knowledge by developing a strategic plan for the company Camposol S.A. for the period 2017-2022.

1. Trade and Investment with China

1.1 Peru-China Trade Relations

Currently, China is the country to which Peru exports the most, with 32.0 % of total exports, and from which it imports the most, with 29.0 % of total imports, in 2021. In 2022, total trade between the two countries exceeded US$ 37.6 billion, generating a surplus of more than US$ 10 billion for Peru (Trade Map 2023).

Figure 1. Peru: Trade with China ($ US) (in thousands) (2002-2021)

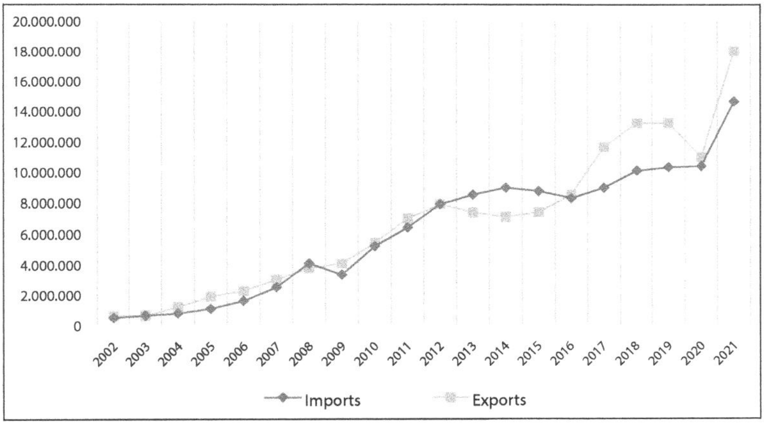

Source: own elaboration based on Trade Map (2023).

It displaced the United States and the European Union as its main trading partners (the US represents 20.3 % and 18 % of Peru's imports and exports to the world). On the import side, countries such as Brazil, Argentina and Mexico are also important partners; and on the export side, Korea, Japan and Canada. Even so, China tops the ranking of the largest trading partner since 2014. This position is held thanks to the FTA between these two countries, which are a new commercial favorite of Peru, despite requiring a few years to take effect, in accordance with the greater understanding of the treaty and the processes to take advantage of the benefits that businessmen are acquiring (Office of Economic Studies and Trade Intelligence CIEN - ADEX, 2023).

Figure 2. Peru: Main Exporters ($US) (in thousands) (2002-2021)

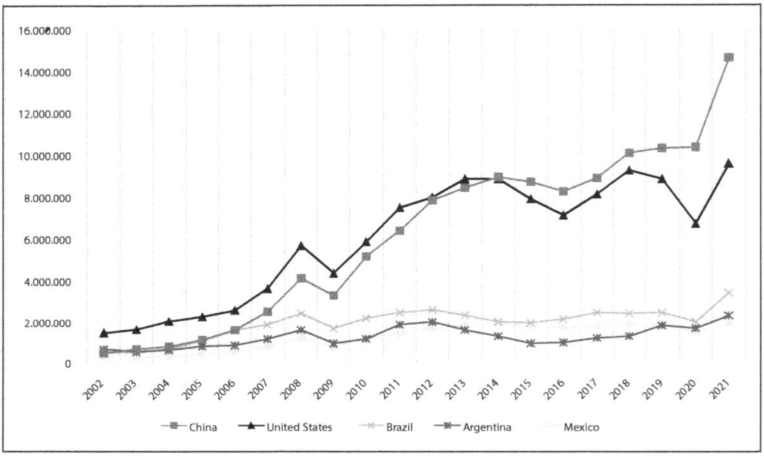

Source: own elaboration based on Trade Map (2023).

Figure 3. Peru: Main Importers (in thousands of dollars) (2002-2021)

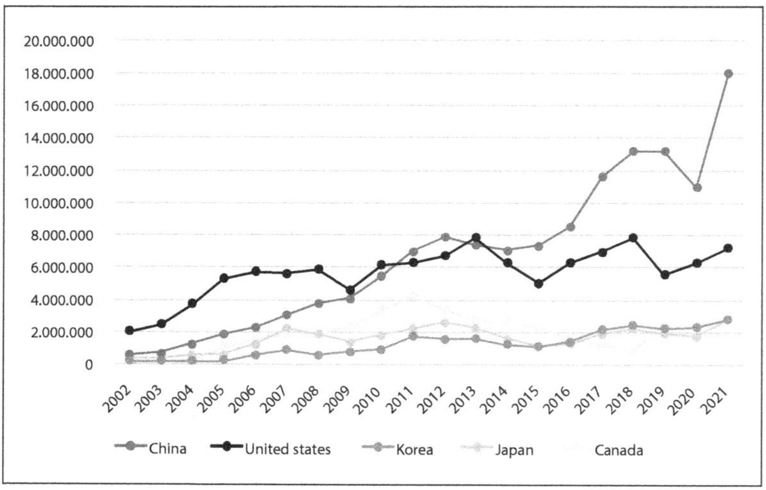

Source: own elaboration based on Trade Map (2023).

Specifically, in the 12 years since the signing of the FTA, from 2010 to 2022, the value of Peruvian exports to China grew by an average of 13.6 % (for traditional products by 13.7 %, and the growth of non-traditional products was 11.3 %). In addition, exports to China generated 622,422 jobs in 2022.

In total, exports to the Asian country accumulated a value of US$ 124,298 million, of which 4 % corresponded to non-traditional shipments. Of these products, those with the highest annual growth were non-metallic mining (65.3 %) and metal-mechanics (27.2 %); in addition, those with the highest share of exported value were the fishing sector with 1.8 % and agriculture and livestock with 1 % of total exports (MINCETUR 2022).

In 2022, the total value of exports to China was US$ 20,277, of which 98.9 % belonged to subheadings included in free access categories. Also, in that year there was an increase of 44.5 % in traditional exports, which account for 96.5 % of total exports. In particular, there were increases in the exportation of fish oil and lead. In addition, the increase in the export value of traditional products such as copper ores and concentrates (US$ 4,339 million) and iron ores and concentrates (US$ 571 million) stands out. These products are among the sectors that generate the most employment. In general, traditional exports create 554,610 jobs; while traditional mining, 491,158; and traditional fishing, 47,538 jobs, in 2022 (Oficina de Estudios Económicos y de Inteligencia Comercial CIEN - ADEX 2023).

On the other hand, non-traditional products increased by 51.2 %; however, they only represent 3.5 % of total exports. These increases were mainly in the fishing sector (US$ 168.8 million), agriculture (US$ 35.8 million), and textiles (US$ 22.2 million). Some examples of products are cuttlefish and small globes; frozen squid and squid (US$ 51.3 million), frozen whole prawns (US$ 45.2 million), frozen livers and roes (US$ 40.6 million) (MINCETUR 2022). Here, non-traditional agriculture is one of the main generators of employment, with 66,871 jobs created in 2022, 10 % more than its value the previous year (Oficina de Estudios Económicos y de Inteligencia Comercial CIEN - ADEX 2023).

Table 1. Peru: Exports to China by Sector ($US) (in millions) (2011-2022)

	2011	2012	2013	2014	2015	2016	2017	2018	2019	2020	2021	2022	2010-2022
Total	5,579	7,321	7,484	7,858	6,652	7,410	9,445	11,453	1,365	13,165	14,012	20,277	124,298
Traditional	5,308	6,939	7,128	7,462	6,186	7,106	9,173	11,503	13,131	12,585	13,546	19,574	119,235
Mining	4,395	5,724	6,367	6,289	5,692	6,079	0	10,027	11,474	0	12,231	18,014	105,892
Fisheries	778	1,219	756	1,109	487,8	950	942	974	1,516	1,007	1,204	1,520	12,462
Oil and natural gas	135	38	-	58	0	59	104	39	131	91	107	32	793
Agriculture	1	3	5	5	6	18	9	14	11	4	4	8	89
Non-traditional	271	337	356	397	466	304	272	400	513	580	466	704	5,064
Fishing	96	170	178	169	229	121	87	129	218	315	174	342	2,228
Farming and livestock	26	34	60	86	109	82	68	113	152	161	188	224	1,302
Textiles	22	20	19	23	32	19	23	62	53	27	24	46	372
Wood and papers	82	57	53	60	62	57	60	57	53	51	27	36	664
Non-metallic mining	0	2	1	0	1	0	1	2	1	0	3	22	33
Chemicals	38	39	31	31	22	9	19	23	30	19	19	21	301
Metal-mechanical	1	3	1	4	1	1	1	2	2	2	4	7	28
Iron and steel	5	10	10	19	5	4	3	4	3	5	16	3	85
Various (including jewelry)	0	0	0	0	0	0	0	1	1	1	1	0	5
Skins and leathers	1	3	2	4	4	11	10	9	1	0	0	0	45
Crafts	0	-	-	-	0	0	-	0	0	-	-	-	0

Source: own elaboration with data from MINCETUR (2022).

During this period, 833 new products were exported to China, for a value of US$ 3,579 million, of which 96.5 % belong to the non-traditional sector, where the metal-mechanical (with a share of 26.3 %), chemical (16.3 %) and textile (15.9 %) sectors stand out. However, while there has been an absolute increase in the non-traditional sector of exports, there has been a decline in their percentage share of total exports. This represents a clear challenge: to improve the relationship, Peru has to increase its exports of non-traditional goods, in addition to manufactured products that can be inserted into Chinese production chains (Santa Gadea 2023).

On the other hand, 1,855 new exporting companies have been registered (US$ 36,432 million), 74.4 % of which were micro exporters and small exporters (MINCETUR 2022). In general, small and micro companies are the ones that have had a percentage growth, with an increase of 0.2 % and 14.0 %, respectively; however, the total value of exports is concentrated in large companies, which by 202, represented 99.7 % of the total, with a value of US$ 20 903 million (Oficina de Estudios Económicos y de Inteligencia Comercial CIEN - ADEX 2023).

Peru's imports to China have grown at an average annual rate of 13.2 % from 2010 to 2022, representing US$ 109,719 million. Purchases of consumer goods grew at an average annual rate of 12.9 % and registered a share of 29.0 %; while, those of raw materials and intermediate products increased at an average annual rate of 15.9 %, and those of capital goods and construction materials, by 11.9 %, with a share of 44.1 % (MINCETUR 2022).

For the year 2022, the value of Peruvian imports from China was US$ 15 192 million (41.3 % with respect to the previous year of the FTA). These were concentrated in capital goods (29.3 % share); raw materials and intermediate products for industry (27.8 %); and consumer durables (15.6 %); in addition, there was an increase in purchases of fuels, lubricants and related products (+187.8 % compared to 2021); and construction materials (68.0 %). However, imports of capital goods for agriculture grew by 67.4 %, while imtports of transportation equipment grew by 66.4 %.

Table 2. Peru: Imports from China by Economic use/destination (millions of dollars) (2011-2022)

	2011	2012	2013	2014	2015	2016	2017	2018	2019	2020	2021	2022	2010-2022
Consumption goods	1,521	2,012	2,316	2,594	2,561	2,471	2,313	2,671	2,979	3,094	3,221	4,108	31,860
Raw materials and intermediate goods	1,390	1,604	1,988	2,001	2,353	2,149	2,151	2,473	2,892	2,845	2,933	47,008	29,479
Capital goods and constructions materials	2,418	3,002	3,628	3,875	4,169	3,902	3,741	3,970	4,351	4,336	4,600	6,384	48,376
Other	0	1	0	0	1	1	0	0	0	0	0	0	4
TOTAL	5,329	6,619	7,932	8,470	9,084	8,523	8,205	9,113	10,222	10,275	10,754	15,192	109,719

Source: own elaboration based on MINCETUR (2022).

Looking to the future, some products that could be used by Peruvian importers, with 98 % of tariff lines at 0 % in 2023, are glass containers and drinking containers; ice making machines, given the high summer temperatures; and inflatable balls, since soccer is so popular in Peru (Oficina de Estudios Económicos y de Inteligencia Comercial CIEN - ADEX 2023).

The behavior of these data shows that the bilateral trade balance between Peru and China is in surplus, especially for mineral exports; however, there are diversification challenges due to the high concentration of exports in the primary sector. Peruvian trading companies are the main agent in the relationship; therefore, an adequate development and creation of a favorable environment will contribute to growth and favorability in China (Oficina de Estudios Económicos y de Inteligencia Comercial CIEN - ADEX 2023).

Peru-China FTA

The Free Trade Agreement with China was ratified on April 28, 2009, in the city of Beijing, and took effect on March 1, 2010. This agreement addresses issues on National Treatment and Market Access, Rules of Origin, Customs Procedures, Trade Defense, Sanitary and Phytosanitary Measures, Technical Barriers to Trade, Trade in Services, Temporary Entry of Business Persons, etc. (MINCETUR 2023).

According to Mincetur, this Treaty means for Peru the possibility of becoming the center of Asian operations in South America by having clear rules of the game, with a transparent and predictable framework that provides the tools for an orderly bilateral trade, which safeguards national interests. In addition, it has made Peru an attractive place for capital investments from China and other countries (MINCETUR 2023).

Among some benefits for Peru there is the possibility of applying the drawback, which allows a percentage of the FOB value and the temporary import and export regimes to be obtained. In addition, trade facilitation is promoted through customs schemes that simplify the procedures to be followed for the entry of goods. Also, Peru may continue with the Price Band System, and China may not maintain, introduce or reintroduce export subsidies.

With respect to imports, Peru granted China immediate access to 63.0% of its tariff portfolio, while the rest of the lines will become duty-free between 5 and 17 years after the signing of the FTA (MINCETUR 2022).

In the case of exports, China offered this in an immediate or determined period of time, removing 94.5% of its tariff lines. It also included a total of 422 tariff lines in category D (without relief), including items of interest to Peru, such as mangoes, poultry, garlic, avocados, etc., which, with the FTA, can enter the Chinese market duty-free immediately and within 5 years (MINCETUR 2022).

However, the benefits of the FTA are not reflected in Peru's investments in China. In addition, there is a large part of the business community that considers that the FTA has not benefited Peru. In this regard, the former Peruvian ambassador to China, Luis Quesada (2022), refers to the asymmetric relations between countries and the difficulty of reversing them despite the efforts made.

Chapter 10 of the China-Peru FTA deals with articles related to investment, such as Article 128: Promotion and Protection of Investment, which states that "each Party shall encourage investors of the other Party to make investments in its territory and shall admit such investments in accordance with its laws and regulations"; it shall also "grant assistance and provide facilities for obtaining visa and work permits to nationals of the other Party involved in activities associated with investments made in the territory of the first Party" (MINCETUR 2023).

Also, in Articles 129 and 131, National Treatment and Most-Favored Nation Treatment, respectively, it is agreed that each country shall accord to investors of the other nation, and to their investments, treatment no less favorable than that which it accords, in like circumstances, to domestic investors. In addition, similarly, Article 132 states that each party shall accord to foreign investors, and to their investments, fair and equitable treatment and full protection and security in accordance with international law.

Other measures ensure the investors' money and its transaction: In Article 135, the transfer of investments and profits obtained in the territories, such as profits, settlement amounts, assistance payments, etc., is guaranteed. Nonetheless, these investing companies are not exempted from the taxation measures of the other country; however, this does not include customs duties, so they can benefit from the trade measures of the FTA. Finally, in order to manage the implementation of these rules, meetings are held to exchange information and transmit proposals on investment promotion.

These rules help firms have a higher level of growth each year, by 10 to 18 percentage points; in addition, firms that access the benefits of the FTA have a reduction of approximately 7 points in the probability of ceasing to export. So, in general, the tariff reduction is beneficial for international trade companies. In aggregate terms, the utilization of the preferences extended by the Peru-China FTA by Peruvian exporters is quite high: 96% of the value of eligible products. The average usage ratio for exporters and importers at the firm level was 74.0% and 38.0%, respectively in 2019 (Novelli and Cusato 2022).

Currently, Peru is working on optimizing the FTA with China, that is, it is seeking to maximize the benefits of the agreement by modernizing investment issues to obtain a clearer framework on the subject and diversify Chinese investment in Peru; incorporating digital aspects into the FTA such as e-commerce and services; facilitating customs procedures; etc. (MINCETUR 2023). In addition, experts on the subject expect that the rules on sanitary and phytosanitary protocols will be revised to allow the entry of some fruits and nuts that Peru has the level to export to China, such as pomegranates, Amazonian walnuts, pecans, pitahayas, etc. (Office of Economic Studies and Trade Intelligence CIEN - ADEX 2023).

3.2 Chinese OFDI to Peru

According to Chinese Ambassador Song Yang (2023/a), China is one of Peru's main sources of investment, exceeding US$ 30 billion, making it the second largest destination for Chinese investment in the region, with nearly 200 companies. BCRP and UNCTAD data are similar; therefore, we can say that during the period from 2000 to 2021, China has invested between US$ 115,229 and US$ 122,021 million, of which approximately US$ 5,908 to US$ 6,201 million were invested in 2021. Although there has been a decline in recent years, it is expected that, with the economic recovery, China will maintain its role as the largest contributor to global economic growth: from 2013 to 2021 its average contribution was over 38.6 % (Song Yang 2023/b).

On the other hand, Pro-Inversion's data show only reported investments, so they are highly subestimated and much lower than those from other sources.

Peruvian authorities have made an effort to attract foreign investment to Peru (MINCETUR 2023). For example, the Ministry of Economy and Finance establishes a policy to promote private investment, for which the Private Investment Promotion Agency (PROINVERSION) exists, it is a specialized technical, functional, administrative body, whose objective is to promote greater private investment within Peru (MINCETUR 2023).

In addition, one of the most noteworthy advances on investments was the enactment, in 2018, of Legislative Decree N.1362, which seeks to regulate the promotion of investment so as to support with the growth of the national economy, contribute to the closing of gaps in infrastructure or in public services, and increase the amount of productive employment and competitiveness in the country.

There is a National Policy for the Promotion of Private Investment in Public-Private Partnerships (PPP) and Projects in Assets (PA), which aims to encourage the participation of the private sector through this type of modalities. The objective is to develop projects that effectively contribute to closing the gaps in public infrastructure and to achieve a higher quality of public services. Additionally, this is intended to have a comprehensive portfolio logic, without discrimination of any kind to the bidders, and in strict compliance with what has been established in the Peruvian Treaties. In addition, under the framework of PPPs and APs, there is the National System for the Promotion of Private Investment (SNPIP), which has regulations to promote and expedite private investment (WTO 2019).

In the mining sector, China ranks first with a portfolio of approximately US$ 19,189 million, representing 33% of total projected investments (US$ 58,346 million). Here the investments that stand out are the expansions of the company Shougang Hierro Perú (US$ 1.5 billion), that of Minera Chinalco (US$ 1.35 billion); in addition, investments in construction such as Las

Bambas (US $10,000 million), Jinzhao Mining with Pampa de Pongo (US$1,500 million); and the Galeno exploration (US$2,500 million) in Cajamarca (Aquino Rodríguez 2019). In addition, by 2023, the main investments were in Las Bambas of Minmetals, Toromocho of Chinalco and Shougang Hierro Peru, which meant an inflow of approximately US$17.6 billion and its production represented 7.6% of the Peruvian GDP; in addition, its accumulated tax payment was over US$6.5 billion, and it generated more than 90 thousand direct and indirect jobs (Song Yang 2023/a/b).

3.3 Chinese Infrastructure Projects in Peru

Infrastructure projects refer to services between a client and a supplier through a contract, in which the ownership belongs to the client (Dussel Peters 2021). The Peruvian Ministry of Foreign Affairs has started to carry out roadshows where it promotes these within the Peruvian territory. Thus, Chinese plans of great magnitude have been possible, which seek to improve the country's transport, telecommunications and energy conditions (MINCETUR 2023). In Peru, from 2005 to 2021, there have been 10 large projects, with an income of US$ 1,185 million and the creation of 6,147 jobs (Dussel Peters 2021).

One of these projects is the Port of Chancay, more formally the project is called "Multipurpose Port Terminal for the port of Chancay". This is an investment contract that in the first instance was agreed with Terminales Portuarios Chancay S.A; but in 2019, the companies Volcan Compañía Minera Perú and Cosco Shipping Ports Limited signed an agreement for the construction of this port, by which the Chinese company became the holder of 60% of the shares of the TPCH (Alferez Murias 2020).

This investment is part of a trend towards the entry of large capital and corporate groups that allocate their money to port investments, which is beneficial for Peru, especially as it has a higher average entry than its Latin American counterparts. In fact, this project is estimated to involve an investment of US$3.6

billion, with which the Peruvian government expects to attract more of the trade between China and South America. In addition, it is expected that Peru will become more competitive, so that it will be similar to the shipping powers in the region. The former director of Proinversion expects that "the Port of Callao will be decongested [...] Chancay will be a mega-port and will help to redirect much of this cargo [...]. And thus increase the availability of the docks, the capacity and speed with which cargo is moved, and the productivity of logistics costs for national production" (Peruvian Association of Shipping Agents 2020).

In addition, it is expected that the Peruvian government will take advantage of the opportunity to orient itself towards the world market hand in hand with Chinese investment based on a holistic perspective, beyond investment in infrastructure, but rather as a long-term connectivity. Therefore, a plan should be developed around this project, to turn the country into a center of industrial and technological production, which will allow us to insert ourselves into value chains in Asia-Pacific (Santa Gadea 2023).

On the other hand, a recent phenomenon has emerged in Chinese investments. They are not only seeking to complement mining activity or to supply infrastructure corridors, but there are now investments in electrical infrastructure projects that aim to participate in this market to supply the national public. The Chinese government encourages its state-owned companies to go out to the international market in search of these alternatives (La Torre 2021).

Thus, another major Chinese investment in Peru has been the purchase by China Three Gorges Corporation for US$ 3,590 million in assets of 83.6 % of Sempra Energy International Holding BV, former owner of the energy company Luz del Sur. The latter's decision was due to a divestment strategy in Latin America, which gave the Chinese company the opportunity to enter the Peruvian market. This purchase demonstrates that Chinese companies are interested in the existing infrastructure market, which makes sense for Peru, as they are less vulnerable to political, social and environmental factors than when starting the project from scratch.

Table 3. Peru: Infrastructure Projects with Investments from Chinese Companies

Sector	Project	Locality	Firm	Type of project	Year of Award of Project	Amount of Project ($ million)	Commentaries
Transportation	Hidrovía amazónica	Loreto	Hidrovías II, integrated by Sinohydro (China) and Construcción y Administración S.A. (Perú).	Public-Private Association (PPA)	September 2017	95	Paralyzed PPA. More than 400 observations
	Improvement of Huánuco - La Unión - Huallanca highway	Huánuco y Áncash	China Railway 20 Bureau Group Corporation		September 2018	450	In progress. Financing by IAD.
	Chancay port	Lima	Cosco Shipping Ports (China) 60% and Terminales Portuarios Chancay (subsidiaria de Volcan Compañía Minera Perú) 40%	Private Investment	January 2019	3,000	First phase amounts of $1,300 million. Multi-purpose port terminal will include two specialized terminals.
Telecommunications	Wifi for Integral and Social Development	Ancash	Joint Venture by YOFC Network (Yangtze Optical Fibre and Cable Company Limited and Yachay Telecomunicaciones SAC)		December 2018	121	In progress.
		La Libertad			December 2018	128	
		Arequipa			December 2018	93	
		San Martín			December 2018		
Energy /electricity	Hidroelectric Power Plant San Gabán III	Carabaya (Puno)	Generación Eléctrica San Gabán S.A. (Perú) and Hydro Global Perú S.A.C. (China Three Gorges Corporation y EDP - Energías de Portugal S.A.)		July 2016	438	In progress.
	Central Hidroelectrical Power Plant Chaglla	Huánuco	China Three Gorges y Energía de Portugal		April 2019	1300 -- 1400	
	Luz del Sur	Lima	China Yangtze Power Co. Ltd. (Subsidiariy of China Three Gorges Corporation)	Private Investment	September 2019	3,590	In operation

Source: own elaboration based on Alférez Murias (2020).

This company, China Three Gorges, has also made the second largest investment in the electricity sector, with the purchase of the Chaglla hydroelectric plant from the Brazilian company Odebrecht, for approximately US$ 1.3 to 1.4 billion. It is important to mention that, while these multi-million dollar purchases could represent a strengthening of a strategic alliance with the Asian giant, they also represent a possible deterioration of Peru's relationship with Brazil, and with the United States, in the area of investments (Alferez Murias 2020).

Currently, the state-owned energy company China Southern Power Grid Co. is considering the sale of 83.3 % of the shares of the Peruvian electricity distribution company Enel Distribución Perú and 100 % of Enel X Perú, which provides advanced energy services. This purchase is valued at US $2.9 billion and, if approved by Indecopi, the Chinese government would own 100 % of the electricity distribution business in Lima, considering that another Chinese company already owns Luz del Sur (Brambilla and Lepido 2023).

Also, in Table 5, we can observe other Chinese infrastructure investments in Peru, which, although smaller than those mentioned above, reflect the continuous and growing rapprochement of the Asian country with Peru.

There are different opinions about investments in hydropower infrastructure. But, authors such as Fan Hesheng (director of the Center for Latin American Studies at Anhui University), points out that cooperation with China is mutually beneficial for the companies and countries receiving the investments, and that they are not intended to increase influence in Latin America. In addition, he says that there is no rivalry between the US and China in the region, rather they promote the interests of both by contributing to the development of the region.

The Chinese Ambassador to Peru, Song Yang (2023/a) has a similar opinion and stated in the Peru-China trade magazine Capechi that, "in the field of infrastructure construction, the National Emergency Operations Center and the Loayza Hospital Maintenance Project, supported by China, have contributed energetically to Peru's progress and the improvement of the welfare of its people. The Bank of China opened a branch in Peru, which will provide greater financial support for trade and investment in Peru and generate greater possibilities for cooperation".

On the contrary, Julia Cuadros (2023), economist and researcher on mining issues at CooperAcción, indicated that after having analyzed several extraction and infrastructure megaprojects of Chinese companies in Latin America, she has observed that they do not comply with the environmental and social protocols of the Chinese state, with respect to the activities they carry out abroad. José de Echave, economist and researcher of the same organization, pointed out that Peru must build standards and regulations to fix the imbalances and non-compliance of these companies.

2.4 Peruvian OFDI to China

There are information limitations, but it has been systematized with the available data.

Taking UNCTAD (2021) as a source, Peru's investments in China have had a volatile behavior between 2007 and 2021. However, by 2021, Peru has invested US $ 188 million in China, 10 % of total investment, from 2017 to 2021 (US $ 1,837 million).

Figure 4. Perú: OFDI to China (thousands of dollars) (2007-2021)

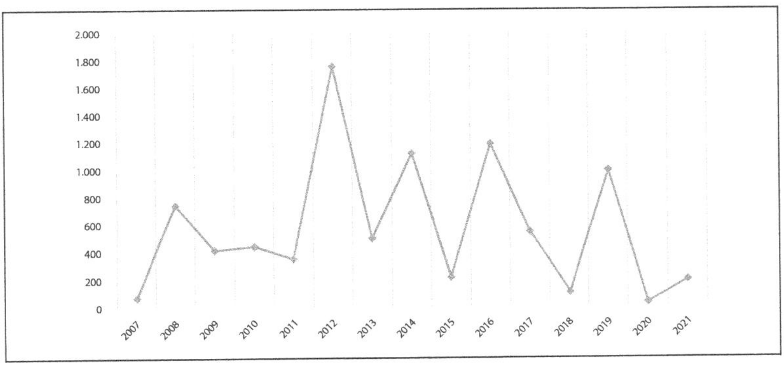

Source: own elaboration based on UNCTAD (2021).

Although there is Peruvian investment in China, it is quite small. There are efforts to promote the entry of foreign investment into China, creating an enabling environment for it. For example, the enactment of the Foreign Investment Law of the People's Republic of China looks after the interests of investors by providing a legal framework for their actions. Thus, this law obliges the state to ensure that foreign companies seeking to invest participate in market competition on an equal footing, aiming to strengthen foreign investment services, and to guide them according to Chinese laws and regulations (WTO 2021).

Another measure for increasing investment has been to reduce the negative list on the access that these investments have; thus, restrictions against foreign participation in transportation companies, in the manufacturing sector, and in the financial sector were eliminated. Not only this, it has also sought to create international platforms for openness and cooperation. So, it has organized international fairs as exhibition platforms to present its opening measures, the China International Investment and Trade Fair (CIFIT) is shown as an opportunity for transnational companies and entrepreneurs to know the Chinese market to implement their investments (WTO 2021). Even the Chinese Ambassador to Peru, in recent remarks at a conference on the Peru-China FTA, Song Yang (2023/b) has extended an invitation to Peruvian companies to the sixth exhibition of the Shanghai fair, where a free exhibition space of 130 meters will be provided, and communications with the Peruvian government will be facilitated (WTO 2023).

Even so, there are currently very few Peruvian companies investing in China (MINCETUR 2023). Since the FTA is not enough for companies to be successful in China, it is also necessary to modify commercial operations so that they are more fluid and rapid. For this, it is necessary for Peruvian businessmen to have knowledge of Chinese business culture, such as communication codes, greetings, business cards, punctuality, conversation topics, clothing, etc., which, while trivial in Peru, are important for doing business with Chinese businessmen. Here, it is also worth mentioning the acquisition of the Chinese language, which is becoming more and more fundamental to increase business with this country: businessmen value knowing their language and customs, because for them it is a sign of a real interest in doing serious business (Tang 2018).

Another important point for achieving successful business in China is to have knowledge of what tools and methodologies to use in the market. Thus, it is necessary to have a clear idea of the processes and costs of trade logistics, in which having an idea of how to use Artificial Intelligence or Big Data analysis can help reduce the risks and probability of failure (Vásquez 2021). In addition, it is important to have human capital with managerial skills, who are clear about the rules of the business, who know the market, its operation, legal system, cultural idiosyncrasies, etc. (Millones Alvarado 2021).

So, we say that the Peru-China FTA has increased the trade relationship between these countries, especially in terms of exports and imports. However, while there has been a large influx of Chinese investment into Peru, the same is not true for Peruvian investment in China. Definitely, both countries have honored the investment clauses of the FTA, through actions that promote foreign investment in their country, from which Chinese mining, fishing and financial companies have been able to benefit; but Peruvian investors in a much smaller amount, because the limitations in the knowledge of the Chinese market (their customs, their methodologies, their language, etc.), have made the insertion much more complicated. Even so, some companies have managed to be successful, and here is a summary of their experience.

3. Case studies

3.1. Intercorp Group

The Intercorp group is composed of a conglomerate of companies, of which Interbank is the one in charge of banking. This, formerly Banco Internacional del Perú, was founded in Lima on May 1,

1897. However, their desire for administrative decentralization led them to expand their agencies, first in Chiclayo and Arequipa, in 1934. This expansion drive became more intense by 1942, with the purchase of new premises, which continued even after the purchase of majority shares by Banco de la Nación in 1970. Then, in 1994, a financial group led by Dr. Carlos Rodríguez-Pastor Mendoza, and integrated by large investors such as Nicholas Brady (former U.S. Secretary of the Treasury), among others, became the main shareholder of the bank by acquiring 91 % of the available shares (Interbank 2023).

This purchase would help with the growth of the company, and the renewal of the way of banking in Peru; thus, with the new name "Interbank", each agency would become an authentic financial store where, upon entering, the client would feel that he/she was accessing an innovative, reliable and solid bank. At that time, the Interbank Tower was inaugurated, but more than that, in 2001, better integrated services and advanced technology began to be used (Interbank 2023).

In addition, in an interview about the process of investing in China, Juan Carlos Ríos (2023), Intercorp's executive director in Shanghai, said that they were driven by the natural entrepreneurial desire to do things differently and better, and decided that Asia would become a business and investment hub for Peru and, since 2006, they began exploring some countries in the region. He indicates that, at that time, it was not difficult to decide on China, since it was the most interesting option for Interbank to set foot in. Because that country had been growing at double-digit rates, there was a policy of investment in infrastructure in railroad networks, ports, highways, airports and hydroelectric plants, hardly comparable with other countries in the world, a marked development of industrial and service "clusters" in multiple first and second line cities, with an average cost of labor force around US $2 per hour. There was no doubt that, in a few years, China would become the world's factory and the world's largest consumer market.

From this, they decided to invest in intangible assets, i.e. to offer B2B services, based on real knowledge, in situ, of how to do business with Chinese investors, suppliers and importers, which generate value to the business of potential customers in Peru. For them, they became their commercial arm and a faster way to reach the Chinese market, with a local team and know-how developed on the basis of pure business experience, having as corporate backing the entrepreneurial, professional and integrity image of the bank, and therefore, of the Intercorp Group in Peru (Ríos 2023).

With this in mind, by 2007 they quickly established the Representative Office in Shanghai and, in 2008, the trading companies Intercorp Perú Trading Co. Ltd. in Hong Kong and Intercorp Perú Trading Shanghái Co. Ltd. in Shanghai, with a capital investment of approximately US $80.8 million and 77 jobs created (FDI Markets 2023). Within these companies there are two main business units: Import (purchases from China) and Export (sales to China), with teams specialized in various categories of each of these business segments.

However, this did not come without its own challenges in a competitive market. Although, at that time it was not very complicated to get stablished in China as the country was open and eager to receive foreign direct investment, the country's speed of change and growth, and the impact that changes in the global economy could have, were shown as challenges (Ríos 2023).

Thus, for example, amid the maelstrom of growth, the Chinese economy was affected to varying degrees by the financial crises in the U.S. in 2008 and in Asia in 2015-16. Similarly, the development of tech giants such as Tencent, Alibaba and others made us all move from a real economy to an essentially digital one between 2016 and 2019. Then, the COVID pandemic, which emerged in China at the end of 2019, has had a very big influence on the contraction of the economy, the business landscape and the behavior of society in China. Finally, the international tensions that have heightened from 2020 to date have caused China to shift from economic pragmatism to one guided by ideology and geopolitics.

Therefore, for those who are in China from any perspective, whether as a market, as a supplier of goods and services or as a source of investment, it is not easy to have the correct reading of where the tide is going and how business strategies should be adapted to these situations and structural changes that have been taking place in that country (Ríos 2023).

Likewise, these processes teach many lessons. In these 16 years in China, they have learned a lot, but it stands out that, to do business with China, you have to stay in China permanently, visit factories, fairs, markets, financial and technological centers and develop a very close relationship with the companies with whom one is going to do business. Information about China exists in abundance, one can identify through the internet almost any need, however, in our experience we believe that to make successful and sustainable business in time we must move "from information about China to knowledge about China and its companies" and that is the main value that he believes his actions provide to his Peruvian clients (Ríos 2023).

In conclusion, Intercorp, together with Banco Interbank, was already looking at the possibility of investing in China since 2006; however, it would not be until 2007 that offices would be established in Hong Kong and Shanghai. According to the executive director of Intercorp in Shanghai, this process would not occur without the difficulties characteristic of a large and dynamic market such as the Chinese one. In spite of this, with an advance in technological, operational and market knowledge, it was possible for them to prosper and become a company that does successful business in China, trusted by their clients. Finally, he pointed out that "the current international situation makes it difficult to have a clear perspective of what the Peru-China relationship will be, where China's geopolitical strategy plays a major role" (Ríos 2023).

3.2. Camposol S.A.

Camposol S.A. is a company focused on the sale of fresh produce, which began operations in the region of La Libertad, Peru, in 1977. In its beginnings it focused on the production of asparagus, which was so successful that a decade later it had more than 3,000 hectares of white asparagus and was the main producer of this product in canned form, which it exported to Spain. However, the drop in asparagus prices in 2007 led him to expand his product portfolio, so he began to sell avocados, which he exported to the United States. Thus, his production grew until he had an avocado plantation of 2,000 hectares, the largest in the world. This growth made the internationalization of the company possible, so that a commercial office was opened in Rotterdam to sell the products to retailers without intermediaries. In addition, Camposol also offers other products such as blueberries, tangerines, grapes, mangoes and shrimp (Ayala Hernández 2019).

About the business model, Camposol is a company divided into three commissions: Camposol Fruits and Vegetables, in charge of agribusiness; Marinasol, which observes the production of seafood; and Camposol International, in charge of making contact with retailers so that direct sales can be made, with a representative office. The latter is in charge of the relationship with Chinese buyers, who are a market segment with different characteristics; for example, they prefer fruits and vegetables for their bright colors and good size, rather than for their taste. Based on this, Camposol gives value to its product, adapting to the needs of Chinese consumers; so, it reserves its larger and more colorful fruits for them, thus ensuring a standard and quality product under its brand (Ayala Hernández 2019).

Camposol International's division in China allows a direct link with retailers, which makes its relationship with customers closer and more personalized, since it offers products that meet the requirements of end consumers, to the point of making them loyal. For a closer approach, the commercial offices in each country are key and become an investment of the company. From this point, Camposol's actions in China are based on a main step of the whole value chain of the company: Marketing and Sales; and a secondary step: Technology (Ayala Hernández 2019).

Camposol Marketing and Sales needs to be recognized for the quality of its products; however, at the beginning it was difficult to achieve this because its customers were distributors who sold the product under their brand to retailers, which puts the company at a disadvantage *vis-à-vis* its end consumers. This changed when they were finally able to open commercial offices in China, where they entered mainly with asparagus and blueberries, and in general in the countries where they sell, since it allows them to sell under their own brand and gain reputation. In addition, having a more direct connection allows them to take advantage of knowledge that can only be acquired by being in a place, such as which fruits are popular or not; thus, they were able to take advantage of the boom in blueberries and avocado, because they are recognized for their healthy properties and good taste associated with Peruvian food (Ayala Hernández 2019).

On the other hand, the promise of quality provided by Camposol required that the technology be adapted to provide the type of products that consumers demanded. Thus, as we have mentioned, in China consumers preferred to buy fruit based on factors such as size and color, so Camposol began to invest in technology in order to have equipment that could separate fruit by size.

Camposol International has found the formula for greater success in China; in fact, Asia is expected to grow from 6 % to 30 % of its sales in approximately 5 years, with greater participation from China. This, considering the strengths of having offices close to consumers: direct contact, knowing the demand, etc, which allow them to take advantage of opportunities, such as the possibility of having knowledge about the market, since Chinese consumers have a preference for avocados and blueberries because of their nutritional properties. However, as we can see in Table 2, this does not exempt them from having weaknesses and threats, such as depending on other business units, which complicates sales because production may be delayed or seasonal due to events that occur in Peru. They can also be affected by external shocks, which, considering the size of the Chinese market, have new and unknown causalities for Peruvian investors; or even by cultural differences, such as the translation of the brand into Chinese.

Table 4. Camposol: SWOT of the Strategic Business Units

	Strengths	Weaknesses
	Direct contact with retailers	Depending on other business unitss to offer their products, particularly by Marinasol.
	Offers according to price and voumen by season	
	Power to offer products by its own trade mark	
	Opportunities	**Threats**
Camposol Internacional	Knowledge of Camposol trademark to final consumers	Decreasing international prices
	Signature of reailer agreements depending on their knwoledge of the ripening of the fruits	Difficulties to translate ubn Spanish of trademarks+
		Exchange of the consumer to elect fot the procuct

Source: own elaboration with data from Ayala Hernández (2019).

So, the agro-industrial company Camposol, through its Camposol International unit, has found a successful way to enter international markets. Specifically in the case of the Chinese market, because of its proximity to consumers it has been able to have a clear recognition of the demands of its consumers, and over time it has learned to adapt to it, through technological renovations. However, even so, there are difficulties due to the rigorous and dynamic Chinese market, such as price changes according to the economy or language differences. Despite this, the company has already made a name for itself and is recognized by loyal customers, which makes it easier for them to deal with any setbacks that may occur and, above all, allows them to move ahead in terms of logistics.

4. On a Balance

The economic relationship between Peru and China is very important. With the signing of the FTA, commercial interaction increased and granted more facilities for the entry of Chinese investment to Peru. There is a significant diversification in sectors such as mining, finance, fisheries, infrastructure and others. Even so, both governments want to expand their relationship and have shown their willingness for a closer relationship; for example, with the invitation to the Shanghai Fair of the Chinese ambassador, or the wishes of MINCETUR to optimize the FTA. In addition, experts in the subject show their opinion and consider two important points for this: the diversification of the products that are exported and the revision of phytosanitary measures to achieve greater exports.

On the other hand, there are still very few Peruvian investments in China. According to some authors, this may be due to cultural factors, not knowing the language, lack of human capital with managerial skills, low productivity of most Peruvian companies, deficiencies in infrastructure and competitiveness, etc., which makes it very difficult for Peruvian companies to enter this demanding and dynamic market. In spite of this, we have managed to find some small cases of Peruvian investment in China: Interbank Group and Camposol. When we analyze these cases, although the sectors are different, both companies mention the difficulty and the demands required to enter the Chinese market. In addition, both Interbank and Camposol point out that these difficulties forced them to understand their clients and customers, in order to offer the best possible product and even the importance of living in China for knowledge and action in situ.

In the first case, the corporation has a financial component, as well as a commercial diversification that allows it to guide Peruvian clients in China and at the same time establish coordination and provide additional information to Chinese companies that are positioning themselves in the Peruvian market, given the links of trust that have been established.

The other case is that of the leaders in the Peruvian agro-industrial boom, whose entry of products into China was facilitated by the FTA. Although the link is fundamentally of primary products, qualitatively it is important and could be the embryo of future diversification.

Indeed, in the medium term, there are other firms seeking to enter the Chinese market. One of them is Danper, which, like Aje Group, is in the agribusiness group of companies. This Danish-Peruvian company has faced difficulties in this market, which have allowed it to improve. Thus, logistically, it has implemented the necessary technology to offer the asparagus demanded by its Chinese customers and, in terms of quality, it has raised it based on the necessary certificates to make the brand stand out, and according to the demand and requirements demanded by China. In addition, its executive director recommended to other Peruvian investors that they understand this market fully so that, they can successfully choose their investment and personnel (Valenzuela Noriega 2018). Its success reflects part of the diversification in Peruvian exports; however, as we have seen in non-traditional products, there is still room for improvement on plans to increase the export of non-traditional goods.

Another company is Aje Group which, although it is already close to the Asian region thanks to its headquarters in India and Singapore, it has not yet been able to enter China, but has been very interested in doing so since 2010, with its products in the food industry, such as beverages (Strategia, 2011). From its observation of the Chinese market, we can note similar difficulties that other businesses have mentioned: the magnitude, complexity and customs of the Chinese market, and it is a company with future investments in China (Bauer 2023).

In addition, another company with plans to invest in China is the Gloria brand, which is in charge of the production and distribution of milk products, therefore, they could benefit from the 0 % tariff that the FTA offers to this type of products: milk and cheese.

In short, we note that the banking and agribusiness sectors have had more investment advances in China, so plans to diversify exports and the revision of phytosanitary measures would be a way to grow exports from these sectors.

Meanwhile, the infrastructure projects mentioned above (such as the port of Chancay) could be an opportunity to create conditions for new investments and greater articulation, including value chains and long-term strategic partnerships with China.

References

Alferez Murias, Jimena del Carmen. 2020. *Panorama y reflexión sobre la inversión china en infraestructura en el Perú: Análisis desde las relaciones internacionales y la política exterior peruana.* Master´s Degree Thesis at Academia Diplomática del Perú Javier Pérez de Cuellar.

Andina. 2010. *Multinacional peruana Ajegroup se alista para ingresar a China e India* . Andina, April 5.

Aquino Rodríguez, Carlos. 2019. "Las relaciones económicas entre Perú y China: comercio, inversión, y cooperación económica." In, Alcalde, Javier, Alden, Chris, Guerra-Barón, Angélica and Méndez, Álvaro. *La Conexión China en la Política Exterior del Perú en el Siglo XXI*. PUCP and IDEI: Bogotá, pp. 76-89.

Asociación Peruana de Agentes Marítimos. 2017. "China y las compras portuarias: un negocio que va más allá de lo simplemente económico". APAM, September 11.

Ayala-Hernandez, Miguel Angel. 2019. *Caso de estudio: Análisis y diagnóstico de una empresa del sector agroindustrial peruano, propuesta de un plan estratégico*. Bachelor Degree Thesis at Universidad de Lima.

Bauer, Augusto. 2023."Exploramos la opción de ingresar a China". Capechi Trade, March.

BBC News. 2022. "Chancay, el megapuerto estratégico para el comercio con Asia que China construye en Perú (y el impacto que ya genera)". *BBC News*, September 8.

Brambilla, Alberto and Lepido, Daniele. 2023. "Enel Sells Peru Assets to China' CSGI for $2.9 Billion". *Bloomberg*, April 7.

CoperAcción. 2023. "La polémica sobre la inversión china en el Perú". *La hora verde*, April 27.

Dussel Peters, Enrique. 2022. *Monitor of China´s OFDI in Latin America and the Caribbean 2022.* Red ALC-China: Mexico.

ECLAC (Economic Commission for Latin America and the Caribbean). 2021. *Latin America and Caribbean FDI 2021.* ECLAC: Santiago de Chile.

Fairlie Reinoso, Alan. 2019. "La influencia del TLC con China en los flujos comerciales del Perú". *Latin American Journal of Trade Policy*, *2*(5), pp. 23-43.

Fajardo, Luis. 2015. "La inusual historia de una bebida peruana que consumen millones en Asia". *BBC News*, May 25.

Interbank. 2023. "Nuestra Historia". Retrived at: https://interbank.pe/nosotros.

La República. 2023. "Familia Añaños: ¿cómo pasó de hacer gaseosas en su patio a liderar una multinacional?" *La República*, May 4.

La Torre Frisancho, Martha Amelia. 2021. *Aumento de la inversión extranjera directa de China en el sector de infraestructura en Perú entre 2016 y 2019.* Bachelor Degree Thesis at Pontificia Universidad Católica del Perú.

León Espinosa, Martín. 2021. "Los lazos comerciales entre Perú y China se fortalecen a pesar de la crisis política". *Diálogo Chino*, December 28.

Mendoza Cóndor, Ricardina Jesusa and Stucchi Tapia, Elizabeth Pierina Geraldine. 2022. *Relación entre la estrategia competitiva de liderazgo en costo y el desempeño exportador de las empresas peruanas de arándanos hacia el mercado de China durante el período 2016-2020.* Bachelor Degree Thesis at Universidad Peruana de Ciencias Aplicadas.

Millones Alvarado, Sonia. 2021. "Retos del Nuevo Gobierno: Objetivo China." *Capechi Trade*, August 12-18.

MINCETUR. 2022. *Estudio del Aprovechamiento del TLC Perú-China: 12 años de vigencia del TLC.* MINCETUR: Lima.

MINCETUR. 2023. *TLC Perú-China.* MINCETUR: Lima.

Moreno Custodio, Leslie. 2020. "Industria textil de Perú doblemente golpeada por el coronavirus y China". *Diálogo Chino*, July 17.

Novelli, Antonio Cusato and Chávez, Jorge F. 2022. "The Utilization of Trade Preferences under the Peru-China FTA". *Working Paper Series* 4 (Centro de Estudios sobre China y Asia-Pacífico), pp. 1-72.

Oficina de Estudios Económicos y de Inteligencia Comercial CIEN – ADEX. 2023. *Relaciones bilaterales y Aprovechamiento del TLC Perú*. ADEX y Alianza del Pacífico: Lima.

OMC (Organización Mundial del Comercio). 2019. *Examen de las Políticas Comerciales: Informe de Perú*. OMC and Universidad del Pacífico/Centro de Estudios sobre China y Asia-Pacífico: Lima.

OMC. 2021. *Examen de la Políticas Comerciales: Informe de China*. OMC: Geneva.

Osterloh, María Isabel. 2019. "Recuento de las inversiones chinas en Perú en el sector infraestructura 2016-2019". *Alert@ Económica*, November 13.

Pro-Inversión . 2023. *Inversión Perú-China*. Pro-Inversión: Lima.

Quesada, Luis. 2022. "Peru's ambassador to China: "The FTA with China is becoming obsolete". *Diálogo Chino*, July 1.

Quintero, Milton David and Villegas, Verónica. 2018. *Internacionalización de AJE GROUP*. Uniempresarial: Bogotá.

Ramírez Díaz, Carlos Alberto, Luna Luna, Manuel Gregorio and Michelena Marín, Marco Antonio. 2021. *Plan estratégico para la empresa Camposol SA período 2017-2021*. Masters Degree Thesis at Universidad del Pacífico.

Ríos, Juan Carlos. 2023. *Intercorp Group (Perú) en China*. Interview by Alan Fairlie, March.

Santa Gadea, Rosario. 2023. *Relaciones bilaterales y Aprovechamiento del TLC Perú-China*. ADEX y Alianza del Pacífico: Lima.

Strategia. 2018. "Ajegroup: de Ayacucho para el Mundo." *Strategia*, pp. 35-37.

Tang, Rubén. 2018. "El reto es que las pymes peruanas pasen a mercados más complejos". *Capechi Trade 1*, October pp. 20-24.

Trade Map. 2023. *Estadísticas del comercio para el desarrollo internacional de las empresas Datos comerciales mensuales, trimestrales y anuales. Valores de importación y exportación, volumenes, tasas de crecimiento, cuotas de mercado.* Retried at: https://www.trademap.org/.

UNCTAD (United Nations Conference on Trade and Development). 2023. *Flows and outputs of chinese investment.* UNCTAD: Geneva.

Valenzuela Noriega, Roberto. 2018. "Las Claves de una Exportación Eficaz según Danper." *Capechi Trade*, October, pp. 20-24.

Vásquez, L. 2021. «Importar y exportar a China: Negocios Seguros.» *Capechi Trade*, Diciembre: 28-29.

Yang, Song. 2023/a. *Relaciones bilaterales y Aprovechamiento del TLC Perú-China.* ADEX y Alianza del Pacífico: Lima.

Yang, Song. 2023/b. *China y Perú son Buenos Hermanos, socios y amigos. El Diario de Lima*, February 8.

ABOUT THE AUTHORS

Rafael Leonardo Arias-Achio is a Ph.D. student and researcher from Costa Rica. His research focuses on the intersection between education and health, as well as Central American foreign policy. He holds a BA in International Relations from the National University of Costa Rica and a Master's in Government and Public Affairs from FLACSO Mexico. He is currently pursuing a Ph.D. at the University of Minnesota in Organizational Leadership, Policy, and Development; and is a Population Studies trainee and research assistant at the Institute for Social Research and Data Innovation at the University of Minnesota.

Rafael Arias Ramírez is an economist and professor at the National University and the University of Costa Rica. He has worked as a professor and researcher at the School of Economics of the National University and the Institute of Research in Economic Sciences of the University of Costa Rica. His master's and doctoral degrees are from the University of Minnesota, with concentrations in Economic Development, Public Policy, and Regional Economics. He has collaborated with the *University Studies Abroad Consortium* (USAC), the University of Chile, the Latin American Faculty of Social Sciences (FLACSO) and other academic institutions internationally.

Chevano Baker holds a Master of Public Policy from the Blavatnik School of Government and an M.Sc. in Economics for Development from the Oxford Department for International Development. Chevano also completed an M.Sc. in Financial Economics at the University of Birmingham and a B.Sc. in Actuarial Science at The University of the West Indies.

Andrés Bórquez is an Assistant Professor at the Institute of International Studies of the University of Chile. He holds a Ph.D. in International Politics from Fudan University, China. His current research interests include China-Latin America relations and the Development Partnership between Chile and ASEAN. He is also the Coordinator of the Master's in Asia Studies at the University of Chile.

Enrique Dussel Peters has a Ph.D. in Economics from the University of Notre Dame (1996). Professor at the Graduate School of Economics, Universidad Nacional Autónoma de México (UNAM) since 1993. Coordinator of the Center for Chinese-Mexican Studies (Cechimex) of the School of Economics at UNAM and of the Academic Network of Latin America and the Caribbean on China (Red ALC-China). Member of Sistema Nacional de Investigadores (level III). Author of chapters and books on political economy, industrial organization, development, processes of segments of global value chains and the socioeconomic Latin America and Caribbean-China relationship in Spanish, German, English, Chinese, and Portuguese. http://dusselpeters.com.

Alan Fairlie is a Tenured Professor of The Economics Department of the Pontifical Catholic University of Peru and Director of the Master's Program in Biotrade and Sustainable Development. Researcher of INTE (Institute of Nature, Land, and Energy) and CISEPA (Center of Social, Economic, Political, and Anthropological Investigations). Former Dean of the Social Sciences Faculty of the Pontifical Catholic University of Peru, during the period from 2011 to 2016. Member of the Latin American Red of Trade Policy (LATN). Member of the workgroups at CLACSO: "Geopolitics, World system, and regional Integration", and "China and the Map of the World Power". Member of the workgroups at GRIDALE: "Harmonization of policies for a multidimensional integration and sustainable development", and "The future of the European Union: Potentials and Challenges". Co-chair of Latin American Studies Association: EU-Latin America. Ex-Andean Parliamentary, in the period from 2016 to 2021 (former president of the Integration and Education Commission).

Celio Hiratuka is a Doctor of Science in Economics of the State University of Campinas (UNICAMP). Professor of Economics at UNICAMP, coordinator of the Center for Industrial Economics and Technology (NEIT) at UNICAMP, Deputy Executive Secretary of the Brazilian National Association of Graduate Studies in Economics (2012-2013) and General Coordinator of Graduate Studies in the Institute of Economics at UNICAMP. He is currently Associate Director of the Institute of Economics at UNICAMP and Coordinator of the Brazil-China Study Group at UNICAMP. His teaching and research themes involve international economy, economic development, international trade and investment, transnational corporations, Brazilian and technological development, and Brazil-China relations. Member of Red ALC-China.

Dorotea López is the International Studies Institute Director and Professor. Economist from the Instituto Técnologico Autónomo de México, Master of Philosophy in Economics, Cambridge United Kingdom, Ph.D. in Social Sciences from the University of Chile. Senior researcher of the Millennium Nucleus on the impacts of China in Latin American countries. Her main areas of interest are trade policy and services.

Jevon Minto is a bilingual award-winning journalist and a 2021-2022 cohort Schwarzman Scholar at Tsinghua University, where he graduated with a Masters of Management Science in Global

Affairs. He also holds an M.A. in Economic Development & International Cooperation from the Meritorious Autonomous University of Puebla, Mexico.

Juan E. Serrano-Moreno is an assistant professor at the Institute of International Studies of the University of Chile. He holds a Ph.D. in Political Science from the University Paris I Panthéon-Sorbonne and has taught at various universities in France, Spain, and Chile. His current research interests include China-Latin America relations and the Chinese political system. He is also an attorney of the Madrid Bar Association, the president of the Association of Spanish Scientists and Researchers in Chile and the coordinator of the Master's in International Strategy and Trade Policy at the University of Chile.

Leonardo E. Stanley is an associate researcher at the Centre for the Study of State and Society - CEDES / School of Economy and Business, National University of San Martin (UNSAM). Professor at UBA and UNTREF. Columnist at Latinoamerica21. HiCue Speakers. His main areas of interest are Global Political Economy, Sustainable Development, International Financial Architecture, and China - Latin America. Leonardo has made several contributions in journals, books, and handbooks, including Routledge Handbook of International Political Economy (2020), Edgar Elgar Handbook on the Politics of International Development (2022), International Studies Association and Oxford Research Encyclopedias International Studies (2022). He is author of "*Emerging Markets and Financial Globalization: Comparing the experiences of Argentina, Brazil, China, India and South Korea*" Anthem Press (2018), and "*Latin America Global Insertion, Energy Transition, and Sustainable Development*", Cambridge University Press (2020).

Noel Young is currently pursuing a Master's of Science in International Public and Development Management at The University of the West Indies, Mona. His research focuses on financial inclusion for small farmers in rural Jamaica. He holds a First Class Honours degree in International Relations with a minor in Economics, specifically in the field of International Political Economy. Noel has diverse professional experience in the financial services sector and diplomacy. Recently, he worked as the Local Economic Affairs Attaché at the Embassy of Mexico in Jamaica.

Universidad Nacional Autónoma de México
Facultad de Economía
Centro de Estudios China-México
Unión de Universidades de América Latina y el Caribe
Red Académica de América Latina y el Caribe sobre China

LATIN AMERICAN AND CARIBBEAN OVERSEAS FOREIGN DIRECT INVESTMENT TO CHINA IN THE TWENTY-FIRST CENTURY

Esta edición se terminó de editar en noviembre de 2023
Su composición se realizó con las familias tipográficas:
Minion Pro 7:10; 8:10; 11:14
Montserrat 7:14; 10:14; 11:14; 12:14; 14:18 18:20; 20:25; 24:32

El cuidado de la edición estuvo a cargo de:
Silvia Jiménez Barba